The Sacred Life of Modernist Literature

The Sacred Life of Modernist Literature

Immanence, Occultism, and the Making of the Modern World

Allan Kilner-Johnson

BLOOMSBURY ACADEMIC
LONDON • NEW YORK • OXFORD • NEW DELHI • SYDNEY

BLOOMSBURY ACADEMIC
Bloomsbury Publishing Plc
50 Bedford Square, London, WC1B 3DP, UK
1385 Broadway, New York, NY 10018, USA
29 Earlsfort Terrace, Dublin 2, Ireland

BLOOMSBURY, BLOOMSBURY ACADEMIC and the Diana logo are trademarks of Bloomsbury Publishing Plc

First published in Great Britain 2022
Paperback edition published 2024

Copyright © Allan Kilner-Johnson, 2022

Allan Kilner-Johnson has asserted his right under the Copyright, Designs and Patents Act, 1988, to be identified as the Author of this work.

For legal purposes the Acknowledgements on p. vi constitute an extension of this copyright page.

Cover design: Rebecca Heselton
Cover image: MasPix / Alamy Stock Photo

All rights reserved. No part of this publication may be reproduced or transmitted in any form or by any means, electronic or mechanical, including photocopying, recording, or any information storage or retrieval system, without prior permission in writing from the publishers.

Bloomsbury Publishing Plc does not have any control over, or responsibility for, any third-party websites referred to or in this book. All internet addresses given in this book were correct at the time of going to press. The author and publisher regret any inconvenience caused if addresses have changed or sites have ceased to exist, but can accept no responsibility for any such changes.

A catalogue record for this book is available from the British Library.

A catalog record for this book is available from the Library of Congress.

ISBN: HB: 978-1-3502-5530-2
PB: 978-1-3502-5534-0
ePDF: 978-1-3502-5531-9
eBook: 978-1-3502-5532-6

Typeset by Newgen KnowledgeWorks Pvt. Ltd., Chennai, India

To find out more about our authors and books visit www.bloomsbury.com and sign up for our newsletters.

Contents

Acknowledgements	vi
Introduction	1
1 Divine reading: Absence and elision as occult form in modernist literature	29
2 The return to ritual: Embodiment and initiation in modernist drama	49
3 The modernist shadow: Psychoanalysis, occultism and the taming of the unconscious	75
4 The making of an overman: The superman and superwoman in modernist literature	95
5 The other East: The *Philosophia Perennis* and the modern pilgrim	127
Conclusion	155
Bibliography	161
Index	175

Acknowledgements

This book first began to take serious shape while teaching a module called 'Magic, Mysticism, and Modernity' at the University of Surrey, and I am indebted and deeply grateful to all of my students who are and will always be endlessly inspiring. I am also particularly thankful to the librarians and archivists at Senate House Library, the Museum of Freemasonry, the Warburg Institute and Gladstone's Library where much of this work was written.

An early version of material which now appears in the introduction and conclusion was previously published in '[God] Is a Flaming Hebrew Letter: Esoteric Camp in *Angels in America*', *Literature and Theology*, Vol. 33, No. 2 (2019), pp. 206–22. Reprinted by permission of Oxford University Press.

A portion of Chapter 4 was previously published as 'Bernard Shaw's Gnostic Genius', *Shaw*, Vol. 41, No. 1 (2021), pp. 35–49. Copyright © 2021 Allan Kilner-Johnson. This article is used by permission of The Pennsylvania State University Press.

Introduction

During the penultimate year of the First World War – against the backdrop of the Battle of Passchendaele, the abdication of Tsar Nicholas II and Woodrow Wilson's declaration of war on Germany – a whimsical and now largely forgotten play by J. M. Barrie premiered at Wyndam's Theatre, then under the management of West End impresarios Frank Curzon and Gerald du Maurier. The curiously named *Dear Brutus* (1917) takes place in a simpler time and place, on midsummer's eve at a remote country house around which a 'strange wood' appears once every year.[1] For the eight guests who have been invited by the estate's mysterious owner, the enchanted forest offers an opportunity to right their ways and to return to a world of their own design. In this respect, the echo of *A Midsummer Night's Dream* (1596) is unmistakable, but the central thematic trajectory of Barrie's play is perhaps even more pointedly rooted in *Julius Caesar* (1599), where Cassius hauntingly remarks to his co-conspirator, 'The fault, dear Brutus, is not in our stars, / But in ourselves, that we are underlings.'[2] At this early point in Shakespeare's play, Cassius imagines that his steadfast rationality elevates him above Caesar, a dangerous error which initiates his downfall and ultimately irreversibly compels his belief in omens and fate. Barrie's *Dear Brutus* similarly captures its characters' conversion from a rational to an enchanted world view (here as a redemptive rather than punitive gesture) suggesting that the dissatisfaction and embitterment they experience can be successfully resolved by a return to the enchanted Neverland of pastoral magic that the modern world had otherwise apparently destroyed.

This was undoubtedly a resonant premise at a time when the devastating events of the Western Front had exhausted confidence in both humanity and

---

[1] J. M. Barrie, *Dear Brutus* (1917; repr. London: Oberon Modern Plays, 2017), p. 14.
[2] William Shakespeare, *Julius Caesar* (1599; repr. London: Penguin, 2015), I.ii.147–8.

the divine. Shortly before *Dear Brutus* premiered to encouraging notices, the first amusing photographs of the Cottingley Fairies were produced, Guillaume Apollinaire coined the term 'surrealism' to label what he described as 'a whole series of manifestations of the New Spirit that is making itself felt today and that will certainly appeal to our best minds',[3] and the occultist Aleister Crowley was at work in America on his notorious novel *Moonchild* (1917). The year was marked by fresh accounts of magical thinking, but, elsewhere, the German sociologist Max Weber had begun to sense, as he memorably explained in his 1917 lecture 'Science and Vocation', that 'the fate of our times is characterized by rationalization and intellectualization and, above all, by the "disenchantment of the world"'.[4] Weber believed that the project of modernity had been initiated by and continued to unfold through the repudiation not merely of enchantment and the divine but through a turn from the Idealism which had once allowed form to the numinous. By the late nineteenth century, the hierarchies of the past were being systematically dismantled by novel world views proposed by Charles Darwin, Karl Marx, Friedrich Nietzsche and Sigmund Freud whose ideas would give rise to a modernity defined by, to use the words of György Lukács, 'the lack of a consistent view of human nature [in which] man is reduced to a sequence of unrelated experiential fragments'.[5] Modernity is best understood as the culmination of several pivotal momentums (e.g. capitalism, liberalism, urbanization, industrialization, Westernization), all of which sought to erase the boundaries of the individual and of small kinship networks in order to move onward to a more rational and seemingly better future. The challenge presented by these developments was the compulsory faith in the teleological progression of Western history which dictated that 'modernity' was new, different and presumably superior even while the world itself seemed, at least from 1914 onwards, to have been fractured into a series of meaningless fragments. While the apparent problems of modernity had in most cases begun some time earlier, it was modernity (and, specifically, modernity as exemplified by the mechanically induced traumas of the First World War) that took the blame. So influential was Weber's argument that Jürgen Habermas opens *The Philosophical Discourse of Modernity* (1985) with an appraisal of Weber's depiction of 'not only

---

[3] Guillaume Apollinaire, 'Programme for *Parade*, 18 May 1917', in *Modernism: An Anthology of Sources and Documents*, ed. Vassiliki Kolocotroni, Jane Goldman and Olga Taxidou (Chicago: University of Chicago Press, 1998), pp. 212–13 (p. 213).
[4] Max Weber, 'Science as a Vocation', in *From Max Weber: Essays in Sociology*, trans. H. H. Gerth and C. Wright Mills (1917; repr. Oxford: Oxford University Press, 1946), p. 155.
[5] György Lukács, 'The Ideology of Modernism', in *The Meaning of Contemporary Realism*, trans. John Mander and Necke Mander (London: Merlin Press, 1963), p. 26.

the secularization of Western *culture*, but also and especially the development of modern *societies* from the viewpoint of rationalization', a key critical position in Habermas's approach to the affordances of the public sphere.[6] Weber was not merely signalling a modernity marked by a retreat from the mystical and sacred but disclosing a systemic hermeneutics of modern suspicion that would progressively and unmistakably emerge in the work of later thinkers.

The Sacred Life of Modernist Literature probes the relationship between modernist literary experimentation and several key strands of occult practice which emerged in Europe from roughly 1894 to 1944. Although the early decades of the twentieth century – the era of cocktails, motor cars, bobbed hair and war – are often described as a period of newness and innovation, many writers of the time found inspiration and visionary brilliance by turning to the mysterious occult past. Well-remembered poets and novelists such as Ezra Pound, W. B. Yeats and Aleister Crowley were tied to occult beliefs, and this book sets these leading figures alongside less well-remembered but equally splendid modernists including Paul Brunton, Mary Butts, Alexandra David-Neel, Florence Farr, Dion Fortune, Hermann Hesse, Somerset Maugham, Bernard Shaw and Rudolf Steiner. Many of these authors are customarily seen to fall outside of the remit of modernist studies. Brunton, David-Neel, Farr, Fortune, Hesse, Maugham, Shaw and Steiner were all undoubtedly products of modernity, but this book aims to demonstrate how their distinctive correlation to occult philosophy and practice brings their textual output unquestionably in line with literary modernism's formal elevation of association, circularity, irreverence and radical subjectivity. The American, Asian and European influences on British occultism have for many years been clear. While the focus of this book is principally British literary culture, it draws into consideration a range of European authors whose impact upon British modernism is evident, without contriving to capture the full cultural and aesthetic range of multiple global modernisms. Occultism was the peculiar yet natural home of a shiftless avant-garde whose aesthetic incitements served as the lasting symbol of the early twentieth century, and *The Sacred Life of Modernist Literature* is premised on the recognition that occultism during the modern period was not a countercultural agitation but the territory of the middle-class intelligentsia, the genteel social reformers and the novelists, poets and playwrights whose work captured a starkly transitional moment. This book makes no attempt to present the historical developments of occult belief

---

[6] Jürgen Habermas, *The Philosophical Discourse of Modernity*, trans. Frederick Lawrence (Cambridge: Polity, 1987), p. 1.

through the methods of the historian, sociologist or theologian, but, instead, to reorientate literary modernism around the occult by bringing the methods and paratexts of modernist studies to bear on the study of occultism, embodying Douglas Mao and Rebecca L. Walkowitz's influential recognition that the 'new modernist studies' is necessarily rooted in methodological expansion.[7] More consequentially, new modernist studies resists the central defining narratives of 'high modernism' and the 'men of 1914' to return attention to the multiplicity of experiences and expressions of those writers falling outside the tightly delineated sphere of white, male, Anglo-American modernism. This book aims to provide further evidence in support of Alex Owen's vital recognition that occultism 'must be understood as integral to the shaping of the new at the turn of the century'[8] by turning to formal features of narrative and style which emerged in the literature of the period. My intended purpose, then, is to examine the historical, textual, political and theoretical underpinning of these writers' works as a means to reflect on how the texts are both a product of their specific occult context and also an historical record of that moment – that is, how writing simultaneously shapes and is shaped by history – and demonstrate how a persistent interest in the occult led to new understandings of the relationship between 'the self' and 'society' during the early twentieth century.

In recent years, the most obvious instances of modernist occultism (most notably Yeats's commitment to what he described as 'the practice and philosophy of what we have agreed to call magic'[9]) have been commonly remarked upon.[10] Previous work on modernism and the occult has, with few exceptions, centred on a conventional male Irish and Anglo-American narrative of W. B. Yeats, Ezra Pound and T. S. Eliot as the tripartite nucleus which enabled and nourished a wider ecosystem of modernist innovation. This has provided an especially convenient approach for scholars of modernist occultism in that these three major figures were each invested at one point or another (and to varying degrees) in occult philosophy. However, there remains the opportunity to examine the lost and forgotten voices of literary modernism and to demonstrate that, beyond simply the attentiveness of canonical modernists to occultism, a significant

---

[7] Douglas Mao and Rebecca L. Walkowitz, 'The New Modernist Studies', *PMLA*, 123.3 (2008), 737–48.
[8] Alex Owen, *The Place of Enchantment: British Occultism and the Culture of the Modern* (London: University of Chicago Press, 2004), p. 15.
[9] W. B. Yeats, 'Magic', in *The Major Works*, ed. Edward Larrissy (Oxford: Oxford University Press, 2001), pp. 344–9 (p. 344).
[10] See, in particular, Leon Surette, *The Birth of Modernism: Ezra Pound, T. S. Eliot, W. B. Yeats, and the Occult* (Montreal: McGill-Queen's University Press, 1993); Timothy Materer, *Modernist Alchemy: Poetry and the Occult* (Ithaca, NY: Cornell University Press, 1995).

strand of less well-remembered modernists complete the picture of a mode which laments the narrowness of consciousness, celebrates gnostic creative insight and imagines the immanence of the sacred. One of this book's principle interventions is to reimagine the contours and boundaries of literary modernism by welcoming into the conversation a number of significant female writers and writers in languages other than English who are often still relegated to the fringes of modernist studies. Returning these less well-remembered modernists to the conversation establishes that the influences of occultism on modernism are both wider and deeper than customarily believed. More crucially, the chapters which follow underline the significant correlation between occult attitudes and many of the key technical innovations of literary modernism: elision as expression, intensification of image, syntactic chaos, fusion of form and substance and a retreat from the textual surface towards the unconscious vagaries of human expression. During the modernist period, the painful absence of a culturally shared spiritual altar remained acutely felt, and a return to magical ways of thinking – to the promise of an enchanted midsummer's eve, a photograph of a fairy or the artistic 'manifestations of the New Spirit'[11] – both stirred and subsequently captured many of the most significant aesthetic and thematic expressions of literary modernism. By uncovering hidden hopes and anxieties that faced a newly modern Western Europe, I demonstrate how literary modernists understood occultism as a universal form of cultural expression which has inspired creative exuberance since the dawn of civilization.

In *Modernity at Large* (1996), Arjun Appadurai recognized that 'one of the most problematic legacies of grand Western social science (Auguste Comte, Karl Marx, Ferdinand Toennies, Max Weber, Emile Durkheim) is that it has steadily reinforced the sense of some single moment – call it the modern moment – that by its appearance creates a dramatic and unprecedented break between past and present'.[12] However, the work of many modern philosophers including Henri Bergson, Martin Heidegger and Ludwig Wittgenstein, among others, found its substance in the mystical apophatic theology of the early middle ages and offers just one of many possible reminders that the sacred was always curiously close to the heart of modern thought. Olav Hammer explains that

> there is a common tendency, probably inherited from the Enlightenment and strengthened in the early days of anthropology, to adopt an exclusivist and

---

[11] Apollinaire, pp. 212–13 (p. 213).
[12] Arjun Appadurai, *Modernity at Large: Cultural Dimensions of Globalization* (London: University of Minnesota Press, 1996), pp. 2–3.

elitist view of Western intellectual development. According to this view, the development of science, of technology and of rationalist philosophies are part of a dynamic modernity, whereas folk religion in various guises, occult and esoteric currents, new religious movements and idealist beliefs from a kind of cultural *arriére-guarde*, stagnant survival of magical thinking or reflexes of pre-scientific speculation.[13]

While many since Weber have viewed mysticism and magic as curiosities which had largely fallen into obsolescence by the turn of the twentieth century, scholars in the twenty-first century have begun to more directly question the accuracy of Weber's *Entzauberung* thesis. In *The Many Altars of Modernity* (2014), Peter Berger argues that what Weber perceived as a rejection of faith was, in fact, 'pluralism, the co-existence of different worldviews and value systems in the same society [which] is *the* major change brought about by modernity for the place of religion both in the minds of individuals and in the institutional order'.[14] In Berger's late work, modernity is defined not by the emergence of disenchantment but by the 'huge transformation in the human condition from fate to choice', a transition in no way antithetical to the pre-eminence of faith and religious fervour in cultural expression.[15] Alex Owen is similarly distrustful of Weber's thesis and imagines instead 'a revisionist history of religion that questions the inevitability of religious decline and [which] is cognizant of diversity and change in the realm of human spirituality'.[16] The primary intervention of Owen's *The Place of Enchantment* (2004), then, is the recognition that 'the "new" occultism of the turn of the century muddies the contemporaneous picture formulated by James Frazer and the Victorian evolutionists of a straightforward magic-religion-science march of culture evolution'.[17] Ken Wilber, an astute yet underappreciated commentator on theology and the project of modernity, treads comparable terrain when he argues that the catalyst for modernity

> was the widespread emergence of Reason (formal operational), not just in a few individuals (which had often happened in the past), but as a basic organizing principle of society itself (which had never happened in the past) – a Reason that

---

[13] Olav Hammer, *Claiming Knowledge: Strategies of Epistemology from Theosophy to the New Age* (Leiden: Brill, 2001), p. xiv.
[14] Peter L. Berger, *The Many Altars of Modernity* (Berlin: De Gruyter, 2014), p. ix.
[15] Berger, p. 5.
[16] Owen, p. 11. Owen's seminal investigation of occultism during the two decades surrounding the turn of the twentieth century appeared before both Wouter J. Hanegraaff's *Hermes in the Academy* (2012) and Kocku von Stuckrad's *Western Esotericism* (2004; trans. 2014), defining texts in the contemporary study of Western esotericism.
[17] Owen, p. 8.

was in fact an actual ascending or transcending of myth, but a Reason that, fed up with a millennium of (frustrated) upward-looking, turned its eyes instead to the glories of this manifest world, and followed that descending God who finds its passion and delight – and its perfect consummation – in the marvels and the wonders of diversity.[18]

Less forgivingly, Michael Saler concludes that the modern retreat from enchanted epistemologies was the product of conspiratorial historians whose rationalist interpretations of modernity serve as prescriptive rather than descriptive accounts of a wide-scale rejection of the magical and divine that had never occurred.[19] It is true that Nietzsche's storied proclamation that 'God is dead' crystallized a growing sense, shared by numerous post-Enlightenment philosophers including Hegel and Schelling, that the relationship between humanity and the divine had been irrevocably transformed.[20] However, the premise of (to return to Wilber's phrase) a 'descending God' consummated by pluralism and diversity by no means precludes the theothanatology of Nietzsche and Weber: the god who had been erased by the Reason of modernity, Berger and Wilber argue, was the patrimonial god of social power, not the many gods of personal devotion and faith. On this point, Carl Jung explained in his epic work of mystical revelation *The Red Book* (1915–30) that 'the other Gods died of their temporality, yet the supreme meaning never dies, it turns into meaning and then into absurdity, and out of the fire and blood of their collision the supreme meaning rises up rejuvenated anew'.[21] Modernity may indeed have predisposed society to value the tangible rather than the elusive; however, modernism, the imaginative and productive manifestation of the social revolution of modernity, was set not on rejecting the sacred but on embodying it in textual form and manifesting the divine.

Although this book's subject is literature and its methods textual, further comment on the theological and philosophical contextualizations of occultism is required before moving forward. The academic study of Western esotericism examines a body of philosophical, mystical and imaginative attitudes originating in late antiquity and stretching to the present which conceal bodies of 'rejected knowledge', the scorned and often subversive ways of thinking

---

[18] Ken Wilber, *Sex, Ecology, Spirituality: The Spirit of Evolution* (London: Shambhala, 1995), p. 370.
[19] Michael Saler, 'Modernity and Enchantment: A Historiographic Review', *American Historical Review*, 111.3 (2006), 692–716.
[20] Friedrich Nietzsche, *The Gay Science*, trans. Walter Kaufmann (1882; repr. New York: Random House, 1974), p. 343.
[21] Carl Jung, *The Red Book: A Reader's Edition*, ed. Sonu Shamdasani, trans. Mark Kyburz, John Peck and Sonu Shamdasani (London: W. W. Norton, 2009), p. 120.

that prevailing cultural forces pushed to the boundaries of respectability. As Wouter Hanegraaff explains, the 'post-Enlightenment tendency of conflating all terms and categories that were seen as contrary to "science and rationality" into one diffuse counter-category had a paradoxical result: it made the domain very hard to pin down because no single term seemed to cover the whole'.[22] The influence of writers including Porphyry, Plotinus, Meister Eckhart, Marsilio Ficino, Giordano Bruno, Paracelsus, Jacob Boehme and Emanuel Swedenborg, among others, persisted well beyond the eighteenth-century's drive towards scientific rationalism and would, in many cases, directly stimulate developments in science, medicine, law, language and the arts that continue to shape our lives in the twenty-first century, even though they were obstructed by ecclesiastical or civil authority and thus relegated to the fringes. The serious contemporary academic approach to this body of material emerged in the wake of the 1960s counterculture with Frances Yates, whose *Giordano Bruno and the Hermetic Tradition* (1964) made the bold but unimpeachable argument that the Hermeticism of late antiquity was foundational to Bruno's thinking and, crucially, was more widespread and accepted in Renaissance intellectual culture than had previously been acknowledged. Marsilio Ficino's 1471 translation of the *Corpus Hermeticum* (a likely second century CE work of mystical insight attributed to the fictional sage Hermes Trismegistus) led to a significant revival of magical ways of thinking in Renaissance Europe, and, as Hanegraaff recognizes, 'Yates' paradoxical interpretation of magic as a force of progress added a touch of genius. It suggested that the hermeticists and defenders of magic had not been locked in the mentality of a superstitious past but had been the real champions of progress all along!'[23] During the 1990s, the Hermetic traditions examined by Yates and her followers were further cultivated by French historian Antoine Faivre who codified 'a diverse group of works, currents, etc., which possess an *air de famille* and which must be studied as part of the history of religions because of the specific form which it has acquired in the West since the Renaissance'. Writing in 1995, Faivre and Karen-Claire Voss included under the rubric of 'Western esotericism': 'alchemy; the *philosophia occulta*; Christian Kabbalah; *Naturaphilosophie* (i.e. Paracelsism and what follows in its wake); theosophy (i.e. Jacob Boehme and his followers); Rosicrucianism (and the various branches of initiatic societies which appeared subsequently); and

---

[22] Wouter J. Hanegraaff, *Esotericism and the Academy: Rejected Knowledge in Western Culture* (Cambridge: Cambridge University Press, 2012), pp. 278–9.
[23] Wouter J. Hanegraaff, 'Beyond the Yates Paradigm: The Study of Western Esotericism between Counterculture and New Complexity', *Aries*, 1.1 (2001), 5–37 (p. 19).

Hermetism (i.e. the reception and influence during the modern period of the writings attributed to the mythical Hermes Trismegistus).[24]

My own approach in the following chapters prefers the term 'occult' over 'Western esotericism' and, thus, defines these diverse devotional practices and philosophical principles by their aestheticized use rather than by their social reception. More specifically, in the context of the literary materials that provide the subject and focus of this book, I take occultism as the hidden or secret (viz. *occultus, occulere*) undertakings whose aims are to realize a form of embodied knowledge, including the intermingling and, at times, competing occult philosophies that offered explication of the relationship between humanity and the divine (e.g. Hermeticism, Neoplatonism and Kabbalah) as well as the actions that might be used seek confirmation of or ascension to a divine state (e.g. ritual, evocation, divination, astrology and alchemy).[25] John Bramble echoes Hanegraaff in defining the 'occult' as 'irregular/heterodox knowledge' and reads the occult practice emerging during and continuing beyond the late-nineteenth-century occult revival as indicative of a particular engagement with the aftershocks of the high imperial and its reconceptualization of 'self' and 'other'.[26] To describe something as 'occult', as Christine Ferguson points out, is 'not a neutral or innocent act',[27] and, indeed, the argument proposed in the following chapters is that the incursion of occult philosophy and practice in modernist writing signals a marked return to an aestheticized godhead whose immanence could be confirmed by the collaborative and productive forms of textual knowledge propagated by modernist experimentation.

Many excellent histories have been written on the interpenetrating occult milieux of the late nineteenth and early twentieth centuries, and in recent decades scholars have been able to reconstruct detailed understandings of the inner workings of organizations once closed off to the eyes of the uninitiated: the Hermetic Order of the Golden Dawn, the Theosophical Society, the Anthroposophical Society, the Quest Society, the Stella Matutina, the Fellowship of the Rosy Cross, the Fraternity of the Inner Light, the Ordo Templi Orientis, the Argenteum Astrum and the Institute for the Harmonious

---

[24] Antoine Faivre and Karen-Claire Voss, 'Western Esotericism and the Science of Religions', *Numen*, 42.1 (1995), 48–77 (p. 49).
[25] On definitions of the occult, see also Wouter J. Hanegraaff, et al., eds, *Dictionary of Gnosis and Western Esotericism* (Amsterdam: Brill, 2006), pp. 884–9.
[26] John Bramble, *Modernism and the Occult* (Basingstoke: Palgrave Macmillan, 2015), p. 1.
[27] Christine Ferguson, 'Introduction', in *The Occult Imagination in Britain, 1875–1947*, ed. Christine Ferguson and Andrew Radford (Abingdon: Routledge, 2018), pp. 1–20 (p. 2).

Development of Man.[28] These occult societies offered their members a number of valuable assurances. While the promise of obtaining occult knowledge was the stated cause, such groups equally offered opportunities for social mobility, leadership roles for women, spiritual practice outside the confines of orthodoxy, access to immense stores of mythological and symbolic imagery, extensive training in mental clarity and focus and the promise of an enticing communitarian approach to art and life. The esoteric traditions standing behind the exoteric practices of the great world traditions were long jealously guarded and almost always excluded women, the poor, the illiterate and any other class of society deemed at the time to be unfit for learning; however, the new organizations of the late Victorian 'occult revival' were, at least in principle, open to all. The Hermetic Order of the Golden Dawn and the Theosophical Society were the most lastingly significant of these organizations and proposed spiritual systems so brazenly protracted that the potential for gaining new knowledge seemed almost unlimited, from the mannerly performance of the Golden Dawn's first-degree initiation ceremony to the divisive trappings of the Esoteric Section of the Theosophical Society.[29] Although both organizations were in significant decline during the early years of the twentieth century (the former had fallen into several fractious splinters by the turn of the century and the latter had been drawn into a series of notorious scandals which tarnished its reputation), they provided the form and substance of many of the most suggestive modernist literary treatments of magical ways of knowing. And it is within these contexts that the world of modernist literature comes most directly and unmistakably into contact with occultism, and where the *compulsory transcendence of god* which has defined much of modern Western history is exchanged for a *radical immanence of divinity* which runs precisely counter to the orthodox theologies of the three Near Eastern monotheistic religions: Judaism, Christianity and Islam.

---

[28] Antoine Faivre, *Western Esotericism: A Concise History*, trans. Christine Rhone (Albany: State University of New York Press, 2010); R. A. Gilbert, *The Golden Dawn Scrapbook: The Rise and Fall of a Magical Order* (York Beach, ME: Samuel Weiser, 1997); Mary K. Greer, *Women of the Golden Dawn: Rebels and Priestesses* (Rochester, VT: Inner Traditions, 1995); Wouter J. Hanegraaf, *Western Esotericism: A Guide for the Perplexed* (London: Bloomsbury, 2013); Ellic Howe, *The Magicians of the Golden Dawn: A Documentary History of a Magical Order, 1887–1923* (York Beach, ME: Samuel Weiser, 1972); Ronald Hutton, *The Triumph of the Moon: A History of Modern Pagan Witchcraft* (Oxford: Oxford University Press, 1999); Owen, *The Place of Enchantment*; Colin Wilson, *The Occult* (1979; repr. London: Watkins, 2003).

[29] The Esoteric Section of the Theosophical Society included among its members William Wynn Westcott, G. R. S. Mead and Rudolf Steiner who would each later go on to found their own widely influential esoteric societies. See Gregory Tillet, 'Modern Western Magic and Theosophy', *Aries*, 12.1 (2012), 17–51 (pp. 20–5).

Literary modernism refers to three interpenetrating strands that gave rise to a distinctive and self-reflexively new literary expression: (1) a historical period covering roughly the first half of the twentieth century which saw war and the loosening of pre-existing forms of social organization through, for example, suffrage, the rise of mass culture and a reimagined international landscape; (2) an aesthetic style which represented a self-conscious repudiation of Victorian form in order to draw attention to human consciousness as captured in a variety of radical techniques including fragmentation, stream of consciousness and the mythic model; and (3) a sociopolitical programme which gave form and purpose to social liberalism, women's growing roles in society and the frank portrayal of sexuality and the body. The aim of the modernists, perhaps more than writers of any prior period, was to capture what their own time meant, what it felt like and what new future might emerge from its depths. While the role of 'modernist zero' has been assigned to figures as diverse as Nietzsche, Wagner, Strindberg, Ibsen and Shaw, Michael Levenson recognizes that 'the emergence of Modernism was not just the result of provoking artifacts and not just a succession of individual careers. Neither a collection of forms and styles nor an array of geniuses, Modernism was a heterogeneous episode in the history of culture.'[30] Together, these heterogenous strands brought about a mode of textual practice which demonstrated thematic and structural interest in the fragmentation of time and identity, a seemingly counterintuitive return to the mythos of the past, an engagement (at times positive and at others downright derogatory) with popular mass culture and a 'modern' attentiveness to new cultural focuses such as technology, feminism and psychoanalysis, oftentimes as an attempt to make order out of chaos. Nothing unimportant is worth knowing, modernism tells us.

In 2013, Hanegraaff pointed out that 'there have been almost no systematic attempts yet to investigate [the esoteric dimensions] for the domain of literature', perhaps gesturing towards an acknowledgement that the methods of literary scholarship do not reveal or provide answers to the most interesting questions raised by esoteric practices and their relationship to language and literary form.[31] Published twenty years before Hanegraaff's reflection on the dearth of work on literature and the occult, Leon Surette's *The Birth of Modernism: Ezra Pound,*

---

[30] Michael Levenson, *Modernism* (London: Yale University Press, 2011), p. 8.
[31] Wouter J. Hanegraaff, *Western Esotericism: A Guide for the Perplexed* (London: Bloomsbury, 2013), p. 149. Elsewhere, Hanegraaff defines the five disciplines in which scholars of Western esotericism usually operate: '(1) historians of science and philosophy, (2) generalists in the humanities, (3) countercultural-religionists, (4) esoteric universalists, and (5) specialists of specific subjects and currents'. Hanegraaff, 'Beyond the Yates Paradigm', pp. 5–37 (p. 24).

T.S. Eliot, W.B. Yeats, and the Occult (1993) was the first major attempt to undercut the prevailing notion that literary modernism was a style and sympathy defined firstly, and perhaps only, by a turn to scientific materialism. Concerned that the occult influences on modernist poetics had been unfairly dismissed by critics as forms of eccentric contamination, Surette returned attention to the significance of what he calls the 'inward gaze' which united outré modernist developments in poetry and occult practice.[32] Gauri Viswanathan describes literary studies' general disregard of the occult as 'partly due to literature's self-definition as a secular vehicle for ideas whose possible religious origins were subsequently effaced as religious sensibility became absorbed into aesthetic form and imagery, especially in modernist writing'.[33] On this point, Surette would undoubtedly agree. He indicates that the 'scholarly phobia of the occult' has produced an academic narrative of literary modernism as a movement of 'sceptical relativists', even while many of its most lastingly influential figures such as Pound, Eliot and Yeats were intellectually (and at time, practically) attracted to occult belief and practices.[34] In doing so, he becomes occupied in a re-examination of the accepted critical position that 'the mythological and Eleusinian elements' of work by, in particular, Eliot and Pound were 'factitious formal and thematic devices' that were rooted in the mythologizing tendencies of literary modernism; in this view, occult beliefs could be acknowledged but then swiftly transmuted into an idiosyncratic aesthetic philosophy easily reasoned away into fairly minor relevance.[35] Such a position continues to be widespread in the twenty-first century: Katherine Ebury reads Yeats's writing and, particularly, the existential model of time as represented by the symbol of the gyre in *A Vision* as symptomatic of key scientific discoveries of the time, and Sinéad Garrigan Mattar similarly reads Yeats's occult beliefs are correlated to contemporaneous developments in science and anthropology.[36] Richard Ellman's pivotal biography of Yeats was willing to admit to the poet's occult influences but, without a clear knowledge of the practices and rituals of the Golden Dawn, was forced to stop short of presenting a comprehensive account of how the philosophical and

---

[32] Surette, p. 85.
[33] Gauri Viswanathan, 'Secularism in the Framework of Heterodoxy', *PMLA*, 123.2 (2008), 466–76 (p. 466).
[34] Surette, p. 161.
[35] Surette, p. ix.
[36] Katherine Ebury, '"A New Science": Yeats's *A Vision* and Relativistic Cosmology', *Irish Studies Review*, 22.2 (2014), 167–83 (p. 168); Sinéad Garrigan Mattar, 'Yeats, Fairies, and the New Animism', *New Literary History*, 43 (2012), 137–57 (p. 146).

spiritual structures of modern Hermeticism found weight and expressive form in Yeats's verse.

For Surette, the term 'occult' provides 'a strong term instead of more honorific terms such as the "wisdom tradition," "Platonism," "symbolism," or even "the literary tradition" – or, simply, and more obscurely, "the tradition"'.[37] This implicit mapping of an inherited literary 'tradition' on to an expansive Western history of occult philosophy, even if only 'obscurely', leads Surette into a revealing claim:

> Occultism draws into itself texts and ideas that have a very long history in Western literary culture. The occultists include in their canon not only the *Corpus Hermeticum* and the works of Paracelsus and Swedenborg, but also the works of Plato, Plotinus, Iamblichus, Dante, Blake, Shelley, and Balzac … Occultism sees itself as the heir of an ancient wisdom – either passed on from adept or rediscovered in each new generation by mystical illumination. This self-perception generates a bookishness within the occult that brings it into contact with imaginative literature and authors at many points.[38]

Surette understands occultism largely as a philosophical perspective largely without practical application; however, he does further indicate that 'the occult can hardly be adequately characterized by theological and philosophical positions. It is much less coherent and perhaps more interesting than that'.[39] Surette does not thus merely contend that occultism is definable by its connection to literature but, rather, that literature and its attendant thematic manoeuvres are an essential component of the historical developments of occultism. But his argument is concerned primarily with the Hellenic inheritances of occultism, and he only partially correctly positions the ceremonial magic of the Hermetic Order of the Golden Dawn as a conceptual inheritance from the mystery traditions of Eleusis and Mithras. This contributes to a conflation of Western historical tradition with occultism and a proposal that the link between modernism and occultism is a shared 'interest in philosophy of history, in secret history, and in the history of religion and mythology'.[40] A decisive paradox emerges from drawing together occult philosophy and literary tradition in this way. The history of the occult is predicated on an enticing nostalgia which emerges as either the reification of a pre-modern 'golden age' in which humanity presumably existed in close communion with the divine or, alternatively, the

---

[37] Surette, p. 5.
[38] Surette, p. 7.
[39] Surette, p. 13.
[40] Surette, p. 23.

longing observance of an increasingly distant time in which this lost treasure of a *priscia theologia* had been reclaimed by a messianic figure able to draw down substantial prophetic insight. 'To be "modern" is not just to be postclassical, still less just to be up to date', Surette later continues, 'To be "modern" in the modernist sense is to have transcended history, to have climbed out of history into an unmediated, incorrigible realm of knowledge, and in that sense to have fulfilled history.'[41] Referring originally to the desire for a lost homeland, the term 'nostalgia' speaks to the recurrent human fascination with belatedness and a sense of having come too late. Svetlana Boym connects this belatedness to a new force of wide-scale nostalgia with both a change in space and a changed understanding of how time articulates our space: 'The nostalgic is looking for a spiritual addressee. Encountering silence, he looks for memorable signs, desperately misreading them.'[42] Surette contends,

> Modernism presented itself as the end, the conclusion – even the fulfilment – of history and therefore as the end of historical writing. It would be difficult to find any modernism flatly expressing such a claim, but the claim is implicit in the *echt* modernist principle of the autonomy of the work of art, which has been deployed within literary scholarship to liberate the work of art from the tyranny of authorial intention and hence from the cult of personality.[43]

'Modernism may have disappeared as a living cultural force', Levenson more recently argued, 'but it maintains its provocation for all who try to understand it. To live within our own modernity is to be anxious about our place in time, the future of culture, and the fate of the changes that the modernists sought to achieve.'[44] To give just one example, it seems clear that the question of what was timeless and what was merely fashionable was at the heart of Yeats's work. His primary focus on Irish nationalism as contained within the shared Celtic experience of Ireland is expressed as early as 'The Wanderings of Oisin' (1889), 'an early testament to Yeats's lifelong struggle to unite his private feelings and esoteric studies with his public role as a mouthpiece for the Irish nation and its cultural tradition'.[45] Throughout his early- and middle-period work, Yeats regularly returned to iconic heroes as saviours for modern Ireland. *The Countess Cathleen* and *Cathleen ni Houlihan* both deal with two ways in which women

---

[41] Surette, p. 4.
[42] Svetlana Boym, *The Future of Nostalgia* (New York: Basic, 2001), p. 8.
[43] Surette, p. 3.
[44] Levenson, p. 1.
[45] Daniel Gomes, 'Reviving Oisin: Yeats and the Conflicted Appeal of Irish Mythology', *Texas Studies in Literature & Language*, 56 (2014), 376–99 (p. 377).

contribute to the progress of society – one is a landowner and the other a peasant – and as Alison Harvey points out in regard to *Cathleen ni Houlihan*, 'National destiny, the play suggests, does not happen where these women are. For the nation, life is elsewhere, in the offstage Celtic twilight, and not in the real space of the home, now broken apart by male devotion to the republican cause.'[46] Yeats was far less concerned with the self-conscious process of modernizing verse (a task more important to Pound and Eliot) and far more interested in the capacity for verse to restore the past.

How does one square this nostalgic tendency with modernism's self-conscious efforts towards newness, innovation and radical social change? The resolution unexpectedly comes from the nostalgia inherent in modernism itself. 'Any distinguishing mark of Modernism', Levenson writes, 'any signs or signature, such as discontinuity, collage, literary self-consciousness, irony, the use of myth, can be traced back to the furthest temporal horizon. To try to identify an elusive beginning or to propose clinching definitions is to play a game with changing rules.'[47] Pericles Lewis points out in *Religious Experience and the Modernist Novel* (2010) that 'modernist novelists frequently imagined their own work as competing with churches in terms of spiritual beauty and emotional power'.[48] More recently, Matthew Mutter's *Restless Secularism* (2017) demonstrates that even among the most apparently secular modernists survived a clear attentiveness to faith traditions, while Eric Tonning's *Modernism and Christianity* (2014) exposes the unexpected emergence of faith in a period of literature that is alternatively remembered for either its stark agnosticism or renewed spiritual fervour. In *Blasphemous Modernism* (2017) Steve Pinkerton defines the sacred as a constituent counter to blasphemy, suggesting that the notion of the sacred is always explicitly tied to the particular features of sacred theological practice which can be profaned. For the often overtly blasphemous modernists, then, reaffirmation of the sacred became a counterintuitively common upshot to a disaffected and disenchanted treatment of modern life:

> [modernist writers] continued to seek in scripture and theology the particular sources of meaning, affect, and literary force that only religion seemed fully capable of providing. With redoubled vigor, they wove the themes and rhetorics of religious tradition into the fabrics of their often highly irreverent poems and

---

[46] Alison Harvey, 'Irish Aestheticism in Fin-de-Siècle Women's Writing: Art, Realism, and the Nation', *Modernism/Modernity*, 21.3 (2014), 805–26 (p. 807).
[47] Levenson, p. 1.
[48] Pericles Lewis, *Religious Experience and the Modernist Novel* (Cambridge: Cambridge University Press, 2010), pp. 1, 5.

fictions, where God endures as a potent object of imaginative appropriate and profanation. For the work of blasphemous modernism, that is, God remains very much alive.[49]

Echoing the sentiment and systematizing aim of T. S. Eliot's Page-Barbour lectures delivered at the University of Virginia in 1933 and collected after as *After Strange Gods* (1934), Pinkerton recognizes that, while the blasphemous always contains within it the suppressed form of the sacred, the sacred must simultaneously deny its own form as a nascent blaspheme. Eliot's consternation in *After Strange Gods* emerged from a recognition of the chaos that ensues when a self-regulating tradition of sacred belief comes in contact with another (and he is predictably quite content to conclude that Christianity is the most reliable of such traditions). However, the issue more pressing to Pinkerton is what happens when modernism is read outside of the centring force of Christianity and surveyed in the context of the broadening social context of modern life – the birth of modernity, after all, does not hinge on the disenchantment of the world but on the disorienting rapidization of heterodox spiritual exchange. Such a question is vital to any approach to the anarchic themes and forms of literary modernism, and the remainder of this introduction will be concerned with its answer.

Like Surette, Helen Sword notices a crucial affiliation between authorship and occult practices which sought or claimed to achieve a numinous wisdom. In her *Ghostwriting Modernism* (2002), modernism is broadly correlated to a spirt of change running roughly one hundred years from the 1860s to the 1960s, from the initial emergences of Spiritualism following the rise of the Fox sisters until the postmodern counterculture a century later that would see the occult and 'occulture' (to use Christopher Partridge's term) return to prominence. 'Writers of imaginative fiction and poetry', she explains, 'have always functioned as spirit mediums of a sort: giving voice and substance to literary characters we cannot see but nonetheless believe to be real; ventriloquizing for the dead; penning elegies and requiems that celebrate the human souls survival beyond death',[50] echoing Surette's earlier point that 'occultism needs a hermeneutic that will explain the general ignorance of an occult revelation contained in various well-known texts. … Much occult writing, then, tends to be very like literary criticism or philology.'[51]

---

[49] Steve Pinkerton, *Blasphemous Modernism: The 20th-Century Word Made Flesh* (Oxford: Oxford University Press, 2017), p. 2.
[50] Helen Sword, *Ghostwriting Modernism* (London: Cornell University Press, 2002), p. 8.
[51] Surette, p. 27.

Whereas Surette employed modernism to define occultism, Sword draws upon the practice of spiritualism to define modernism as, principally, a practice of authorship which enables opportunities for channelling the powers of a unified field and bringing this to bear on literary production. 'Not coincidentally', Sword later points out, 'many of the best-known female mediums of the modernist era came from literary backgrounds or undertook literary careers quite separate from their mediumistic vocations. ... In some cases, ghostwriting for the dead served as a logical extension of their own authorial talents; in others, no doubt, it served as a substitute.'[52] Pamela Thurschwell similarly takes a long nineteenth-century approach, centring her attention on the decades from 1880 to 1920. This leads to a focus on psychical research as metaphor for 'wider reconceptualizations of the borders of individual consciousness' and questions of 'what separates one mind from another and what separates the living from the dead'.[53] More recently, Leigh Wilson has pushed this conversation further to argue that the occult influences on modernist writers are neither eccentric embarrassments nor sterile philosophizing but critical elements in the conceptualization of literary production and dissemination. Wilson tracks two dominant threads in modern occultism – spiritualism and theosophy (both emblematic in this context of the wider discourses surrounding supersensible contact and a contemplative turn to practical comparative religion rather than, specifically, the Spiritualist movement or the precepts of the Theosophical Society) – which come together to be defined as 'a magic that fundamentally understood that the mimetic is able to produce, not just an inert copy, but an animated copy powerful enough to enact change in the original'.[54] Wilson demonstrates that the experimental forms of literary modernism were both dependent upon and dictated the need for a vision of a world which could be restructured through the opportunities afforded by occult philosophy and practice. In her reading, theosophy and spiritualism emerge as the predominate esoteric discourses of the modernist period because they 'resisted the transgressive associations of magic. Where they went instead, of course, is to science.'[55] In *Mythic Thinking in Twentieth-Century Britain* (2013), Matthew Sterenberg highlights the modernist return to a myth-making attitude which 'constituted a new mode of making meaning that appealed to the imagination by making the claim that myths

---

[52] Sword, pp. 13–14.
[53] Pamela Thurschwell, *Literature, Technology, and Magical Thinking, 1880–1920* (Cambridge: Cambridge University Press, 2001), p. 2.
[54] Leigh Wilson, *Modernism and Magic: Experiments with Spiritualism, Theosophy and the Occult* (Edinburgh: Edinburgh University Press, 2012), p. 1.
[55] Wilson, *Modernism and Magic*, p. 5.

communicate timeless truths that cannot be apprehended through reason or science'.⁵⁶ Christine Ferguson and Andrew Radford's recent edited collection *The Occult Imagination in Britain, 1875–1947* (2018) similarly positions occultism as a source of diffuse cultural and aesthetic interest and, although not ostensibly centred on the literary domain, includes chapters on the modernist occultists and writers Florence Farr and Dion Fortune. For Ferguson and Radford, the seven decades stretching from the founding of the Theosophical Society in 1875 to the death of Aleister Crowley in 1947 are 'a particularly fertile period of occult activity in Britain during which the influences, texts and legacies of the revival's early phase were being disseminated and put to new use within an expanding and fragmenting public sphere'.⁵⁷

'Modern occultism', Randall Styers piquantly concludes, 'demonstrates the deep level at which the "secular" and the "sacred," the "rational" and the "irrational," refuse separation'.⁵⁸ The modernist tradition of spiritual scholarship emerging from contributors to the famed Eranos conferences including Mircea Eliade, Carl Jung, Gershom Scholem and Henry Corbin returned legitimacy to the domain of symbol and myth, elaborate systems of meaning and belief which had been progressively equated with superstition. As Eliade maintains in *Patterns in Comparative Religion* (1958), 'a thing becomes sacred insofar as it embodies (that is, reveals) something other than itself'.⁵⁹ In his later *The Sacred and the Profane* (1959), Eliade expands on this point of sacred manifestation with the term 'hierophany': 'It is a fitting term, because it does not imply anything further; it expresses no more than is implicit in its etymological content, *i.e.*, that *something sacred shows itself to us.*'⁶⁰ The religionism of Eliade, Corbin and Scholem – that is 'the conviction that a universal, hidden, esoteric dimension of reality really does exist'⁶¹ – has fallen out of favour in contemporary religious studies, but the notion of an inner reality (and one, furthermore, which might reach towards inspiration beyond itself) remains a viable and at times necessary route into consideration of the formation of meaning in literary texts and in the act of readership. Hanegraaff points out that the scholars of the Eranos tradition

---

[56] Matthew Sterenberg, *Mythic Thinking in Twentieth-Century Britain: Meaning for Modernity* (London: Palgrave Macmillan, 2013), p. 3.
[57] Ferguson, pp. 1–20 (p. 2).
[58] Randall Styers, *Making Magic: Religion, Magic, and Science in the Modern World* (Oxford: Oxford University Press, 2004), p. 19.
[59] Mircea Eliade, *Patterns in Comparative Religion*, trans. Rosemary Sheed (Lincoln: University of Nebraska Press, 1996), p. 13.
[60] Mircea Eliade, *The Sacred and the Profane: The Nature of Religion*, trans. Willard R. Trask (New York: Harvest, 1959), p. 11.
[61] Hanegraaff, *Western Esotericism*, p. 11.

'were concerned about the necessarily antithetical relation between history and (metaphysical or esoteric) Truth. They understood that the relativism ingrained in strict historical thinking would ultimately undermine *any* belief in a deeper meaning or a more universal dimension of human life.'[62] Religionists such as these did not view occultism as a form of forbidden knowledge but evidence of supersensible qualities of intuition, connection and value-making that atrophied in humans during the few thousand years of civilization and the few hundred years of modernity.

The Swiss philosopher Jean Gebser, though largely underestimated today, provides a crucial point of reference in the development of twentieth-century immanentist philosophy. Partially echoing Weber's sense that modernity was defined by a self-conscious repudiation of enchantment and the sacred, Gebser's *The Ever-Present Origin* (1985) argues that human consciousness has developed through periods of radical transformation and upset, progressing through a series of structures of consciousness: (1) archaic, (2) magic, (3) mythical, (4) mental and (5) integral. It is a cultivation and extension of Frazer's magic/religion/science taxonomy, which had begun to look increasingly outmoded through the anthropological and sociological advances of the twentieth century. Wilber explicitly draws upon this framework to read the development of modernity along Gebserian lines: 'The first trend that defined modernity was "No more myth!" (and the Enlightenment philosophers would use exactly that phrase in describing their own endeavors). The Enlightenment mentality, with its rational demand for *evidence*, burst asunder the closed circle of the mythological world and deconstructed its culture worldspace in no uncertain terms.'[63] Recognizing an enticing correlation to Gebser's fellow countryman and contemporary Jean Piaget's theory of cognitive development, Wilber understands the macro-level developments articulated by Gebser as taking place simultaneously on the micro levels described by Piaget because, 'every child still has to negotiate the archaic worldview, then deconstruct that with the magical worldview, then deconstruct that with the rational (on the way to the transrational)'.[64] Wilber forcefully maintains that

> the evidence disclosed by rationality will indeed be able to outcontextualize, and thus outtrump, the evidence disclosed within the horizons and the structures of mythic awareness (just as mythic masterfully outtrumped and outcontextualized

---

[62] Hanegraaff, *Western Esotericism*, p. 121.
[63] Wilber, p. 371.
[64] Wilber, p. 251.

magic). It is not that a great and absolute truth overthrows a falsehood, so much as that a great truth supersedes a lesser truth (no epoch lives, or can live, simply on falsehoods). And this is what the Age of Enlightenment brought to bear upon the Age of Myth: a new horizon of evidence that outcontextualized the old.[65]

The evolvement of each individual, for Wilber, is equally the progress of all humanity, and the generative and adaptive powers of consciousness are presented as the actual source of the sacred, an innate core in each individual that is unshakable by even the rationalizing forces of modernity. As Thurschwell indicates, the flourishing of magical ways of thinking in the years surrounding the turn of the twentieth century 'inagurate[d] shifting models of the permeability and suggestibility of the individual's mind and body' which offers 'a powerful tool to expand the potential effects of consciousness and the possibilities for intimate ties and identifications'.[66] The project of modernity has, since its original formulations in the inquisitive rationalism of the eighteenth century, sought to undertake the extraordinary process of resituating the individual in the realm of the rapidly expanding world, often with an unerring recognition that portions of this rapidly expanding world remain always out of the grasp of humanity. Martin Heidegger's notion of *dasein* – the rootedness of humanity which implies both our mundane construction and our simultaneous experiential elaboration – finds its roots in the negative theology of the fourteenth-century Dominican mystic Meister Eckhart: as Terry Eagleton writes of this work, 'We emerge as subjects from inside a reality which we can never fully objectify, which encompasses both "subject" and "object", which is inexhaustible in its meanings and which constitutes us quite as much as we constitute it.'[67] Gilles Deleuze's body of work, in Peter Hallward's estimation, is fixated on the process of immanent creation and manifestation, which implies:

> (a) that all existent things or processes exist in just one way, as so many distinct acts of creation or so many individual *creatings*; (b) that these creatings are themselves aspects of a limitless and consequently singular creative power, a power that is most adequately expressed in the medium of pure thought; (c) that every creating gives rise to a derivative *creature* or created thing, whose own power or creativity is limited by its material organisation, its situation, its actual

---

[65] Wilber, p. 377.
[66] Thurschwell, pp. 2, 7.
[67] Terry Eagleton, *Literary Theory: An Introduction* (Oxford: Basil Blackwell, 1983), p. 62. See also John D. Caputo, *The Mystical Element in Heidegger's Thought* (New York: Fordham University Press, 1986); Catriona Hanley, *Being and God in Aristotle and Heidegger: The Role of Method in Thinking the Infinite* (Oxford: Rowman & Littlefield, 2000).

capacities and relations with other creatures, and so on; (d) that the main task facing any such create is to loosen and then dissolved these limitations in order to become a more adequate or immaterial vehicle for that virtual creating which alone individuates it.[68]

The embodiment of the divine, in spite of the pessimism and secularism of modernity, echoes the movements from a transcendental Enlightenment philosophy to an immanentist modern philosophy and ethics, which, as later chapters will show, serve as the instigating force of many of the key technical developments of literary modernism. Strangely yet unmistakably, occultism and literary modernism are united by a set of shared intentions: making order out of chaos; formulating change, growth and newness; fusing form and content; and intensifying mundane expression into a form of immanent contemplation.

In *The Occult* (1971), the novelist and popular philosopher Colin Wilson influentially wrote about what he describes as 'Faculty X', the 'sudden feeling of *meaning*, which human beings sometimes "pick up" accidentally, as your radio might pick up some unknown station'.[69] The ability to tune into this 'feeling of *meaning*' is 'the key to all poetic and mystical experience; when it awakens, life suddenly takes on a new poignant quality'.[70] Wilson stops just short of attributing any mystical power to this 'Faculty X' but recognizes its crucial contribution to literary art and creation: 'The poet is a man in whom Faculty X is naturally more developed than in most people. While most of us are ruthlessly "cutting out" whole areas of perception, thus impoverishing our mental lives, the poet retains the faculty to be suddenly delighted by the sheer *reality* of the world "out there."'[71] Aleister Crowley (on whom Wilson wrote a great deal) famously pronounced that 'Magick is the Science and Art of causing Change to occur in conformity with Will' – a definition which Dion Fortune was happy to accept with the addition of the phrase 'causing change of consciousness' – and even the most incredulous literary scholar would be inclined to accept that change in consciousness is both the subject and the upshot of much modernist writing.[72] It is a similar sentiment strikingly captured by Joseph Conrad in his comments on Henry James: 'All creative art is magic, is evocation of the unseen in forms persuasive, enlightening, familiar and surprising, for the edification of mankind,

---

[68] Peter Hallward, *Out of This World: Deleuze and the Philosophy of Creation* (London: Verso, 2006), p. 2.
[69] Wilson, *The Occult*, p. xxxiv.
[70] Wilson, *The Occult*, p. 73.
[71] Wilson, *The Occult*, p. 111.
[72] Aleister Crowley, *Magick in Theory and Practice* (1929; repr. New York: Castle Books, 1970), p. xii.

pinned down by the conditions of its existence to the earnest consideration of the most insignificant tides of reality.'[73]

In *Restoring Paradise: Western Esotericism, Literature, Art, and Consciousness* (2004), Arthur Versluis argues that

> we must begin to go beyond historical research in order to understand not only who or what esoteric works, figures, or groups have been overlooked or marginalized, but also, and perhaps even more critically, how esotericism is transmitted in the West. This is a vast and almost totally unexplored field, and one that has ramifications in many directions, not least of all for the understanding of art and literature.[74]

Versluis identifies and resists something akin to what American philosopher Thomas Nagel would later describe as 'psychophysical reductionism', the explication of complex psychological or imaginative processes as matters of clear and verifiable fact.[75] To escape this form of reductionism, Versluis reaffirms the interpretive directive of the humanities and notices that 'the Western esoteric traditions, despite their often almost bewildering variety, are fundamentally about reading: about reading nature, about reading the stars, about reading as discovering esoteric knowledge of ourselves and of the cosmos'.[76] For Versluis, the powerful bond forged between author and reader – a bond which is necessary for any meaning to be derived from the text – begins an initiatory process whereby this knowledge can be instilled and, perhaps, shared. 'The mystery of reading is, of course, also about union', Versluis writes, 'When we read a novel, we enter into another's world; we feel as someone else feels, imaginatively enter into different lives.'[77] The initiation of textuality emerges not from the agonistic relationship between younger and older writers (to paraphrase Harold Bloom's well-known argument) but through the relationship between author and reader, or at least those readers 'who enter into a work imaginatively' or 'see the work as mirroring a process that they seek to undergo in themselves'.[78] This invitation to contemplate the 'how' rather than the 'what' of occult practice and transmission was taken up by Jeffrey Kripal in *The Flip: Epiphanies of Mind and*

---

[73] Joseph Conrad, 'Henry James: An Appreciation', in *Notes on Life and Letters*, ed. J. H. Stape (Cambridge: Cambridge University Press, 2004), pp. 15–20 (p. 16).
[74] Arthur Versluis, *Restoring Paradise: Western Esotericism, Literature, Art, and Consciousness* (Albany: State University of New York Press, 2004), p. 1.
[75] Thomas Nagal, *Mind and Cosmos: Why the Materialist Neo-Darwinian Conception of Nature Is Almost Certainly False* (Oxford: Oxford University Press, 2012), pp. 4–5.
[76] Versluis, p. 3.
[77] Versluis, p. 4.
[78] Versluis, p. 14.

the Future of Knowledge (2019), where he argues for a necessary return to the experiential – and, in that sense unutterable – creation and transmission of knowledge, meaning and purpose:

> A radically new real can appear with the simplest of 'flips', or reversals of perspective, roughly, from 'the outside' of things to 'the inside' of things, from 'the object' to 'the subject'. And this can occur *without surrendering an iota of our remarkable scientific and medical knowledge about the material world and the human body*. The general materialistic framework of the sciences at the moment is not wrong. It is simply half-right.[79]

Thinking along comparable lines, John Bramble points out that 'to be able to know the world differently – as a kind of Gnostic, a stance which entailed mystical nihilism as much as affirmative transcendence – was an asset for modernism's quarrel with positivism, uniformity, bourgeois master-narratives, materialist progress and the Westernization of the earth'.[80] This does not come in the form of religiosity or even in the nature mysticism of the Romantics, but in a recuperation of an ancient recognition that the sacred may reside in the hidden pathways of the mind. With these contexts in mind, it bears echoing Marina Warner's recent question of 'how do we live with the intrinsic, problematic irrationality of our consciousness? How do we make a helpful distinction between religious adherence and an acknowledgement that myth and magic have their own logic and potential, independent of belief in higher powers?'[81] This book attempts to go some way towards squaring these questions, while recognizing, also, that the questions themselves are counterintuitive and rhetorical.

What literary modernism indicates – beyond simply the clear and undeniable thematic reliance on a heterodox vision of the sacred – is an immanentist approach to the creation of meaning through literary form. As Elaine Scarry points out in *Dreaming by the Book* (1999), 'verbal art, especially narrative, is almost bereft of any sensuous content. Its visual features, as has often been observed, consist of monotonous small black marks on a white page.'[82] Scarry understands the act of reading fiction as a conjuring act in which the elements of life are brought forth into the mind of the reader to create an illusion of volume, dimension and time. What intrigues Scarry, and what will inspire the readings

---

[79] Jeffrey Kripal, *The Flip: Epiphanies of Mind and the Future of Knowledge* (New York: Bellevue Literary Press, 2019), p. 12.
[80] Bramble, p. 3.
[81] Marina Warner, *Stranger Magic: Charmed States & the Arabian Nights* (London: Chatto & Windus, 2011), p. 22.
[82] Elaine Scarry, *Dreaming by the Book* (New York: Farrar, Straus and Giroux, 1999), p. 5.

that comprise the remaining chapters of this book, is the question of 'by what miracle is a writer able to incite us to bring forth mental images that resemble in their quality not our own daydreaming but our own (much more freely practiced) perceptual acts?'[83] For Scarry, narrative is a form of magical creation, a dreamy reverie in which the reader is worked upon to enter into collaborative creation with the spell of language:

> Just as Anacreon's lyrics give Hephaestus or another craftsman a set of directions about the object to be produced, and just as Huysmans' Des Esseintes issues elaborate specifications to the craftsmen of his walls and floors, so the verbal arts at every moment address the reader as a Hephaestus who is to undertake an explicit work of construction.[84]

The notion that language can possess definitive, unambiguous meanings is a distinctly modern development that emerged alongside the early emergences of the professional disciplines such as science and law.[85] Scarry's inherent romanticism is, in large part, a forceful riposte to the scientific materialism that shaped modernity and which has long been assumed to have shaped literary modernism as well. The roots of Scarry's method lie implicitly in the receptivist models laid out in Roman Ingarden's *The Literary Work of Art* (1931) and Roland Barthes's *The Pleasure of the Text* (1973): literature presents us with a labyrinth which we must navigate using resources of languages, culture and inference in order to construct a meaning that is all our own. Rather than a literature compelled towards the rebellious dynamics of the unconscious in a disenchanted material world, modernism emerges as an enraptured attempt to give form to the creative principles of the divine to the figure of the reader-god. It was a similar conclusion, albeit one achieved through different means, which Bernard Shaw reached in a 1911 lecture on 'The Religion of the Future':

> We are all experiments in the direction of making God. What God is doing is making himself, getting from being a mere powerless will or force. This force has implanted into our minds the ideal of God. We are not very successful attempts at God so far, but I believe that if we can drive into the heads of men the full consciousness of moral responsibility that comes to men with the knowledge that there never will be a God unless we make one – that we are the instruments through which that ideal is trying to make itself a reality – we can work towards

---

[83] Scarry, p. 7.
[84] Scarry, p. 34.
[85] Versluis, p. 18.

that ideal until we get to be supermen, and then super-supermen, and then a world of organisms who have achieved and realized God.[86]

For Shaw, as for many of the other modernists examined in this book, the promises of newness issued by the modern world emerged alongside models of living and modes of writing that recognized a form of non-dualism and the possibility of humans manifesting the sacred. Modern occult practices resisted the rationalism of the eighteenth century, the materialism of the nineteenth century and the ever-pressing rapidization and cynicism of the twentieth century. Shaw believed that 'we are all experiments in the direction of making God'[87] and so too is modernist literature an experiment in the direction of the sacred.

The following chapters are organized along the lines of literary milieux which were united towards specific textual aims through a diverse entanglement with various occult expressions. Roughly speaking, the chapters focus on, in sequence, stylistics, drama, psychoanalysis, social transformation and internationalization; however, much of what was happening both historically and textually regarding these topics occurred in synchronous fashion. To give just one example of the complex networks and affinities that are woven through these five chapters: Golden Dawn initiates Florence Farr and W. B. Yeats would collaborate with Bernard Shaw in the 1894 Avenue Theatre season, underwritten by tea heiress and Golden Dawn financer Annie Horniman; Farr and Shaw would soon after contribute to A. R. Orage's *The New Age* at a time when fellow contributor Ezra Pound was mingling with figures like Evelyn Underhill and Rabindranath Tagore at the Quest Society, an esoteric Christian offshoot of the Theosophical Society, and editing T. S. Eliot's deeply arcane *The Waste Land* (1922); Orage would entice his friend and *New Age* contributor Katherine Mansfield to pursue the occult philosophy of G. I. Gurdjieff, and she would eventually move to Gurdjieff's Institute for the Harmonious Development of Man outside Fontainebleau, France, where she died tragically young in 1923. At the very same time, while London was awash with *nowness* and the flash of the new, writers like Alexandra David-Neel and Paul Brunton were travelling through India and Tibet, finding answers to ancient questions as well as new questions that had never been imagined. The full expression and influence of occult practice in literature cannot be traced through individual traditions (or

---

[86] Bernard Shaw, 'The Religion of the Future', in *The Religious Speeches of Bernard Shaw*, ed. Warren Sylvester Smith (University Park, PA: Penn State University Press, 1963), p. 35.
[87] Shaw, p. 35.

even through specific genres or geopolitical remits), and any thoroughgoing study of such influence must account for the dizzying array of networks, affiliations and relationships that conduct the materials of literary production.

Chapter 1, 'Divine Reading', opens by reading the occult impulse of modernity along the standard lines of Anglo-American literary modernist history to demonstrate not only that occult modes of thought existed at the very heart of modernist innovation but also that the interest in immanence and the reader-god created a new form of readership that would come to define the modernist text. To a certain extent, this chapter carries on from the arguments posed by Surette and others in order to take stock of the full developments of literary approaches to the occult while also bringing into this discussion Mary Butts, whose substantive absence from the history of literary modernism has only recently begun to be corrected. At a time when the swell of mass culture was affecting a retreat from the masses, writers were drawing upon models of curious elision and obscurity in the form of the apocryphal Rosicrucian fraternity of healing monks and the Matter of Britain stories of a sacred healing Grail, images which held unmistakable vitality and significance in the years following the First World War. This chapter argues that the infamous difficulty of modernist writing is a means by which writers sought to implant meaning in the minds of their readers, engaging the reader as an active participant in creation of order to restore cooperative forms of knowledge that had become increasingly outmoded through the supposed epistemological advances of the nineteenth century.

In Chapter 2, 'The Return to Ritual', the argument turns to the unremarked-upon occult beliefs and practices of modern theatre practitioners including Antonin Artaud, Jerzy Grotowski and Michael Chekhov to demonstrate that the rise of 'Method Acting' and the forms of drama subsequently produced are unmistakably rooted in an immanentist method of drawing down dramatic characters into the consciousness of the actor. The chapter opens by examining of the rise of the 'Method' in actor training and production as a return to ancient ritual and contemporary ceremonial magic before considering how the mystical and deeply resonant playtexts of Florence Farr and Rudolf Steiner sought to capture the transcendent capacity of the individual to reach beyond known knowledge into a higher realm of possibility.

The historical correspondences between the ambitions, practices and implicit social order of psychoanalysis and modern occultism are detailed in Chapter 3, 'The Modernist Shadow'. Psychoanalysis represents a modern containment of mystical dogmata and developed along lines that either sought to outright deny occultist influences or integrate supersensible realms into a picturesque account of the unconscious. The Doctor Taverner stories of novelist, psychoanalyst and occult leader Dion Fortune serve as a key focus of this chapter, alongside the work of Hermann Hesse, a follower of the ornate mystical views of Carl Jung and a writer who has recently fallen somewhat out favour following a heyday of popularity in the 1960s and 1970s. The fiction of Fortune and Hesse is distinctly fixated on the soullessness and despair which lingered for decades after the First World War and presents a retreat to the numinous unconscious as the most valuable remedy to these pains.

Chapter 4, 'The Making of an Overman', looks initially at the Nietzscheanism and Fabianism which ran through the pages of A. R. Orage's *The New Age* and which introduced a modern ideal of the super-evolved sage of the modern world. Bernard Shaw knowingly positioned himself as one such sage and, through his characters such as John Tanner and Saint Joan, meditated upon the possibilities of the individual bringing through knowledge that existed beyond themselves as a remedy to the degeneration that was feared to be plaguing society. Emerging from a different ambiance but influenced by the same materials, Dion Fortune's *The Sea Priestess* (1938) is a shrewd culmination of the modern faith in the arrival of the superman, here portrayed as an ancient Atlantean priestess who is able to cure the ails of a myopic country estate agent, an Everyman of modern life. The principal aim of this chapter is to demonstrate that the modernist discourse surrounding the superman is richly rooted in occult philosophy and magical ways of knowing, and while the central motion put forward by Nietzsche was the image of an earthly liberator in a godless world, the superhuman and supersensible quality of an overman necessarily relied upon occult philosophy.

Finally, Chapter 5, 'The Other East', turns to examples of modernist writing undertaken outside of the geopolitical topography of European modernism to consider the resounding influence of India and Tibet on modern occult writing and practice. Travel writers including Alexandra David-Neel and Paul Brunton understood Asia to hold the *philosophia perennis*, the presumed source of all faith traditions which was believed to have become increasingly lost in the theological elaborations over the past few millennia. Somerset Maugham also travelled to India in search of spiritual enlightenment, a quest which he would allegorize in his 1944 novel *The Razor's Edge*, the latest primary text which this study examines. David-Neel, Brunton and Maugham were well aware that gnostic wisdom gleaned from gurus and lamas could never be conveyed through textual form and developed a series of compelling narrative strategies which boldly aimed at embodying something which the structures of language can never enclose.

From the little magazines where occultism and Fabianism were comfortable companions, to consulting rooms of psychoanalysts where archetypes were revealed to be both mystical and mundane, to the forbidden mountain trails that led to formidable spiritual teachers, the conditions of modernism were invariably those conditions which inspired a return to the occult traditions that many thinkers believed had long evaporated. Indeed, in many ways these traditions were the making of the modern world. What is ultimately at stake in this book is the hypothesis that modernism was not, precisely speaking at least, new but rather a flourishing of Neoplatonic ideals and apophatic mysticism which transmuted the theurgic impulse into the textual surface and allowed for the possibility of the immanence of divinity. Existing criticism accepts the visibility of modernism as, simultaneously, a historical period covering roughly the first half of the twentieth century, a literary style grounded in radical innovation and a sociological programme which gave rise to growing equality and social liberalism. But what has not been considered fully is that the modernism is also a conceptual thought experiment – a problematic and unfulfilling one at that – that puts in place the conditions for the promotion of individual subjectivity in order to judge it as destructive. 'Socrates *wanted* to die –', Nietzsche famously contends in *Twilight of the Idols* (1889), 'it was not Athens, but it was *he* who handed himself the poison cup, who compelled Athens to hand him the poison cup'.[88] Modernism accepted its poisoned cup but, in spite of what Nietzsche imagined, flourished because of it.

---

[88] Friedrich Nietzsche, *Twilight of the Idols and the Anti-Christ*, trans. R. J. Hollingdale (London: Penguin, 2003), p. 44.

1

Divine reading: Absence and elision as occult form in modernist literature

In all kinds of ways, the figuratively absent kitchen table of Virginia Woolf's *To the Lighthouse* (1927) offers the paradigmatic expression of a modernism invested in magical ways of knowing:

> Whenever she 'thought of [Mr Ramsay's] work' she always saw clearly before her a large kitchen table. It was Andrew's doing. She asked him what his father's books were about. 'Subject and object and the nature of reality', Andrew had said. And when she said Heavens, she had no notion what that meant. 'Think of a kitchen table then', he told her, 'when you're not there'.[1]

Andrew describes to the painter Lily Briscoe the manoeuvres of a modern phenomenologist (one who, like Husserl and Heidegger, recognizes that matter is in a state of formation) in a domestic allegory, one which he presumably imagines she will grasp. But Lily, whose own creative practice requires the existence of tables, people and chairs, bristles at the sophistry until, later, her artistic sensibilities lead her to a representational style similarly established by elision. The haunting allegory becomes even more poignant when the reader is forced to think of Andrew when *he* is not there following his death in the First World War or to think of Mrs Ramsay, also, when she is not there. William R. Handley says of this famously absent kitchen table that Woolf 'is laughing … at Mr. Ramsay as a philosopher who cannot see the objects in front of him, paradoxically including his wife'.[2] Alex Zwerdling draws attention to Woolf's juxtaposing of psychological interiority and the 'real world', that is, the dangerous gap between what people 'want and what is expected of them',[3] and Allen

---

[1] Virginia Woolf, *To the Lighthouse* (1927; repr. New York: Harcourt, 1981), p. 23.
[2] William R. Handley, 'The Housemaid and the Kitchen Table: Incorporating the Frame', *To the Lighthouse' Twentieth Century Literature*, 40.1 (1994), 15–41 (pp. 15–16).
[3] Alex Zwerdling, *Virginia Woolf and the Real World* (London: University of California Press, 1986), p. 5.

McLaurin aligns Woolf's portrayal of domestic space such as this alongside the notions of fellow Bloomsbury thinker Roger Fry: 'In many ways Virginia Woolf tries to right the balance between the literary and visual by allowing a great deal of the spatial element in her art – as much, indeed, as words can accomplish in this direction.'[4] There is no mistaking that the kitchen table 'when you're not there' offers a composite emblem of both Mr Ramsay's failings as a modern *paterfamilias* and the negotiation of loss which Woolf's text mediates. But also, and more urgently, this famous scene condenses Woolf's primary method of conveying meaning through elision and of hovering at the void of signification, a technique at the very heart of modernist literary experimentation. The table allegory might accurately capture the daunting philosophy of a modern thinker, but, by the text's final lines, Lily's opportunity to enter into a collaborative production of meaning where the world says none exists becomes too enticing for her to resist.

Woolf should no means be described as an occultist, but her inspired engagement with the abstractness of language and expression unmistakably calls upon occult modes of thought that seek to engage with the participant in a form of collaborative understanding that emerges from the active involvement in the creation of meaning. 'If one were to catalogue the various types of "mystical" experience appearing in the writings of Virginia Woolf', Julie Kane points out, 'the list would be virtually indistinguishable from the topics of interest to the Theosophists and spiritualists of her day: telepathy, auras, astral travel, synaesthesia, reincarnation, the immortality of the soul, and the existence of a Universal mind'.[5] In *Modernism and Magic*, Leigh Wilson echoes this point when she recognizes that 'Woolf's attempts to articulate what happens during artistic creation hover around the transformations of magic'.[6] Woolf, although publicly inimical towards mystical thought, understood synchronic and collective forms of knowledge in ways markedly similar to occult groups of her time and recognized that the most powerful way to capture the ineffable qualities of human experience is to not even portray them at all but, instead, to offer the reader opportunities to ruminate on arrays of language and meaning that build towards a personally realized design. It is precisely this invitation to the reader to

---

[4] Allen McLaurin, *Virginia Woolf: The Echoes Enslaved* (Cambridge: Cambridge University Press, 1973), p. 91.
[5] Julie Kane, 'Varieties of Mystical Experience in the Writings of Virginia Woolf', *Twentieth Century Literature*, 41.4 (1995), 328–49 (p. 328).
[6] Leigh Wilson, *Modernism and Magic: Experiments with Spiritualism, Theosophy and the Occult* (Edinburgh: Edinburgh University Press, 2012), p. 12.

enter into the co-construction of meaning that is so often at the centre of charges against modernism of elusiveness, snobbery and impenetrability.

This chapter examines the occult intimations of the modernist turn to elision and absence, and, more specifically, the role that this semantic and conceptual refusal of meaning played in the development of modernist sensibilities. The rarefied elusiveness of literary modernism, both then and now, may have excluded many readers, but its principal aim was to invest within the reader a quality of cooperative knowledge production in a radically reshaped global landscape. Delicately observed, Terry Eagleton explains that the modernists 'were developing their own closed symbolic systems, in which Tradition, theosophy, the male and female principles, medievalism and mythology were to provide the keystones of complete "synchronic" structures, exhaustive models for the control and explanation of historical reality'.[7] As Vicki Mahaffey contends of this 'closed' nature of much of literary modernism, 'stylistically such obfuscation may serve to express the elusiveness and even the horror of reality; one could argue that it symbolically forces its readers to bear witness to the unspeakable incoherences and violence nonsense of the real'.[8] Eliot's objective correlative, Joyce's epiphanies, Hemingway's iceberg theory and Woolf's moments of being, each in their own way, highlight the affective potential of absence and elision and emphasize a sacred reading practice which exists as the 'end-result of a dynamic, generative paradox or antimony (a stark contradiction between two principles) that structures and in some sense determines the invention of difficult or strange language'.[9] Perhaps the most pressing influence of occultism on modernist literature is not subject and imagery but the reconstitution of the literary text as an object of immanent creation in which gaping holes of denotation provide the richest sites of meaning and purpose.

Throughout much of the history of Western literature, textual art has been viewed as a mimetic form of communication, with the artist ascribed the task of recreating the universe; imitation of life was not only the method but also the goal of the writer. And within the Anglo-American literary tradition, fictional prose to a great extent and lyric poetry to an even greater extent have been evaluated on the degree to which the textual image conjures a scene or sensibility that is, if not familiar, at least partly recognizable. However, 'the post-Jamesian artist or intellectual', Christopher Knight points out, 'has made it something

---

[7] Terry Eagleton, *Literary Theory: An Introduction* (Oxford: Basil Blackwell, 1983), p. 110.
[8] Vicki Mahaffey, *Modernist Literature: Challenging Fictions* (Oxford: Blackwell, 2007), p. 14.
[9] Joshua Gunn, 'An Occult Poetics, or, the Secret Rhetoric of Religion', *Rhetoric Society Quarterly*, 34.2 (2004), 29–51 (p. 31).

akin to a practice to imagine the work as incomplete, except as this completion is understood as taking place in a realm outside of, or invisible to, common understanding'.[10] William Franke positions the apophatic burden of modernism as less inherently rooted in the implications of a new literary style but merely a reminder that 'periodically in intellectual history, confidence in the *Logos*, in the ability of the word to grasp reality and disclose truth, flags dramatically'.[11] But it bears pointing out that literature has also been powerfully associated with the imaginary and visionary throughout literary history, particularly during periods of providential innovation and change. Sharing in this recognition, Anthony L. Johnson explains that in the context of literary elision, 'the reader is called upon to become actively involved in bridging the gaps so created and in devising morpho-syntactic, semantic or pragmatic by-passes to reconstitute textual continuity. Since internal fragmentariness disrupts discursive unity-cum-continuity, it invariably "vertically" attracts readerly attention away from a text's discursivity (a series of sign-events *in praesentia*) towards retrievals of sense.'[12]

Within the context of these discussions of stylistic elision, the common claims regarding the 'esoteric' language (as in, comprehensible only to those with specialist knowledge) of modernists such as Pound, Joyce and Woolf deserve further attention. In *Am I a Snob?: Modernism and the Novel* (2003), Sean Latham points out that 'modernism has thrived on a smug sense of cultured superiority ... for modernism's mythologized autonomy derives from the illusion of disinterestedness, from the conviction that aesthetic pleasure exists in a realm completely antithetical to the vulgar self-promotion of the marketplace'.[13] Pushing such claims further, Andreas Huyssen reads the forbidding quotient of modernist writing more polemically as 'a conscious strategy of exclusion, and [evidence of] anxiety of contamination by its other: an increasingly consuming and engulfing mass culture'.[14] Joshua Gunn specifically explores the parallels between occultism and the 'esoteric' language of the modernists:

[10] Christopher Knight, *Modern Apophaticism from Henry James to Jacques Derrida* (Toronto: University of Toronto Press, 2010), p. 5.
[11] William Franke, *On What Cannot Be Said: Apophatic Discourses in Philosophy, Religion, Literature, and the Arts*, vol. 2 (London: University of Notre Dame Press 2007), p. 9.
[12] Anthony L. Johnson, '"Broken Images": Discursive Fragmentation and Paradigmatic Integrity in the Poetry of T. S. Eliot', *Poetics Today*, 6.3 (1985), 400.
[13] Sean Latham, *Am I a Snob?: Modernism and the Novel* (Ithaca, NY: Cornell University Press, 2003), p. 2.
[14] Andreas Huyssen, *After the Great Divide: Modernism, Mass Culture, Postmodernism* (Bloomington: Indiana University Press, 1986), p. vii.

Occult discourse – which I define broadly as the study of secret or previously secret knowledge, which subsumes the revelations of so-called 'New Age' literature – can be understood as the end-result of a dynamic, generative paradox or antimony (a stark contradiction between two principles) that structures and in some sense determines the invention of difficult or strange language.[15]

Tellingly, Gunn's initial example is the Scylla and Charybdis episode of *Ulysses* (1922), in which Stephen Dedalus comes head-to-head with the Theosophical raillery of the mystic and poet AE (George William Russell), to whom he is indebted financially and perhaps aesthetically as well. John Bramble similarly imagines an innate affinity between the projects of modernism and occultism, which both sought to push away the seemingly repressive and levelling forces of modernity: 'To be able to know the world differently – as a kind of Gnostic, a stance which entailed mystical nihilism as much as affirmative transcendence – was an asset for modernism's quarrel with positivism, uniformity, bourgeois master-narratives, materialist progress, and the Westernization of the earth.'[16] Gnosticism holds on to the view that there exist sparks of innate divinity within the individual which are seeking to return to the greater source, and this form of embodied knowledge, which is neither communicable nor verifiable, becomes a useful symbol for modernist stylistic sensibilities. While certainly not all modernists were occultists, modernism celebrates the hidden and can be comprehended in refreshed ways through attention to the occult compulsions that delineate boundaries of meaning. The innovations of literary modernism are dependent upon the collective consciousness, that is, the shared reasoning (or performative and productive nonreasoning) that burst forth as nodes of creative output. As the readings of Marinetti, Pound, Eliot and Butts that follow intend to demonstrate, literary modernism is punctuated by moments of striking absence and elision that open up the productive powers of the reader-god alongside occult-aligned thematics.

F. T. Marinetti's Futurism offers an intriguing example of how occult forms of thinking and the possibility of divine revelation found expression in even the most unlikely places. While British interest in Futurism began wane by 1914, the key tenants of Marinetti's movement provided a crucial foundation for the evolving British creative spirit: favouring intuition over intellect; celebrating the incantatory power of verbs and nouns; undertaking, in Marinetti's terms, an

---

[15] Gunn, pp. 29–51 (p. 31).
[16] John Bramble, *Modernism and the Occult* (London: Palgrave Macmillan, 2015), p. 3.

'attitude of daily heroism';[17] and perceiving technology as a new god which must be protected at all costs. Yet in spite of his unwavering insistence on progress, newness and destruction of the old, Marinetti wrote of his project in the terms of a modern divinely inspired mystic and introduced it to the world as such. 'The Founding and the Manifesto of Futurism' (1909) echoes in several crucial ways three early-seventeenth-century German tracts known collectively as the Rosicrucian manifestos: *Fama Fraternitatis* (1614), *Confessio Fraternitatis* (1615) and the *Chymical Wedding of Christian Rosenkreutz* (1617). The manifestos were published anonymously (although at least the *Chymical Wedding* is attributable to the Lutheran theologian Johann Valentin Andrae) and together reported the existence of a secret fraternity led by a Father Christian Rosenkreutz who shared with his circle of healing monks a secret divine wisdom that enabled them to heal the sick. That there were political aims in this esoteric ludibrium now seems clear: in *The Rosicrucian Enlightenment* (1972), Francis Yates reads the appearance of the *Fama* and *Confessio* as an elaborate political response to the marriage of Frederick V, Elector Palatine of the Rhine, and Prince Elizabeth, daughter of James I. Furthermore, the manifestos

> would appear to be proclamations of enlightenment in the form of an utopist myth about a world in which enlightened beings, almost assimilated to spirits, go about doing good, shedding healing influences, disseminating knowledge in the natural sciences and the arts, and bringing mankind back to its Paradisal state before the Fall.[18]

Excitement grew across Europe as people sought out entrance to the apocryphal order. Pamphlets proliferated, several supposed Rosicrucian societies emerged and the belief that humans could access direct knowledge of the divine caught in the fertile minds of early-seventeenth-century Europe. The enticing combination of magic, Christian Cabala and alchemy generated by Rosicrucianism would stimulate new modes of thought which emerged during the Enlightenment, and this wide-ranging influence seems most directly tied to the curiously conjoined invitation and exclusion offered by the Rosicrucian manifestos: they made public knowledge of a secret society that could never be joined, both because it did not in actual fact exist and because, if it did, it was necessarily hidden.

---

[17] F. T. Marinetti, 'Destruction of Syntax – Wireless Imagination – Words-in-Freedom' (1913), in *Modernism: An Anthology*, ed. Lawrence Rainey, trans. Lawrence Rainey (Oxford: Blackwell, 2005), pp. 27–34 (p. 28).

[18] Frances Yates, *The Rosicrucian Enlightenment* (1972; repr. St Albans: Paladin, 1975), p. 250.

Rosicrucianism offers a resonant demonstration of the creation of meaning as a response to absence and the willingness of readers to imagine a great deal when presented with very little. In his 'The Founding and the Manifesto of Futurism', Marinetti seems to be especially aware of how to build a movement initially out of absence, offering his readers the opportunity to join a Rosicrucian-like fraternity of the future: the unmistakable aim of his 'Manifesto' is to reveal the existence of a fraternity of art and innovation which, through allegorical exertion, has received an inspired revelation of the future of civilization:

> 'Let's go!' I said. 'Let's go, my friends! Let's leave! At last the mythology and the mystical ideal have been superseded. We are about to witness the birth of the Centaur, and soon we shall see the first Angels fly! ... We have to shake the doors of life to test their hinges and bolts! ... Let's leave! Look! There, on the earth, the earliest dawn! Nothing can match the splendor of the sun's red sword, skirmishing for the first time with our thousand-year-old shadows.'[19]

In part to underscore his opposition to 'the mythology and the mystical ideal' of the past, Marinetti's lexis is rich with mystical language, with filigreed 'mosque lamps' and 'opulent oriental rugs' representing an enchanted past and the sounds of 'the famished automobiles roaring beneath the windows' signalling a new future, captured in an indescribable moment of gnostic revelation.[20] Several years later, Eliot's pitiable Prufrock would issue a similar invitation to go into the night in search of the ultimate reality which remains just outside of his grasp, but Marinetti is the fulfilled prophet that Prufrock could never become and is wholly convinced of his divine insights. Describing the nature of the prophetic poetic character, Louis L. Martz notes that 'the voice of the prophet tends to oscillate between denunciation and consolation, between despair and hope, between images of desolation and images of redemption, between the actual and the ideal. He does not tell a story, as the epic bard does; he relates visions of good and evil, and he does so in what we call prose and what we call poetry.'[21] The prophet is not the teller of the future but the radical commentator on the present, and their revelations hold the potential to, through unsettling and empowering the populace, create change in the future. While the central aim of Marinetti's ventriloquized speaker is to repudiate the organic superstition of history, the zeal with which he and his allegorical companions rush to communicate their

---

[19] F. T. Marinetti, 'The Founding and the Manifesto of Futurism', in *Modernism: An Anthology*, ed. Lawrence Rainey, trans. Lawrence Rainey (1909; repr. Oxford: Blackwell, 2005), p. 3.
[20] Marinetti, 'The Founding and the Manifesto of Futurism', pp. 3–6 (p. 3).
[21] Louis L. Martz, *Many Gods and Many Voices: The Role of the Prophet in English and American Modernism* (London: University of Missouri Press, 1998), p. 4.

insight is nothing short of the divine raptures of gnosis, a 'techgnosis', to use Erik Davis's term for mechanized mysticism.[22] In 1958 the sociologist Edward Shils returned to the questions raised by José Ortega y Gasset in *The Revolt of the Masses* (1930; English trans. 1932) in order to propose that modernity and mass culture relied urgently on the emergence of an intellectual class that remains intrinsically connected to the sacred and divine:

> In every society however there are some persons with an unusual sensitivity to the sacred, an uncommon reflectiveness about the nature of their universe, and the rules which govern their society. There is in every society a minority of persons who, more than the ordinary run of their fellow-men, are enquiring, and desirous of being in frequent communication with symbols which are more general than the immediate concrete situations of everyday life, and remote in their reference in both time and space. In this minority, there is a need to externalize this quest in oral and written discourse, in poetic or plastic expression, in historical reminiscence or writing, in ritual performance and acts of worship. This interior need to penetrate beyond the screen of immediate concrete experience marks the existence of the intellectuals in every society.[23]

The easy movement Shils makes towards the notion of an intellectual with 'a need to externalise this quest [to] penetrate beyond the screen of immediate concrete experience' unambiguously highlights a spiritual class of intellectual prophets and sages, figures for whom the materials of reality become purified and perfected through esoteric means. These figures, Shils contends, provide the only possible way through the dehumanizing campaign of mass culture and give voice to the unspeakable, intangible and wholly forgotten. Such is Marinetti's aim. Marinetti's techgnosis continues into 1912's 'Technical Manifesto of Futurist Literature' in which an eleven-point manifesto is divinely dictated to him by a 'swirling propeller … as I sped along at two hundred meters above the powerful smokestacks of Milan' during his first and only airplane flight.[24] Whereas poets had once received divine address from the gods, Marinetti receives his sublime dictates from an emblem of modernity and technological advancement, an airplane. Here he powerfully resists Enlightenment subjectivity, defined by the logic-function of intelligence and the graffiti of civilization's combined

---

[22] See Erik Davis, *Techgnosis: Myth, Magic, and Mystery in the Information Age* (Berkeley, CA: North Atlantic Books, 2015).
[23] Edwards Shils, 'The Intellectuals and the Powers: Some Perspectives for Comparative Analysis', *Comparative Studies in Society and History*, 1.1 (1958), 5–22 (p. 5).
[24] F. T. Marinetti, 'Technical Manifesto of Futurist Literature', in *Modernism: An Anthology*, ed. Lawrence Rainey, trans. Lawrence Rainey (1912; repr. Oxford: Blackwell, 2005), pp. 15–19 (p. 15).

knowledge, and remains firmly committed to the potentials of an intuitive revelation rooted in the shapes and machines of the modern world.

Marinetti's celebration of intuition extends into his later essays, developing into a sustained celebration of allegory as an inherently intuitive form of communication that captures meaning in the undelimitated space between two seemingly separate propositions. It was this which Marinetti referred to as the 'wireless imagination', that is, 'the absolute freedom of images or analogies, expressed with disconnected words, and without the connecting syntactical wires and without punctuation'.[25] The new age heralded by the 'Founding and Manifesto' is defined by 'the beauty of speed' and its adjacency to struggle and destruction, a wilfully nihilistic spirit that recognizes that radical social rapidization renders everything, including the individual, fit for no purpose higher than resisting the status quo of the old world order. 'Time and space died yesterday. We already live in the absolute, for we have already created velocity which is eternal and omnipresent.'[26] Marinetti may be pushing aside the mysticism of the past, but mystical nevertheless he remains: the old impotent gods have been replaced with new machines whose immanence is unmistakable.

Futurism in many ways set the model for the modernist coterie, a group of transdisciplinary artists, writers and thinkers, which, whether or not they were working towards the aims of a published manifesto, were, nevertheless, operating as a confederacy of thinkers. Of course, Marinetti's perspectives do not encapsulate the styles and sympathies of modernism and modernity at large, but they do gesture towards the wider critical concerns that modernists evolved regarding the shifting constitution of 'in-groups' and 'out-groups' and how lines of power and influence had begun to reform. While the political inheritance of Futurism is deeply problematic, its resolute accent on the potential of a new divine immanence captured in language and art can be observed in refreshed ways in British Vorticism, a mode perhaps best remembered for its 'hype and provocation'.[27] In one of the most influential narratives of the development of Anglo-American modernism, Lawrence Rainey argues that the origins of modernism 'were somehow to be discerned in the early formulations of Ezra Pound, formulations who premises had been deepened and extended by Eliot's work, ultimately bringing about a profound change in the literary and cultural climate of the age'.[28] In Ezra Pound's 'Vortex', published in the first edition of *Blast*

[25] Marinetti, 'Destruction of Syntax', p. 30.
[26] Marinetti, 'The Founding and the Manifesto of Futurism', p. 4.
[27] Raphael Ingelbien, 'Metres and the Pound: Taking the Measure of British Modernism', *European Review*, 19.2 (2011), 285–97 (p. 288).
[28] Lawrence Rainey, *Modernism: An Anthology* (Oxford: Blackwell, 2005), p. xxi.

as a Vorticist manifesto, the American émigré's distinctive interest in the defiant capacity of language to invest meaning within the spirit of the reader is apparent. In *Modernist Alchemy* (1995), Timothy Materer recognizes that, for modernist poets, 'belief in the occult world is necessary, yet at the same time, a modern poet who lacks a sense of irony when exploring this world may seem hopelessly naïve'.[29] Pound seemed to find that crucial balance between irony and belief. At the same time that Pound was elucidating the structures of Vorticism, his occult interests had led him to the Quest Society, a mystical Christian splinter group of the Theosophical Society founded by G. R. S. Mead. The society's distinctive focus was not only on Christian mysticism as a reparative response to the focus on Eastern mysticism in the Theosophical Society but also, more specifically, on the value of mystical thought to the production of art and literature. Pound would publish work in the society's journal *The Quest: A Quarterly Review* alongside figures including W. B. Yeats, Evelyn Underhill, A. E. Waite and Rabindranath Tagore, and it would be the Quest Society, as Demetres Tryphonopoulos has shown, that had the most significant influence on Pound's occult knowledge.[30] In his famous essay originally published in *The Quest* on 'Psychology and Troubadours', Pound argues that 'an art is vital only so long as it is interpretive, so long, that is, as it manifests something which the artist perceives at greater intensity and more intimately than his public'.[31] This interpretative element, Pound imagines, is what creates the vitalization of writing, in the sense that it is not static and attenuated, but living and vibrant, able to cast new light and shade for each successive reader. Where Pound takes this proposition next is more speculative: 'Did this "close ring," this aristocracy of emotion, evolve, out of its half memories of Hellenistic mysteries, a cult? a cult stricter, or more subtle, than that of the celibate ascetics, a cult for the purgation of the soul by a refinement of, and lordship over the senses?'[32] He is speaking here ostensibly about the troubadours, but the ultimate extension of his argument is that the 'aristocracy of emotion' of modern poetics can find its roots in the richest formulations of Hellenistic mysteries, now divided between the hedonic and chivalric.

From the Imagistic apparition of 'In a Station of the Metro' (1913) to the volatile labyrinths of the *Cantos*, Pound's poetry remains committed to knowing more than it says, covering more than it reveals and challenging more than

---

[29] Timothy Materer, *Modernist Alchemy: Poetry and the Occult* (Ithaca, NY: Cornell University Press, 1995), p. 4.
[30] Demetres Tryphonopoulos, *Celestial Tradition: A Study of Ezra Pound's* The Cantos (Waterloo, ON: Wilfrid Laurier University Press, 1992), p. 82.
[31] Ezra Pound, 'Psychology and Troubadours', *The Quest: A Quarterly Review*, 4.1 (1912), 37–58 (p. 37).
[32] Pound, 'Psychology and Troubadours', p. 42.

it welcomes. *Hugh Selwyn Mauberley* (1920) is a love letter to London which captures the Ulyssean struggle to modernize the mind of the poet, here shown through the paired images of the poet surrogate 'E.P.' and the abject aesthete Mauberley whose agonistic frenzy in greeting the poetic past leads to his exclusion from literary circles. When one reads the poem 'Medallion' which comes as the conclusion to the sequence and which is taken to represent the output of Mauberley's creative mind, one can clearly see why Mauberley has replaced silence with the voices of others. The contrasting voices of *Hugh Selwyn Mauberley* offer a curious demonstration of Harold Bloom's model of poetic influence and transmission in *The Anxiety of Influence* (1973). For Helen Sword, Bloom's archetype of agonistic struggle bears indications of a deeply esoteric mediumship, one in which the role of the author is as much about summoning and vanquishing a spirit as it is concerned with the creative production of new material: 'Only by calling the dead back to life, Bloom suggests, can living poets appropriate their literary masters' voices and usurp their authorial powers.'[33] Consideration of the practices and beliefs of spiritualism, Sword continues, 'can also provide a useful paradigm for probing the mechanics of Bloom's Oedipal *apophrades,* a return of the literary dead that ultimately empowers rather than diminishes the living'.[34] The Kabbalistic schematism of Bloom's Ratios of Revision presupposes a numinous factor in the development of the poet (the 'ephebe') through a form of impassioned initiation at the hands of an older and wiser writer; anxiety begins when this figurative apprenticeship fails to come to its natural end and is replaced with an agonistic struggle. It is this psychic drama of creation and understanding that is curiously played out across Pound's poem. Through the first three poems of *Hugh Selwyn Mauberley* the rapidization of modern life reaches fever pitch, with the speaker attempting to reconcile and justify the changes surrounding him and his place in aesthetic history through self-evaluation alongside the models of classical Greece. (Incidentally, Pound's 'Canto I' (1917) opens with a similar gesture, in a free translation of Book XI of the *Odyssey,* whose existence and translation are brought into question in the final lines when the speaker reveals that he is working through a Latin translation of the original, thus fracturing again the possible hold on the original source.) But the effort is unfulfilled, and the voice of E. P. disintegrates until the beginning of '*Siena mi fe': deisfecemi Maremma*' when he is able to cautiously erect his own vision of literary history from the monuments of past, now

---

[33] Helen Sword, *Ghostwriting Modernism* (London: Cornell University Press, 2002), p. 32.
[34] Sword, p. 40.

hampered by the debauchee Monsieur Verog, Brennbaum the aesthete and the passé man of letters Mr Nixon. The second half of the poem, 'Mauberley', might be taken as the fruition of E. P.'s own growing poetic sensibility, now overflowing into a second double, a further refraction of Pound's own sense of the future modern poetry, who, willing yet unable to deduce his correct place in the history of letters, imagines his own watery dissolve. The promise presented by *Hugh Selwyn Mauberley* of modern poetry as a shifting elusive frame of meaning, not a monument, is realized in the *Cantos* where modernist poetics reaches its most crystalline form in the shape of an ever-growing, never-ending opus that refuses all containment and, in doing so, offers a knowing reflection of the immanence of the divine.

This solution to the problem of flattening out the holographic form of life and fitting it into the narrative of poetic history on which Pound's poem centres is markedly redolent of that described by T. S. Eliot in 'Tradition and the Individual Talent' (1919) and to which Stephen Dedalus comes to in rather more despairing style in the Nestor episode of *Ulysses*. That both Pound and Eliot – both in their own ways, but, passionately nevertheless – were invested in magical ways of thinking, in the possibility of a shared global spiritual system and in the occult milieu of their time reminds us that the traditional narrative of Anglo-American literary modernism has unmistakably occult beginnings. The Matter of Britain stories of Arthur, knights errant and the mysterious Grail would take on a new resonance and vocabulary shortly after the end of the First World War.[35] As Emma Jung explains in *The Grail Legend*, completed by Marie-Louise von Franz:

> The grail legend is an especially stimulating subject for psychological consideration because it contains so many features that are also to be found in myths and fairy-tales. Moreover, it has lost far less of its fascination for contemporary men and women than have the latter, which may indicate that it still embodies a living myth.[36]

In Chrétien de Troyes's *The Story of the Grail* (*c.*1180), the earliest extant treatment of the Grail motif, a wounded king presides over the Grail castle and the intense magic that it holds. But Chrétien died before he completed his romance, leaving unanswered the question of what special powers the Grail actually possessed.

---

[35] On the full scale of these developments, see Allan Johnson, *Masculine Identity in Modernist Literature: Castration, Narration, and a Sense of the Beginning, 1919–1945* (London: Palgrave Macmillan, 2017), chapter 1.
[36] Emma Jung and Marie-Louise von Franz, *The Grail Legend* (Princeton, NJ: Princeton University Press, 1960), p. 9.

While the first recorded account of the Grail legend is Chrétien's, it is certain that he was not writing original material and was almost certainly drawing upon a vast body of oral tradition. The role in this famous narrative of the wounded Fisher King, long since sidelined, was returned to prominence in Weston's *From Ritual to Romance* which aimed, drawing upon the methodologies of both J. G. Frazer and G. R. S. Mead, to unravel the 'sometimes partially understood, sometimes wholly misinterpreted, record of a ritual, originally presumed to exercise a life-giving potency, which, at one time of universal observance, has, even in its decay, shown itself possessed of elements of the most persistent vitality'.[37] Frazer's *The Golden Bough*, though unquestionably one of the most influential works of nineteenth-century scholarship, has nevertheless been met with a fair measure of distrust. Frazer's central thesis that forgotten pre-modern traditions can be reconstructed through examination of currently surviving practices would be accepted by the Cambridge Ritualists and the Folklore Society, but, as contemporary historian of ritual and folk tradition Ronald Hutton reminds readers, there are far too many outliers and uncertainties in the historical record to make any such claim of direct transmission.[38] Weston's argument that the legend of the incurable Fisher King's wound represents the survival of an ancient ritual of regicide first took shape in the pages of *The Quest*, where the methods of Frazer and the Cambridge Ritualists had expanded towards the enthusiastic approach to defining a unifying current of occult wisdom connecting all spiritual traditions. While Weston's argument was incorrect, it nevertheless had a significant influence on modernist literary formulations and Surette argues that 'Eliot could not have failed to notice the occult nature of Weston's book, and that he submitted his long poem to Pound's scrutiny specifically because he knew Pound to have some competence in occult theories and beliefs'.[39]

Critics have generally underestimated the influence of Mead and his Quest Society on Jessie Weston's infamous *From Ritual to Romance*, and, more problematically, they have customarily avoided the relationship of young Unitarian Eliot to these ideas, which gave rise to the patently occult foundations of *The Waste Land*. The editorship of Pound ('the greater craftsman', according to Eliot's dedication) allowed *The Waste Land* to revel in vitally charged voids which offer an invitation to the reader to partake in a ceremony of production and

---

[37] Jessie L. Weston, *From Ritual to Romance* (1920; repr. New York: Anchor, 1957), p. 113.
[38] Ronald Hutton, *Stations of the Sun: A History of the Ritual Year in Britain* (Oxford: Oxford University Press, 2001); *The Triumph of the Moon: A History of Modern Pagan Witchcraft* (Oxford: Oxford University Press, 1999).
[39] Leon Surette, *The Birth of Modernism: Ezra Pound, T. S. Eliot, W. B. Yeats, and the Occult* (Quebec: McGill-Queen's University Press, 1993), p. 227.

reproduction heralded by the Grail. Surette recognizes that Eliot was drawing something quite distinctive from his reading of *From Ritual to Romance* and contends 'that Eliot sought Pound's advice not – as criticism has long assumed – because he was uncertain about the rhetorical structure of his poem, but rather because he was uncertain about its *thematic* coherence and clarity, given his unfamiliarity with the occult materials that I am suggesting he self-consciously employed in the poem'.[40] Pound's incursion into the editing of the poem leads to what Anthony L. Johnson refers to as the text's 'paradigmatic coherence' which charts meaning and purpose across breaks and elisions: 'Eliot's procedure is such that syntagmas are seen to fit into a coherent pattern if but only if a paradigmatic reading strategy is adopted.'[41] Elizabeth Schneider understands this method as definable by its requirement of a 'double vision' on the part of the critic – that is, the ability to simultaneously distinguish and understand the units of meaning captured within every poetic moment as well as the radial fragmentation and replication of allusive tropes across the work as a whole. One such example is the attraction and repulsion demonstrated towards failed fortune tellers across the poem, which appears in both pointillistic detail and in the very form of the poem itself. The first appearance of one such soothsayer comes in the epigraph, drawn from Petronius's first century CE verse-novel the *Satyricon*, in which the Cumaean Sibyl has requested eternal life without having the foresight to request eternal youth, leaving her to subsequently wither and to beg for death. The first section of the poem, 'The Burial of the Dead', is focalized by a series of speakers who, likewise, are caught in a deathly stasis and are unable to break free from the horrors of the world. The speaker of the first seven lines, for instance, is buried beneath the ground and becomes fearful of the plant life that feeds on the nutrients of the soil; the Countess Marie Larisch is left lonely and cold with only her books and distant memories of a happy aristocratic childhood to keep her company; and Stetson's thousand-yard stare signals to his interlocuter an entrapment in a living death brought on by what is now known as post-traumatic stress disorder.[42] Within this world of

---

[40] Surette, p. 227.
[41] Johnson, 'Broken Images', pp. 399–416 (p. 404).
[42] There are a number of variations in the use of inverted commas among the magazine publications in the *Criterion* and the *Dial* and the print publications by Boni and Liveright, Hogarth Press and in *Poems, 1909-1925* (1936). The *Criterion* edition most regularly implements inverted commas, turning both the Marie sequence and Madam Sosostris set piece into dialogue. Although the *Criterion, Dial* and Hogarth Press editions avoided the running quotation marks at the beginning of lines in 'A Game of Chess', the relationship between speaker and silent listener has remained stable across editions of the passage. There is fair reason to imagine a break after the Belladonna scene into the dialogue; however, voices merge in the poem and perhaps they do here as well.

failed fortunes and dashed hopes for death, the possibility of finding answers in Madame Sosostris's deck of tarot cards seems especially ironic. What she sees in her spread is fundamentally general and mundane, except for the one enticing moment of revelation which remains to her forbidden. Of this famous poetic set piece, Betsey Creekmore argues that the querent has asked the question of 'may I die?', returning explicitly to the question of the Cumean Sybil in the epigraph.[43] Johnson points out that 'Eliot's incompetence in sustained narrative sequencing is richly compensated for by a prodigious excellent in paradigmatic dynamics',[44] and the resonance of this particular example captures both the theme and sentiment of a poem whose meaning and import emerge as much from the absence of awareness as it does from direct engagement with coherent plotting.

The Waste Land is one of the most widely remarked-upon offspring of Weston's theosophically adjacent *From Ritual to Romance*, but the legend of the Fisher King and his incurable wound would be used elsewhere by modernist writers to allegorize the search for meaning and the possibility of entering into a collaborative co-creation of significance. In Charles Williams's *War in Heaven* (1930), the Grail becomes something of a Mcguffin that draws into sharper resolution the dissolute materialism of the modern world, which can only be saved by the confederation of a middle-class publisher and members of the aristocracy and clergy. Mary Butts's *Armed with Madness* (1928) would similarly turn to an evocative correlation between the healing Grail and the absence and elision of modern life. Her intricately conceived avant-garde style is rooted in free association and, as Sam Wiseman points out, 'is marked by a quintessentially modernist tension, the struggle to reconcile a deep sense of attachment to a regional English home with the intellectual and experiential allure of cosmopolitan modernity'.[45] In addition to moving in circles right at the heart of modernist thinking and art (Pound, Wyndham Lewis, Ford Madox Ford and Roger Fry were among her friends), Butts was a passionate follower of occult philosophy and practice; during 1921 she spent several months living at Aleister Crowley's Abbey of Thelema in Cefelù and contributed to Crowley's *Magick, Liber ABA (Book 4)* under the magical name Soror Rhodon. Butts's high modernist fiction is invested in a deeply seated and deeply personal mystical

---

[43] Betsey B. Creekmore, 'The Tarot Fortune in *The Waste Land*', *ELH*, 49.4 (1982), 911. See also Robert Currie, 'Eliot and the Tarot', *ELH*, 46.4 (1979), 722–33.
[44] Johnson, 'Broken Images', p. 401.
[45] Sam Wiseman, 'Cosmopolitanism and Environmental Ethics in Mary Butts's Dorset', *Twentieth-Century Literature*, 61.3 (2015), 373–91 (p. 373).

world view which sees enchantment and textuality as indispensable companions, and her *Armed with Madness* is unmistakably imbued with the recognition of the continual unfolding of divinity and the possibilities of modernist innovation to invite the reader into a spell of invocation. *Armed with Madness* portrays a period of providential change in the lives of several young members of the fast set for whom the emergence of a purported Grail offers the only possible escape from meaninglessness and malaise: 'There was something in their lives spoiled and inconclusive like the Grail story', the narrator muses.[46] The shrewd thematic parallels to *The Waste Land* are unmistakable, and Andrew Radford argues that her characters 'apprehend the same existential anguish that Eliot describes, but they remove themselves physically from modern urban society so as to inaugurate a "sacred game" elevated to the realm of living sacrament'.[47] In Butts's text, the invitation to describe and rationalize a curious chalice that comes into their possession sets up a thunderous commentary on the co-construction of scared meaning out of mundane language.

Butts's opening gambit in *Armed with Madness* is an extraordinary discontent silence that has settled on a comfortable country house where 'the equivocal, personal silence of the wood' is only partially cancelled out by the gramophone which the residents of the house had been 'playing to the wood after lunch, to appease it and to keep their dancing in hand'.[48] Absence is everything at the outset of the text, and even clothing is missing in these opening scenes when brother and sister Scylla and Felix (who 'belonged to the house and the wood and the turf and the sea'), along with their friend Ross, are nude sunbathing.[49] The odd absence that hovers about the text is connected not merely to the desire to connect and to understand but also to the dangerous implications of the modern world's

> sense of broken continuity, a dis-ease. The end of an age, the beginning of another. Revaluation of values. Phrases that meant something if you could mean them. The meaning of meaning? Discovery of a new value, a different way of apprehending everything. ... There was something wrong with all of them, or with their world. A moment missed, a moment to come. Or not coming. Or either or both. Shove it off on the war; but that did not help.[50]

---

[46] Mary Butts, *Armed with Madness* in *The Taverner Novels* (New York: McPherson, 1992), p. 66.
[47] Andrew Radford, 'Defending Nature's Holy Shrine', *Journal of Modern Literature*, 29.3 (2006), 126–49 (p. 137).
[48] Butts, p. 13.
[49] Butts, p. 14.
[50] Butts, pp. 17–18.

The simultaneous arrival of the American visitor Dudley Carston and the appearance of 'an odd cup of some greenish stone ... rather like pea-soup carnelian' offers an enticing salve to the vanity fashioned by the 'broken continuity' of modern life and, at least for the moment, a sense of the 'different way of apprehending everything' that is so urgently needed.[51] Carston emerges as a serviceable foil to the gentry-pagan goings-on of the house and its visitors, and, while he is an intuitive reader of history and the human mind, his concentration is turned principally towards his romantic feelings towards Scylla and how his American courtesy feels impotent in this radical set. Wiseman reads *Armed with Madness* as indicative of Rebecca Walkowitz's notion of 'cosmopolitan style',[52] and, in the increasingly imagistic and incorporeal panorama captured by Butts's novel, the elusiveness of high modernist fragmentation and stream of consciousness develops knowingly alongside a thematic fascination with objects and consciousnesses that carry only one portion of a divine story. Jane Garrity points out that the text 'attempts to contrast imitation and authenticity by pitting the contemporary urban wasteland against the presence of a rural-supernatural order',[53] and it is from this appositional purview ('a moment to come. Or not coming. Or either or both') that both the difficulty and the significance of the text emerges.

For the dwellers in the house – who talk about the history of the Celts and Saxons 'as if there was no time, no progress, no morality'[54] – the supposed Grail cup is construed and reconstrued in a collaborative form of interpretation. It is portrayed, variously, as 'a shallow little green dish',[55] 'the stone of exile',[56] the 'joy-stone'[57] and a 'Keltic mass-cup'.[58] What the cup represents, more allusively, is the arrival of revivified modern faith and a sensibility that is at once ancient and new, and, in this way, it represents the physical manifestation of the modern and the collaborative formulation of meaning which this new world demands. When the group tries to piece together what they know of the story of the Grail, Scylla instructs them that 'the best way to get that story out is for everyone to say what he thinks or feels or remembers. The Freud game really'.[59] Unsurprisingly,

---

[51] Butts, p. 22.
[52] Wiseman, pp. 373–91 (p. 373).
[53] Jane Garrity, *Step-Daughters of England: British Women Modernists and the National Imaginary* (Manchester: Manchester University Press, 2003), p. 189.
[54] Butts, p. 23.
[55] Butts, p. 23.
[56] Butts, p. 31.
[57] Butts, p. 31.
[58] Butts, p. 36.
[59] Butts, p. 34.

the collective reconstruction of what each thinks, feels and remembers about the Grail is rooted in the textual unconscious of poetry and myth. Felix, for instance, believes that the Celtic Twilight emblematized by Tennyson is 'a false way of telling about something that exists'.[60] To his mind, Tennyson captured the meaning but not the significance of the Grail legends.

Scylla understands that the power and significance of the cup inheres entirely in the process of shared imaginative discourse: 'If that cup is anything at all, if it was once an old cup of the sacrament people called "big magic," if it's anything or nothing, we can't hurt it, and it can't hurt us. We have our courage and our imagination. We have to be as subtle as our memories.'[61] The account of the discovery of the cup is cut by Carston's parenthetical recognition that '(Scylla seemed to be the only woman in the group, a point for reflection)', and the sexual implications of co-creation offer a somewhat sombre romantic through line within the text.[62] Garrity points out that '*Armed with Madness*'s thematic radicalism is located in its suggestion that the female body and the Grail are equivalent conduits to an authentic English past, a move that situates women's agency as central to the nation's cultural regeneration'.[63] 'Where Eliot's work', she continues, 'is saturated with images of reproductive sterility, Butt's fiction dramatizes the procreative and regenerative aspects of the spiritual Grail quest, linking it to ritual practice, the cycles of nature, and – crucially – the female body'.[64] The Grail becomes also Scylla, a childbearer among a group of men, so the quest to ascertain the rights and status of the recovered chalice becomes a rather unambiguous counterpoint to the themes of sexual selection in a mythical vein: 'Butts's conception of a questing mythical femininity both absorbs and interrogates the seminal research of the Cambridge Ritualists of the early twentieth century.'[65] Scylla's nominal correlation to Homer's sea monster turns her into 'a kind of *vagina-dentata* figure' whose potential role in procreation is not only necessary for the furthering of this society but also fearsome and seemingly impossible.[66] Equally significant, however, is that the ambiguity and elusiveness of the text allows portrayals of homosexuality, bisexuality and loose morals to be largely unnoticed by early reviewers (Virginia Woolf nevertheless

---

[60] Butts, p. 34.
[61] Butts, p. 46.
[62] Butts, p. 22.
[63] Garrity, p. 211.
[64] Garrity, p. 209.
[65] Andrew Radford, 'Excavating a Secret History: Mary Butts and the Return of the Nativist', *Connotations: A Journal for Critical Debate*, 17.1 (2007), 80–108 (p. 87).
[66] Garrity, p. 210.

apprehended the full depth of Butts's project and resolutely condemned the novel's impropriety).[67]

In Butts's novel the anxieties of creation strike male characters as well. Like Woolf's Lily Briscoe, Clarence's most desperate challenge is to define an artistic style that is able to channel the divine spark of inspiration into material form, capturing something that seemed, to both Lily and Clarence, to be wholly ineffable and therefore most urgently in need of artistic representation. The challenge of representation is his defining battle. 'He drew in a tree-shape rather hard. The white haze gathered. The more he looked, the less he saw. Instead, he began to see shapes in his head, not outside it, an exercise he avoided, because it interfered with precision of hand.'[68] The nature of making meaning out of emptiness provides Scylla with her clear sense of affinity with life; she explains to Carston that 'if the materialist's universe is true, not a working truth to make bridges with and things, we are set of blind factors in a machine. And no passion has any validity and no imagination. They are just little tricks of the machine.'[69] The narrative captures its characters' sense of possibility of meaning in a world that was simultaneously destroying meaning through classification and through modernization. The creation of meaning out of absence is not merely the method by which these characters make sense of themselves but a method by which the inherited mythical traditions of England offer up the possibility of a renewed hope and future.

Too often modernist scholars read the elusive quality of literary experimentation as a form of epistemological scepticism, a sort of proto-postmodernism in which words have already been emptied of meaning, leaving behind a great abyss of connotation and consequence. However, it seems clear that this node of techniques oriented towards removing rather than revealing, for the most part, was in no way indicative of a loss of faith in divine presence or in the capacity of words to communicate, but, rather, underscored a profound reliance on the creation of cooperative and shared forms of meaning. The *via negativa* of modernism calls on the egoic reader and the author-god to battle to fill the empty space. What modernism reminds us of is that literature provides, firstly, an object of study, one whose boundaries, limits and delimitations open it up to a huge array of possibilities, and an opportunity to *become* rather than merely to observe oneself as an object to the world.

---

[67] Garrity, p. 192.
[68] Butts, p. 29.
[69] Butts, p. 85.

2

The return to ritual: Embodiment and initiation in modernist drama

The previous chapter addressed the proposition that elision served modernism as a key stylistic resource for engaging readers in the cooperative creation of literary meaning and that this recourse to a mystical apophaticism urged readers towards an intuitive and spontaneous approach to embodied understanding. Through the effort of readership, the sacred (in these contexts, referring to that which existed beyond the rationalism of scientific materialism) could be made partly manifest as a liniment to ease the burdens of war and radical social change. Modernist drama was, likewise, concerned with a re-evaluation of the relationship between subject and object, and the potential for locating the divine spark inherent in human consciousness. While the techniques were different, the ambition of arousing the spirit of the audience and provoking them towards a direct and unmediated sense of purpose was clearly present. This chapter draws attention to the certain but unremarked-upon correlations between occult philosophy and the rise of modernist drama as developed by Konstantin Stanislavski, Vseolod Meyerhold, Michael Chekhov, Antonin Artaud and Jerzy Grotowski, among others. At times deliberately and at other times incidentally, these directors and teachers framed the 'New Drama' in uncannily occult terms with elaborate systems of training which sought to reaffirm the actor's divine capacity for channelling and embodying sensation. Twentieth-century actor training drew on a distinctly esoteric framework, and the method through which contemporary Western actors have been understood to transmute a written text into an embodied performance has long been connected to mysticism. While the most significant mode of occult performance of the mid-nineteenth century was the improvisational theatre of the dining room seance, the lines between professional theatre and occult ritual would become blurred by the century's end. Beginning with an account of the nineteenth-century rise of ritual studies and the affinities between ritual and the new forms of acting, playwriting and actor training which began to emerge near turn of the twentieth century, the chapter then scrutinizes the impact of these developments through readings of several largely forgotten modernist plays by the occultists Florence Farr and Rudolf Steiner: two short ritualistic dramas set in ancient Egypt written by Farr in collaboration with Olivia Shakespear and a cycle of four mystery dramas that Steiner worked on up until the outbreak of the First World War. While Farr and Steiner seem initially to be wilfully resistant to the styles and objectives of the 'New Drama', they nevertheless render categorically modernist playtexts that attempt to disengage the egoic, rational mind to enliven the instinctual response through non-analytical means.

Nineteenth-century conceptualizations of the vast human inheritance of ritual were various, and thinkers including Max Müller, William Robertson Smith and Andrew Lang saw, each in their own way, the role of ritual in either creating, perpetuating or legitimating religious belief; for them, ritual was understood to be an enactment of inherited myth, with the ritualized actions providing a crucial personified reminder of a shared cultural source. But it was Robertson Smith's student and friend J. G. Frazer who, in his magisterial *The Golden Bough*, argued that myths are reverse engineered in order to explain inherited rituals whose purpose and function had long been forgotten. For Frazer, humans are fundamentally a ritualistic rather than mythological creature, implying that the transmission of cultural history and knowledge comes through the actions that we undertake rather than from the stories that we use to justify these actions. It was from this position that the Cambridge Ritualists including Jane Ellen Harrison, Gilbert Murray and Francis Cornford continued to explore the curious and often idiosyncratic transmission of knowledge through ritualized actions that aimed to lessen the distance between humanity and the divine. Émile Durkheim's *Elementary Forms of the Religious Life* (1912) portrayed the function of ritual to be the unification of community through a shared knowledge process, a materialist reading of religion and ritual which ran counter to William James's more mystical provocations in *The Varieties of Religious Experience* (1902). Claude Lévi-Strauss would contest such a notion in his 1962 study of structural anthropology, *The Savage Mind*, where he defined myth as the constitutive substance in the transmission of cultural experience, thus relegating ritual to the method of its mechanical communication. 'The value of the ritual as meaning seems to reside in instruments and gestures: it is a *paralanguage*', Lévi-Strauss explains. 'The myth, on the other hand, manifests itself as a *metalanguage*; it makes full use of discourses, but does so by situating its own significant oppositions at a higher level of complexity than that required by language operating for profane ends.'¹ Contemporary ritual studies scholar Catherine Bell defines ritual as 'a set of activities that does not simply express cultural values or enact symbolic scripts but actually effects changes in people's perceptions and interpretations'.² Bell maintains that 'ritual does not mold people; people fashion rituals that mold their world',³ a sentiment later echoed in Roger Grainger's recognition that 'ritual, like theatre, is an inhabitable metaphor, a state of mind they can enter and leave, a place to be; it is a unique coming together of subject and object in which each reaches out and subjectifies the other; is the place of discovery and encounter'.⁴

A resonant and deeply influential example of modern occult ritual is the ornate Hermetic Order of the Golden Dawn initiatory system which represents, in the words of Golden Dawn historian Ellic Howe, 'an important reservoir of "hidden knowledge" based upon an ingenious construction of arbitrary relationships between different symbolical systems, e.g. the Cabbalistic Treat of Life, astrology, alchemy, the Tarot trumps and so on [which] represented the equivalent of a Hermetic University, with an exacting series of examinations leading to the equivalent of a post-graduate degree in the Theoricus Adeptus Minor grade'.⁵ Founder William Wynn Westcott – a coroner by trade and a theosophist and Freemason by conviction – arranged for the manufacture of a sheaf of encoded documents which detailed five quasi-Masonic rituals to initiate and then raise candidates through the degrees of Neophyte ($0° = 0°$) to Philosophus ($4° = 7°$). Crucially, tucked inside was the address of one Fräulein Sprengel, purported head of an occult organization called *Die Goldene Dämmerung* who would give permission to consecrate a new Isis-Urania Temple of the Golden Dawn in London (conveniently, Westcott would report the untimely death of Fräulein Sprengel shortly after). The rituals were unquestionably created by Westcott, and 'Fräulein Sprengel' was no more than a fictional justification for spiritual authority.⁶ Westcott brought with him to the endeavour Samuel MacGregor Mathers and William Robert Woodman, both fellow Freemasons and, crucially, fellow members of the Socitas Rosicruciana in Anglia (SRIA), an esoteric

---

[1] Claude Lévi-Strauss, *The Savage Mind* (London: Weidenfeld and Nicolson, 1966), p. 66.
[2] Catherine Bell, *Ritual: Perspectives and Dimensions* (Oxford: Oxford University Press, 1997), p. 74.
[3] Bell, p. 73.
[4] Roger Grainger, *Ritual and Theatre* (London: Austin Macauley, 2014), p. 62.
[5] Ellic Howe, *The Magicians of the Golden Dawn: A Documentary History of a Magical Order, 1887–1923* (York Beach, ME: Samuel Weiser, 1972), p. xxii.
[6] For a full account of the provenance of the cypher manuscripts and the ensuing fictional letters exchanged, see R. A. Gilbert, *The Golden Dawn Scrapbook: The Rise and Fall of a Magical Order* (York Beach, ME: Samuel Weiser, 1997), 21–33; Howe, chapter 1; Carroll Runyon, *Secrets of the Golden Dawn Cypher Manuscripts* (Silverado, CA: Church of the Hermetic Sciences, 1997).

Masonic side order founded in 1866 similarly through the reported discovery of lost occult documents.[7] The names of the nine degrees of the SRIA were borrowed in their entirety, and by the time that Mathers began to write the rituals for the Inner Order of the Rose of Ruby and the Cross of Gold (R.R. et A.C.), he had moved beyond the Fräulein Sprengel story and based his work upon a purported connection to the 'Secret Chiefs', a Golden Dawn counterpart to Helena Blavatsky's Mahatmas.

Between its founding in 1888 and the start of its gradual decline a decade later, the Golden Dawn initiated 315 members across its five temples in London, Weston-super-Mare, Bradford, Edinburgh and Paris, including Annie Horniman, W. B. Yeats, Florence Farr, Maud Gonne, Constance Wilde, Arthur Machen, Algernon Blackwood, Mina Bergson, Aleister Crowley, Allan Bennett and A. E. Waite.[8] As Edmund Lingan points out, 'Many occultists related their theatrical practices to the dramatic mysteries of a primordial tradition [and] several such occultists suggested that their performance practices bore an affinity to the initiatory dramas of ancient cults.'[9] The rituals of the Golden Dawn were published across four volumes beginning in 1937 by Israel Regardie, an initiate of R. W. Felkin's Golden Dawn-splinter Stella Matutina and a one-time secretary to Aleister Crowley. Regardie's introduction to the first edition is still one of the most rigorous and nuanced treatments of the Golden Dawn rituals and deserves a substantial quotation:

> We can epitomise in a single word the entire teaching and ideal of those rituals. If one idea more than any other is persistently stressed from the beginning that idea is in the word *Light*. From the candidate's first reception in the Hall of the Neophytes when the Hierophant adjures him with these words: 'Child of Earth, long hast thou dwelt in darkness. Quit the night and seek the day', to the transfiguration in the Vault ceremony, the whole system has as its objective the bringing down of the Light. For it is by that Light that the golden banner of the inner life may be exalted; it is in light where lies healing and the power of growth. Some vague intimation of the power and splendour of that glory is first given to the aspirant in the Neophyte Grade when, rising from his knees at the close of the invocation, the Light is formulated above his head in the symbol of

---

[7] Howe, p. 27. While many scholars tend to view Mathers as the primary spiritual innovator of the Golden Dawn, Westcott's personal writing reveals the rich and nuanced occult learning that he possessed. See R. A. Gilbert (ed.), *The Magical Mason: Forgotten Hermetic Writings of William Wynn Westcott, Physician and Magus* (Wellingborough: Aquarian Press, 1983).

[8] Howe, p. 49.

[9] Edmund Lingan, *The Theatre of the Occult Revival: Alternative Spiritual Performance from 1875 to the Present* (London: Palgrave Macmillan, 2015), p. 7.

the White Triangle by the union of the implements of the three chief officers. By means of the Adeptus Minor ritual, which identifies him with the Chief Officer, he is slain as though by the destructive force of his lower self. After being symbolically buried, triumphantly he rises from the tomb of Osiris in a glorious resurrection through the descent of the white Light of the Spirit. The intervening grades occupy themselves with the analysis of that Light as it vibrates between the light and the darkness, and with the establishment within the candidate's personal sphere of the rays of the many-coloured rainbow of promise.[10]

The rituals for the first five degree of the Golden Dawn system follow a typically Masonic order of admitting the candidate, performing a circumambulatory trial, undertaking an oath or pledge and then receiving the symbolism of the new degree. The intended aim was to initiate the participant into a direct connection with the sacred, progressively moving to deeper and more multifaceted recognitions of the sacred through each degree ceremony. Theosophist and Co-Freemason Annie Besant defined initiation as 'a certain series of events through which the man passes; actual events and experiences taking a certain amount of time, not a vague indefinite series of feelings, but actual communications and thoughts and actions gone through by a man out of the physical body'.[11] In this process are three stages – '(1) The Path of Purification of Purgation; (2) the Path of Illumination; and (3) the Path of Union with Divinity'[12] – which map neatly on to Arnold van Gennep's later 1908 categories of separation, transition and incorporation in *Les rites de passage*: an initiation is, in several key ways, a rite of passage. Howe explains in *The Magicians of the Golden Dawn* (1972) that 'in some respects the ritual ceremonies were like complicated theatrical performances', perhaps something of an understatement in considering just how theatrical the rituals are.[13] The initiation into the Inner Order of the Rosea Rubea et Aurea Crucia (5° = 6°), for instance, draws upon the Christian Rosenkreutz legend to portray an eight-sided room covered in magical sigils called the Vault of the Adepti in which stands a coffin to represent the mystical burial place of the legendary Father Rosenkreutz.

The theatrical rituals of the Golden Dawn would influence many initiatory groups throughout the twentieth century. As occult writer and practitioner Gareth Knight points out, 'Ritual scripts, like theatre scripts, require a

---

[10] Israel Regardie, *The Golden Dawn: The Original Account of the Teachings, Rites and Ceremonies of the Hermetic Order of the Golden Dawn*, 6th edn (St Paul: Llewellyn, 1989), pp. 23–4.
[11] Annie Besant, *Initiation: The Perfection of Man* (London: Theosophical Publishing House, 1918), p. 76.
[12] Besant, p. 1.
[13] Howe, p. 67.

particularly concentrated method of study. Not of the intellect, but of the pictorial imagination, taking it all in slowly and deeply. Then what may appear banal or repetitive on the printed page can come across as a powerful subjective and even mystical experience.'[14] A largely forgotten contribution to the history of ritual is W. B. Yeats's collection of initiatory rituals, now known either as the 'Celtic Mysteries' or the 'Castle of Heroes', which had been initially formulated in a series of 'visions' or trance-induced group meditations in early 1898 and private automatic writing produced around the same time.[15] The form of the rituals follows Freemasonic and Golden Dawn structure of bringing a blindfolded candidate into a scene of inexplicable language and sounds, with a guide who will speak for the initiate initially until the initiate becomes an active participant in the ritual. Having thus been made a part of one's own ritual, privileged information is received, and one is prepared to begin progressing towards the intellectual, spiritual or ethical requirements for the next degree. In one of the few extended readings of the rituals, Lucy Kalogera argues that through this work Yeats 'hoped to create a specifically Irish esoteric-visionary society'.[16] 'In them', she continues, 'Yeats hoped to find new symbols for literature, as he believed that folklore and myth created from the same racial memory from which his rituals would be drawn were the keys to all great literature, expressing the content and character of the soul rather than merely the intellect'.[17] The structure provided by the Golden Dawn rituals remained largely intact, now with a new veneer of Celtic godforms influenced by the writings of Fiona Macleod (William Sharp) and other writers of the Celtic Revival. The ritual system of the Golden Dawn would provide inspiration to other modernist writers as well. In Dion Fortune's rituals *The Rites of Isis* and *The Rites of Pan*, for instance, an opening apostrophe to a deity figure is followed by the embodiment of Pan by the ritual's Priest and Isis by the ritual's Priestess. Knight explains of Fortune's rituals that 'by means of a set rite we obtain prolonged attention, and by means of the "conditioned symbols" that make up the rite, we generate emotion. ... Thus by the use of that all-important factor, the pictorial imagination, the attention is held, a mood is achieved, and spiritual realisation or exaltation can follow.'[18] Rather than enacting sacred invocation and embodiment of deity, Aleister Crowley's *Rites of Eleusis* (1910) is an astrological masque of seven rituals covering the

[14] Gareth Knight, *Dion Fortune's Rites of Isis and of Pan* (Cheltenham: Skylight, 2013), p. 40.
[15] Lucy Kalogera, 'Yeats's Celtic Mysteries', unpublished doctoral dissertation, Florida State University, 1977, appendices 1 and 2.
[16] Kalogera, p. 5.
[17] Kalogera, p. 6.
[18] Knight, p. 11.

seven classical planets of antiquity: Moon, Sun, Mercury, Venus, Mars, Jupiter and Saturn. Characters represent and are named after zodiacal signs, so the rituals present an embodied representation of planets in signs and the outward expressions of such. 'The Rite of Venus', for instance, includes the characters Venus, Taurus, Libra, Pisces, Luna in Taurus and Saturn in Libra. The rituals of the Hermetic Order of the Golden Dawn form a corpus of occult drama that was meant for selected eyes only, but there is clear evidence that this theatricality and flair would influence key developments in the exoteric drama intended for public audiences.

At this point it is important to re-establish the lines between exoteric and esoteric ritual, between (1) ritualized practices intended to publicly transmit tangible material in the form of morals, knowledge or sensations (what Bell identifies as rites of passage, calendrical rites, rites of exchange and communion, rites of affliction, feasts and political rites) and (2) the jealously guarded rituals of initiatory groups that intended to transmit morals, knowledge or sensations sense through the mechanism of unmediated gnosis. Although 'the boundaries between occultism and theatre blurred during the Occult Revival', Lingan maintains the important distinction between ritual theatre that was created in connection to specific occult organizations and theatre that draws upon occult images and ways of thinking; the conceptual contributions of Eliphas Lévi, Helena Blavatsky and Edouard Schuré perpetuated the primeval 'dynamic relationship' between theatre and occult philosophy.[19] In *Way of the Actor* (1987), Brian Bates describes how the shamanistic contexts and form of early ritual continue to impact upon both the training and performance of contemporary actors, who are regularly understood to either be possessed by a character outside of themselves or transformed into another being. Like shamans, actors have 'abilities to change their states of mind and body, and to ascend to the sky or descend to the underworld where lie the worlds of spirits and gods – the agents of perennial truth and knowledge'.[20] Modern drama, as Bates argues, is built upon this 'inside-out' model of shamanistic embodiment, marking a clear distinction from the 'outside-in' focus on diction and delivery that had predominated in theatre up until the late nineteenth century.[21] The professionalization of performance through training, 'methods' and an emphasis on 'technique' is a twentieth-century development that must not be underestimated. As Alison

---

[19] Lingan, pp. 15, 27.
[20] Brian Bates, *The Way of the Actor* (London: Century Hutchinson, 1987), p. 21.
[21] Bates, pp. 32–5.

Hodge suggests, actor training 'has come to inform both the concept and construction of the actor's role, and consequently the entire dramatic process'.[22] These systems of actor training originated from a series of directors who, both in their own time and in the warm regard they continue to be held in the theatre world, take on the persona of great mystics and spiritual leaders: one could describe herself as a *follower of Stanislavski* or a *disciple of Growotoski* without attracting much, if any, puzzlement. These directors and teachers explicitly relied on the mystical premise that character could be channelled into mind of the actor, purified and prepared through exercises and preparations that would look at home in the training materials of an occult organization.

Konstantin Stanislavski founded the Moscow Arts Theatre in 1898 and would, a decade later while rehearsing Turgenev's *A Month in the Country*, codify his grammar of acting and actor training centred on sense memory into what is now described as the Stanislavski Method or simply the 'Method', the term preferred by later teachers such as Lee Strasberg, Stella Adler and Harold Clurman who emerged from the American Laboratory Theatre. As Stanislavski points out in *An Actor Prepares* (1936), 'All external production is formal, cold, and pointless if it is not motivated from within', so actors were encouraged to find cyphers for the emotion within themselves.[23] In some cases, members of the Moscow Arts Theatre were practicing occultists. Michael Chekhov, nephew of Anton Chekhov and student of Stanislavski, was a follower of Rudolph Steiner's Anthroposophical Society and integrated Steiner's vision of the Higher Self into his practices until 1928 when he was expelled from the Moscow Arts Theatre for what was perceived as explicitly occultist actor training.[24] Chekhov approvingly quotes Steiner throughout his *On the Technique of Acting*, where he lays out an unmistakably hermetic approach in the laws of triplicity, polarity and transformation as methods for understanding and interpreting drama, and his 1931 Paris production of his own Symbolist play called *The Castle Awakens* utilized Steiner's eurhythmy.[25] Growtowki presents a similar sensibility in *Towards a Poor Theatre* (1968) when he points out that

> the education of an actor in our theatre is not a matter of teaching him something; we attempt to eliminate his organism's resistance to this psychic process. The

---

[22] Alison Hodge, 'Introduction' to *Twentieth-Century Actor Training*, ed. Alison Hodge (London: Routledge, 2000), pp. 1–9 (p. 1).

[23] Constantin Stanislavski, *An Actor Prepares*, trans. Elizabeth Reynolds Hapgood (London: Geoffrey Bliss, 1937), p. 164.

[24] Maria Carlson, *No Religion Higher Than Truth: A History of the Theosophical Movement in Russia, 1875–1922* (Princeton, NJ: Princeton University Press, 1993), p. 177.

[25] Mel Gordon, 'Mikhail Chekhov's 1931 Occult Fantasy', *Performing Arts Journal*, 17.1 (1995), 110–12.

result is freedom from the time-lapse between inner impulse and outer reaction in such a way that the impulse is already an outer reaction.[26]

Grotowski used distinctively spiritual terms to describe acting: the 'holy actor' sacrificed his or her whole body to the role in a ritual of dead and rejuvenation, and, as he concludes, his method of work at the Theatre Laboratory is 'a via negativa – not a collection of skills but an eradication of blocks'.[27] Peter Brook, whose own creative practice was heavily influenced by Grotowski, notes that 'Grotowski's actors offer their performances as a ceremony for those who wish to assist: the actor invokes, lays bare what lies in every man – and what daily life covers up. This theatre is holy because its purpose is holy; it has a clearly defined place in the community and it responds to a need the churches can no longer fill.'[28] Grotowski ultimately works towards rejecting the superficiality of the theatre – costumes, sets, lights – because the singular and most definitive aspect of theatre is 'the actor-spectator relationship of perceptual, direct, "live" communion'.[29]

In his beguiling and forceful *The Theatre and Its Double* (1938), Antonin Artaud understood that theatre audiences had become desensitized to the obscurities of human character through the relentless stylization of a stock dramatis personae. Modern drama's transition from an 'outward-in' emphasis on declamation and carriage to an 'inward-out' realism had begun several decades earlier – first in Russia, then in Norway, Sweden, England and beyond – but Artaud keenly sensed that an even more comprehensive reconstitution of the dramatic arts needed to take place, one which saw cruelty cast into the foreground to trigger metamorphic change. It was for this reason that Artaud proposed that an ideal modern theatre finds its most redolent prototype in the medieval craft of alchemy:

> Where alchemy, through its signs, is like the mental Double of an act effective on the level of real matter alone, theatre ought also to be considered as the Double not of this immediate, everyday reality which has been slowly truncated to a mere lifeless copy, as empty as it is saccharined, but another, deadlier archetypal reality.[30]

---

[26] Jerzy Grotowski, *Towards a Poor Theatre* (London: Methuen, 1968), p. 16.
[27] Grotowski, p. 17.
[28] Peter Brook, *The Empty Space* (1968; repr. London: Penguin, 2008), p. 67.
[29] Grotowski, p. 19.
[30] Antonin Artaud, *The Theatre and Its Double*, trans. Victor Corti (1938; repr. Croydon: Alma Classics, 2014), p. 34.

Throughout *The Theatre and Its Double*, Artaud rejects a reproductive model of drama, thinking instead of theatre as a process of alchemical dissolution, separation and distillation which opposes the long-prevailing Aristotelian view of dramatic characters as icons (initially of gods and heroes and latterly of the everyman and the downtrodden) who play out the inevitability of their archetype. As Aristotle memorably maintained in the *Poetics* (c.335 BCE), 'An action implies personal agents, who necessarily possess certain distinctive qualities both of character and thought ... By character I mean that in virtue of which we ascribe certain qualities to the agents.'[31] But Artaud was not willing to take characters as stock-still emblems acted upon by forces outside of their control but, rather, as active participants in the creation of meaning; here alchemy is not simply an enticing metaphor but a radical proposition. For Artaud, drama is an art form of the supersensible, one that necessarily transcends human experience in its creation even while it is this very human experience which it intends to capture. Drama, he suggests, is the natural alchemy of the soul:

> We ought to note the strange proclivity all books dealing with alchemy maintain for theatre terms, as if their authors had from the start felt everything *productive*, that is to say everything theatrical, in the whole series of *symbols* by which the Great work occurs mentally, while waiting for it to occur substantially in real life, as well as in the digressions of an uninformed mind, of all the acts and in what one might term the 'dialectic' sequence of all the wanderings, apparitions, mirages and hallucinations which those who attempt to perform such acts *by purely human means* cannot fair to encounter.[32]

Tellingly, he is not using the model offered by alchemy as a way to explore drama but, rather, proposing that it was alchemy which found its symbolic framework from drama. Thirty years after *The Theatre and Its Double*, Peter Brook picked up on the esoteric impulse of 'inward-out' modernist drama in *The Empty Space* (1968) where he imagines the 'Theatre of the Invisible-Made-Visible', 'the notion that the stage is a place where the invisible can appear has a deep hold on our thoughts.'[33] For Brook, a committed follower of Artaud, the materialization of a post-Stanislavski modern drama is a natural and expected response to the desire for ritual, an innate human drive which had been progressively precluded by the rationalizing forces of scientific materialism:

---

[31] Aristotle, *The Poetics of Aristotle*, trans. S. H. Butcher (London: Macmillan, 1902), p. 25.
[32] Artaud, *The Theatre and Its Double*, p. 34.
[33] Brook, p. 47.

> We have lost all sense of ritual and ceremony – whether it be connected with Christmas, birthdays or funerals – but the words remain with us and old impulses stir in the marrow. We feel we should have rituals, we should do 'something' about getting them and we black the artists for not 'finding' them for us. So the artist sometimes attempts to find new rituals with only his imagination as his source: he imitates the outer form of ceremonies, pagan or baroque, unfortunately adding his own trappings – the result is rarely convincing. And after the years and years of weaker and waterier imitations we now find ourselves rejecting the very notion of the holy stage.[34]

While both Artaud and Brook are remembered for their perturbing and unruly dramaturgy – Brook's 1964 staging of Peter Weiss's *The Persecution and Assassination of Jean-Paul Marat as Performed by the Inmates of the Asylum of Charenton under the Direction of the Marquis de Sade* (1963) for the Royal Shakespeare Company is a typical example – their dramatic aims remained unwaveringly tied to generating ritualized transcendence which offered a glimpse of the sacred divinity of the spirit. Vseolod Meyerhold, like Steiner and Gurdjieff, taught movement 'études' as a form of warm up and centring, an occult technique which was knowingly and ruthlessly parodied in Leanora Carrington's 1976 novel *The Hearing Trumpet*. These esoteric precepts were by no means unique in modern drama, where, in spite of the obvious turn to the New Drama of Ibsen, Strindberg and Chekhov, the occult and supersensible became key figurations in both the substance and form of work by modernist playwrights including Florence Farr and Rudolf Steiner.

The significant association between occult ritual and the rise of modernist drama comes perhaps into clearest focus in the work of actress, director, playwright and journalist Florence Farr, who viewed modern theatre as a powerful tool to act upon the sensibilities of the audience and performers. Farr had gotten her start playing bit roles at the Folly Theatre near Charring Cross, a popular music hall where opera bouffe was the order of the day.[35] She would satirize her early theatrical experience in the novel *The Dancing Faun* (1894), published in the same year in which she both was promoted to Praemonstratrix in the Golden Dawn and produced Bernard Shaw's first commercially successful gesture towards the New Drama in a season at the Avenue Theatre, now the Playhouse Theatre at Embankment. Although it would still be a full decade before the founding of the Royal Court Theatre gave a permanent home to the

---

[34] Brook, p. 51.
[35] Josephine Johnson, *Florence Farr: Bernard Shaw's New Woman* (Gerrards Cross: Colin Smythe, 1975), pp. 19–20.

New Drama, Farr's 1894 Avenue Theatre Season offered a potent taste of what was to come.[36] Golden Dawn initiate Annie Horniman invested the capital and Aubrey Beardsley, then serving as art editor for *The Yellow Book*, designed the poster for the season which included plays by Yeats and John Todhunter (both initiates of the Golden Dawn) alongside the later addition of Shaw's *Arms and the Man* which ran for fifty performances over eleven weeks and featured Farr in the role of Louka.[37] When *Arms and the Man* was later published in *Plays Pleasant*, Shaw credited Farr and Horniman for helping to get his first major production to the West End.[38]

When Farr was initiated into the Hermetic Order of the Golden Dawn in 1890, she took the magical name *Sapientia Sapienti Dono Data* ('wisdom is a gift to the wise'), suggesting that she saw both the accumulation and passing on of wisdom as the core focus of her life's work. Farr understood an obvious and unambiguous relationship between the worlds of occultism and theatre. In addition to her membership in the Golden Dawn, she ran the Fellowship of the Three Kings, an occult theatre group which included among its members Yeats, Edith Craig, Thomas Sturge Moore and Pamela Coleman Smith and met at 8 Adelphi Terrace when Shaw lived at number 10.[39] It seems possible, although no documentary evidence exists, that the Fellowship of the Three Kings maintained an informal, outer circle relationship with the Golden Dawn and was used as a drama training ground where the overlap between ritual and stagecraft could be explored. Farr's dramatic work looked both backwards to the long history of drama as a form of religious ritual and forwards to the pressing new theatrical developments of the twentieth century, and, furthermore, sensed that theatre could move beyond passive transfer of meaning and sentiment to offer, instead, an opportunity for the audience to embody within them the world of the play and the wisdom it contained. One particular route in this direction was a form of vocalization Farr taught called 'cantillation', the semi-chanting of verse accompanied by a string instrument called a psaltery tuned to the speaker's voice, in a clear gesture towards the religious associations of choral chanting in the earliest development of classical Greek theatre. Musician and instrument

---

[36] On the developments of the new drama from 1904 onwards with the opening of the Court Theatre, see Wallace Martin, *The New Age under Orage: Chapters in English Cultural History* (Manchester: Manchester University Press, 1967), chapter 4.

[37] Johnson, p. 62. Horniman would finance an even more famous moment in the history of modern drama several years later when she purchased the Abbey Theatre in Dublin (and four years later in 1908 she would purchase the Gaiety Theatre in Manchester).

[38] Bernard Shaw, *Plays Pleasant* (1898; repr. London: Penguin, 2003), p. 7.

[39] R. F. Foster, *W. B. Yeats: A Life, Volume 1: The Apprentice Mage* (Oxford: Oxford University Press, 1998), p. 257.

maker Arthur Dolmetsch designed the psaltery, to which Farr chanted lines of poetry that she believed 'could magically bridge the inner essence or soul and outer reality of physical form'.[40] Farr's experiments with the theatrical form aimed to bring life to a new mode of modern drama, by returning audiences' attention to theatre as a form of spiritual embodiment.

Material for her own dramatic writing would come in December of 1895 when Farr claims that she was contacted by one of the disincarnate 'Secret Chiefs' of the Hermetic Order of the Golden Dawn who gave her privileged knowledge about both ancient Egypt and a possible redemptive future for humanity. Following this, Farr's interest in Egyptology intensified and the following year she published one of her major works of non-fiction, *Egyptian Magic* (1896), which identifies a vision of an ideal society built upon knowledge and initiation, a new form of public organization which, it seemed to Farr, could coexist quite happily with the genteel social reform of the Fabian Society and the artistic, liberally minded conclave of Bedford Park in West London. Farr positions the magic of Egypt as uniquely modern, an almost rationalist explication of the innerworkings of the systems which shape the individual's place within society and connection to divinity:

> In studying Egyptian Magic one has at once a thoroughly scientific satisfaction. One is troubled with no vogue theories, but receives precise practical details; we observe that every square inch of the Upper and Under Worlds is mapped out. The strength that such a system inherently contains was proved by the long duration of the Egyptian civilization.[41]

The work was fairly widely cited during its time, and, because she published it under her magical name, S. S. D. D., Manly P. Hall, in his classic 1928 *Secret Teachings of All Ages*, would assume that the writer of *Egyptian Magic* was male. Publication of *Egyptian Magic* came shortly before Farr's departure from the Golden Dawn during a tumultuous year which saw the increasing disintegration of the order, and her Egyptian visions would be put to dramatic use early in the new century when she collaborated with Olivia Shakespear on two modernist one-act plays that depicted elaborate rituals of the Egyptian New Kingdom around 1500 BCE: *The Beloved of Hathor* (1902) and *The Shrine of the Golden Hawk* (1902). Josephine Johnson argues that Farr wrote much of the material for the plays (Shakespear's 'style was less direct than Florence's, more decorative,

---

[40] Barbara Acker, 'The Verse Delivery Experiments of William Butler Yeats and Florence Farr', *Voice and Speech Review*, 5.1 (2007), 192–200 (p. 193).
[41] S. S. D. D. (Florence Farr), *Egyptian Magic* (1896; repr. Whitefish: Kessinger, n.d.), p. 2.

and her subject matter rather more romantic', Johnson reasons[42]), and it is clear that the plays demonstrate a significant culmination in Farr's ritual practice and use of cantillation, which continued to provide in this context a potent tool in the creation of a heightened, ritualized theatre. In what seems initially to be the preamble to a play about masculine potency and valour, *The Beloved of Hathor* opens with the female characters Ranoutet and Ouny discussing the decisive final battle that the storied warrior Aahmes will lead against the Hyksos the following morning. However, the play powerfully and ironically upends these patriarchal formulations to show that it is Ranoutet, the priestess of the temple, whose divine connection to the maternal goddess Hathor will ensure victory in battle and shape the lives of men. Aahmes may be the titular 'beloved of Hathor', but it is the mystical interventions of Ranoutet which maintain his spiritual marriage to the goddess and ensures his military might. In the early moments of the play, Ranoutet remains intently focused on preparations for the culminating ritual of supplication to Hathor, the success of which is dependent upon Aahmes's chastity and devotion to his patron deity:

> RANOUTET: The foretelling of this victory has been long in our ears; when it comes to pass we of the temple will receive [Aahmes] with great honour. He is the beloved of Hathor, and her will has been his pleasure. If he can withstand temptation in the supreme hour of earthly triumph, she will receive him into the great mysteries.
>
> OUNY: Can Aahmes still be tempted – Aahmes, the lover of Hathor?
>
> RANOUTET: The hour is at hand which is to try his strength of purpose.[43]

Although Ranoutet can ceremonially bless him in his undertakings, she cannot ensure his fidelity to the goddess, which, by extension, demands his human fidelity to her as the deputy of Hathor. 'After the battle fought for Egypt comes the enlightenment', she explains to him, 'Then comes the supreme vision. This flesh shall fall from you. You shall be no more the warrior of Egypt, but shall know yourself to be the Lord of Space and Being!'[44] It is through the sacred erotic union with Ranoutet following the battle that he will achieve 'the supreme vision' that will elevate him to the priesthood, a task shown within the world of the play to be unobtainable by men whose rootedness in the material plane requires the interventions of women to enable spiritual transcendence. When the

---

[42] Johnson, p. 90.
[43] Florence Farr and Olivia Shakespear, *The Beloved of Hathor and the Shrine of the Golden Hawk* (Croydon: privately printed, 1902), pp. 7–8.
[44] Farr and Shakespear, p. 15.

enchantress Nouferou arrives in the inner sanctum of the temple, she mistakes Aahmes's masculine authority for the source of sacred power and incorrectly assumes him to be the direct conduit to the forms of spiritual wisdom that she is seeking. 'I burn for knowledge', she pleads, 'for the freedom of the bird upon the wing. I am weary of the speech of the wise, who have not wisdom; who would tell me that Egyptian women must always be discreet and secret.'[45] She seduces him with incantations, physically and psychically commanding the great warrior and, in doing so, ruins his hope for divine union with Hathor. When Ranoutet returns to discover that the kingdom's hope for redemption has been devastated by the unrestrained passions of a man, she proclaims,

> This plant of failure, Aahmes, which you have sown, bears a flower which to the outward seeming is of splendid color and a sweet smell, and its name is Power. Put it upon your heart, and be strong to rule our people; but know that such a blossom is arid, and holds no promise of immortal fruit. Have power and the ruling of the kingdom, but have sorrow also, and eternal grief; because the doors of Hathor's sanctuary open to you no more.[46]

The battle is ultimately won, but, now decoupled from the divine grace of Hathor and her priestess, the 'victory be to the flesh alone'.[47] With the two intimations of *The Beloved of Hathor* – that it is women who hold on to the spiritual endowment of the kingdom and that men are the intemperate but necessary vessels for its continuation – Farr and Shakespear offer an acerbic and unmistakably satirical commentary on the 'Woman Question' that remained central in public discourse at the time. The late Victorian tropes of the fallen woman and seductress are powerfully redeployed in a new constellation of power which resists the scientific materialism of the time to portray a world in which the spiritual domain of women offers the only access to knowledge and power.

The thematic shape of *The Beloved of Hathor* is echoed in its companion play, *The Shrine of the Golden Hawk*, which portrays the incursion of a woman into a male priesthood which is connected firmly to the elemental nature of the world but less immediately attached to the transcendent realm of immanent divinity. Faced with threat of famine, the priest Gebuel invokes elemental powers through the god Heru into a golden breastplate fashioned in the shape of the hawk. Nectoris, a woman who has 'been guided by some star that smiled on my nativity, which was darkened until this day in obedience to a wisdom higher

---

[45] Farr and Shakespear, p. 13.
[46] Farr and Shakespear, p. 19.
[47] Farr and Shakespear, p. 28.

than its own', comes to seek wisdom by entering into direct communication with Heru.[48] Her ancestral mission is to capture the golden hawk in order to become a priestess and queen, and when her entrance into the shrine leads to an ecstatic revelation of her soul, Gebuel recognizes the futility of the masculine undertakings of the priests who have been concerned with the material rather than the spiritual implications of the divine. Mary Greer reads *The Shrine of the Golden Hawk* as a commentary of Farr's then-recent split from the Golden Dawn and repudiation of the limitations that men continued to place on her spiritual expression.[49] Like Ranoutet, Nectoris is endowed with sacred power because she is able to undertake one task that men are not: unmediated access to the divine. Farr placed great significance on the transformational power of initiation within an established occult lineage, and it was this interest in the embodiment of wisdom which united Farr's diverse interests across theatre, Western occultism, Egyptology and women's suffrage. The plays themselves are evocative in their simplicity and yet still forcefully capture change in a rapidly evolving world. Farr would later become a member of the Theosophical Society, and her vision gradually changed in two ways: her esoteric interests moved away from Western mystery traditions to the living spiritual practices of Asia, and her political support for suffrage and women's rights became more pronounced and, at least in sentiment, more revolutionary.

While the Method first developed and taught in Moscow would become the predominant mode of theatrical training and production in Western theatre, the modernist era was littered with rebels. One such case was Farr's attempt to restore incantatory power of dramatic speech to the training of actors, and another equally suggestive return to the initiatory roots of theatre emerges from the new performance style known as eurhythmy created by the spiritual leader, philosopher, educationalist and playwright Rudolf Steiner. In eurhythmy, movement supports voice, inner feeling and outward expression, and the total experience was understood to lift the performance to heights unobtainable in the naturalism of Stanislavski's Method (although it bears remembering that Steiner's eurhythmy would later influence Michael Chekhov at the Moscow Arts Theatre). Shortly before the outbreak of the First World War, Steiner designed and began construction on a temple to the theatrical arts called the Goetheanum in Dornach, Switzerland, a grand project hearkening back to

---

[48] Farr and Shakespear, p. 39.
[49] Mary K. Greer, *Women of the Golden Dawn: Rebels and Priestesses* (Rochester, VT: Inner Traditions, 1995), p. 267.

Wagner's theatre-temple at Bayreuth.[50] In addition to housing productions of his four illuminating but demanding mystery dramas – *The Portal of Initiation* (1910), *The Soul's Probation* (1911), *The Guardian of the Threshold* (1912) and *The Soul's Awakening* (1913) – the Goetheanum was to become the headquarters of his Anthroposophical Society and, as David Adams explains, 'a dramatic illustration of the principles of a new style of architecture, simultaneously organic and functional' as a total presentation of Steiner's spiritual beliefs.[51] The mystery dramas are imposing constructions – verging on the overwritten and clearly emerging from a Teutonic tradition of spectacle and totality – which become enamoured of the human capacity for bringing through new knowledge and insight from supersensible realms. But the plays are also among the most startling works of modernist drama in terms of their intensity of thought and innovation in presentation. Christian Clement argues that, for Steiner, 'the ultimate purpose of drama is initiation. Theatre is supposed to not only entertain and educate, but to subject the viewer to a process of radical inner transformation through aesthetic means.'[52] Covering a span of approximately fifteen years, the mystery plays follow a collection of bohemian artists, philosophers and mystics who have gathered around a formidable spiritual teacher called Benedictus and particularize both the mundane properties of these characters' lives – love, marriage, creative prospects and death – and their increasing access to supersensible realms of reflection and divine connection that they are able to enter through their spiritual practices.

Steiner was a prolific writer and lecturer who spoke widely about the mystery dramas throughout this career, using them to illuminate key features of his spiritual faith exemplified by his Anthroposophical Society. Both the mystery dramas and the Goetheanum which housed them were the embodiment of his spiritual independence from the Theosophical Society. He was leader of the German section of the Theosophical Society from 1902 to 1912, before the Section's charter was withdrawn by Annie Besant, who had become president of the Theosophical Society at Adyar, India, in 1907. Steiner's emphasis on esoteric Christianity was at odds with the prevailing narrative of Theosophy, which maintained that the primordial religions of Hinduism and Buddhism carried the

---

[50] Robb Creese, 'Anthroposophical Performance', *Drama Review*, 22.2 (1978), 45–74 (p. 47).
[51] David Adams, 'Rudolf Steiner's First Goetheanum as an Illustration of Organic Functionalism', *Journal of the Society of Architectural Historians*, 51.2 (1992), 182–204 (p. 182).
[52] Christian Clement, 'Weimar Classicism and Modern Spiritual Drama: Rudolf Steiner's Theatre of Spiritual Realism', in *Weimar Classicism: Studies in Goethe, Schiller, Forster, Berlepsch, Weiland, Herder, and Steiner*, ed. David Gallagher (Lewiston, NY: Edwin Mellen Press, 2011), 135–54 (p. 144).

wisdom of a single perennial tradition connecting all faith systems; in this view, Christianity was merely a copy of a copy, and the Theosophists sought to return to what they viewed as the earliest and thus most authentic spiritual traditions. More directly, Besant's pronouncement that a young Indian boy named Jiddu Krishnamurti was the incarnation of Maitreya – the messianic bodhisattva who would become a new 'World Teacher' – raised ire with Steiner, who viewed the singularity of Christ's birth as an immutable article of faith. Many German-speaking Theosophists would follow Steiner to his new Anthroposophical Society, and Krishnamurti would eventually reject his role as the new World Teacher and break ties with the Theosophical Society and its Order of the Star of the East in 1929 (although he remained an active spiritual teacher until his death in 1986 and remains widely admired).

Steiner's expulsion from the Theosophical Society would offer him the opportunity to crystallize his distinct spiritual vision along the lines that he intended. Steiner's 1892 doctoral thesis, published two years later as *Wahrheit und Wissenschaft* (*Truth and Knowledge*), delivered a brief but well-formed account of Kant and Fichte, but it would be Goethe who would fertilize Steiner's richest thinking. Steiner found in the work of Goethe evidence of the supersensible residing in the mundane world and, following a tenure working in the Goethe archives in Weimar, published *The Theory of Knowledge Implicit in Goethe's World-Conception* (1886) and *Goethe's Worldview* (1897). As Edouard Schuré argues in *The Genesis of Tragedy*, 'On the whole, the romantic theatre regarded the marvellous simply as a diverting sort of utopia, a disorderly chimera. For the introduction of order and clarity there was needed the mighty genius of Goethe', and it was undoubtedly Goethe whom Steiner would turn to in the writing of his mystery dramas.[53] The 'wisdom of god' (viz. Theosophy) would become Steiner's 'wisdom of humans' (viz. Anthroposophy), indicating the practical and material components of his spiritual tradition, which included, in connection with his School of Spiritual Science, biodynamic farming, Waldorf early-childhood education (named after the Waldorf-Astoria cigarette factory which funded the first Waldorf School), eurhythmy, music, drama and architecture.[54] Together these human arts constituted a spiritual *Gesamtkunstwerk*, or, as Steiner described it, an 'esoteric science' of life. 'We will do justice to the term *esoteric science* as

---

[53] Edouard Schuré, *The Genesis of Tragedy and the Sacred Drama of Eleusis*, trans. Fred Rothwell (London: Rudolf Steiner, 1936), p. 70.
[54] Mark Grant, 'Steiner and the Humours: The Survival of Ancient Greek Science', *British Journal of Educational Studies*, 47.1 (1999), 56–70 (p. 59). On the historical developments of Waldorf education, see also P. Bruce Uhrmacher, 'Uncommon Schooling: A Historical Look at Rudolf Steiner, Anthroposophy, and Waldorf Education', *Curriculum Inquiry*, 25.4 (1995), 381–406.

it is used here', Steiner explains in *An Outline of Esoteric Science* (1909), 'if we think of what Goethe had in mind when he spoke of the "revealed mysteries" in the phenomena of the universe'.[55] If, on one hand, *Gesamtkunstwerk* refers to an aesthetic ideal and ambition, it equally presented the possibility of healing a vague trauma or, as Olivier Schefer describes it, the 'mending of a modernity that was frequently charged with egoism, individualism, and materialism by the very people that were inventing it'.[56] But on New Year's Eve 1922, following an evening eurhythmy performance, the wooden Goetheanum was burnt to the ground in what was reported by the *New York Times* as a case of arson.[57] There is perhaps no clearer signal of the end of the modernist *annus mirabilis* than when, in the final hours of 1922, Steiner's grand theatre burnt to the ground. A second building, known as the Second Goetheanum, was completed in concrete three years after Steiner's death and continues to serve as the spiritual home of Anthroposophy and a monumental example of Expressionist architecture.[58]

As Robb Creese argues, Steiner's mystery dramas 'cannot be fully understood with the intellect. They can be described, but their full impact is felt only by an audience with an active, well-developed inner life.'[59] Alternating between scenes of stark realism and fantastical mysticism, the plays allow the characters to journey to supersensible realities, including portrayal of their past lives which saw them initially join together as members of a mysterious Rosicrucian brotherhood. Steiner's plays work in the tradition of the medieval mystery dramas, thematically sparse but conceptually sophisticated works which aimed to prompt recognition of the uncommunicable *mysterium fidei* of Christian faith (the sacred mystery of Christ's Apotheosis, for instance, is the culmination of the day-long passion play which has been performed at Oberammergau since 1634). Lingan offers an extended reading of the mystery plays in Anthroposophical terms, but, otherwise, few English-language critics have paid any serious attention to the works, and even fewer theatre practitioners have found reason to mount the plays, although there remains a small but committed

---

[55] Rudolf Steiner, *An Outline of Esoteric Science*, trans. Catherine E. Creeger (1909; Hudson, NY: Anthroposophic Press, 1997), p. 12. Previous English-language editions translated the title as *An Outline of Occult Science*.
[56] Olivier Schefer, 'Variations on Totality: Romanticism and the Total Work of Art', in *The Aesthetics of Total Artwork: On Borders and Fragments*, ed. Anke Finger and Danielle Follett (Baltimore, MD: Johns Hopkins University Press, 2011), p. 32.
[57] 'Home of Theosophy Burns: Incendiarism Suspected in Destruction of Steiner's Temple Near Basle' [sic], *New York Times*, 2 January 1923.
[58] Carol M. Cusack, '"And the Building Becomes Man": Meaning and Aesthetic in Rudolf Steiner's Goetheanum', in *Handbook of New Religions and Cultural Production*, ed. Carole M. Cusak and Alex Norman (Leiden: Brill, 2012), pp. 173–92.
[59] Creese, p. 52.

contemporary following among Anthroposophists.⁶⁰ *The Portal of Initiation*, the first play in cycle, turns on three interlocking frames of dramatic presentation which underscore and, ultimately, complicate the play's thematic interest in reality, belief and individuation of the soul. The first of these frames is provided by a prologue and interlude in which young mothers Estella (*stella*, 'star') and Sophia (σοφία, 'wisdom') discuss two plays that will be performed that evening. Estella intends to see *Entrehrten des Leibes und der Seele* (rendered in English-language translations by Harry Collison as *Outcasts from Body and from Soul* and by Ruth and Hans Pusch as *The Uprooted*) but Sophia remains committed to attending a performance that her own occult society will be presenting. The main playtext of *The Portal of Initiation* seems to be a combination of both, featuring the 'didactic-allegorical' presentation of Sophia's play with the humane Romanticism of Estella's. In the interlude, Estella describes having seen a very similar play to this, one which contained 'moments when all the human suffering I have ever known or observed seemed to take shape before me. ... The dramatic construction was wonderful. The playwright shows how a young painter loses his creative joy when he begins to grow uncertain in his love for a woman.'⁶¹ At least initially, this is an ironic moment of self-reflection in which Steiner invites a character to comment on the sincerity and excellence of his own dramatic work. Estella is resistant to stylized, spiritualized drama, arguing to her friend that 'art can only reach to such heights by being faithful to the whole of life. The moment it departs from this, it becomes untrue.'⁶² For her part, Sophia believes that emotional intensity requires a heightening of dramatic expression: 'When you have perceived the complete reality of life, there comes into your heart a feeling of a certain poverty in works of art. For, of course, the greatest artist is only a bungler, compared with the perfection of Nature.'⁶³ The framing device situates the audience in a reliable temporal frame of modern theatre-going but also offers distinctive commentary on Steiner's views of modern drama and the potentials that it could hold in the modern world.

The verse play that follows this prologue centres on the artist Johannes who, fearing that 'all former fire / has disappeared out of my soul', struggles to situate his artistic practice and spiritual sensibilities within the boundaries of the modern world.⁶⁴ The Johannes narrative – the central focus of the first two

---

⁶⁰ Lingan, pp. 74–89.
⁶¹ Rudolf Steiner, *The Portal of Initiation* in *Four Mystery Dramas*, trans. Ruth and Hans Pusch (Great Barrington, MA: Steiner Books, 2007), p. 123.
⁶² Steiner, *The Portal of Initiation*, p. 124.
⁶³ Steiner, *The Portal of Initiation*, p. 125.
⁶⁴ Steiner, *The Portal of Initiation*, p. 22.

plays in the cycle and the thematic hallmark of the cycle at large – reasserts a typically Steinerian perspective that spiritual development is a requirement for artistic success, or, as Steiner explained in a lecture shortly after the play's debut that 'that which inspires all theosophical life can also pour itself out into Art'.[65] Although the spiritual development of the characters Capesius and Strader will play an increasingly significant role in the final two of the four plays, the artistic development of Johannes offers the most significant through line connecting all of the plays and underlines Steiner's view of the equivalency between artistic expression and spiritual insight, both of which are required for real initiation. Each scene is rooted in a distinctive form of cognition, from the waking life of the first scene through to dream association, contemplative meditation and spiritual ecstasy. Characters, too, become associated with distinguishing ways of knowing, such as Theodora's capacity for seership and Felicia's frequent recourse to fairy tales. The first scene opens with a cacophony of words and ideas following a lecture by the occult teacher Benedictus (lit. 'blessed'). Each figure has left the lecture with a different perspective: Capesius takes the view that 'alone through reason is the soul approached', a position which explains his later frustration that 'superstition is mixed up / with logic and with reason';[66] Strader, achieving the same ends through different means, contends that 'no outer cause has made me / devote myself to thought';[67] the seer Theodora is incited to deliver a rambling discourse on the meaning of the soul. From this crowd, Maria emerges as the most influential influence on Johannes, and the one who has most effectively captured the meaning of Benedictus's teachings. By the end of the first scene, Johannes recognizes that his artistic and spiritual journeys are united and must be simultaneously overcome through the symbolic struggle between the forces of Lucifer and Ahriman. In Steiner's cosmology, Lucifer is the embodiment of pride and satisfaction, as well as a tangible exemplar of the dangers of these vices; Ahriman, a Zoroastrian deity aligned with trickery and destruction, becomes an indication of the overt celebration of the rational and mechanistic, tricking humans into abandoning their own inner perceptions in favour of the visible and touchable. Maria describes Ahriman as 'the father of deceit',[68] an echo of what Steiner explains in 'The Ahrimanic Deception':

---

[65] Rudolf Steiner, 'Self-Knowledge in Relation to the Mystery Play *The Portal of Initiation*, trans. G. A. Kaufmann, 1910, http://wn.rsarchive.org/Lectures/19100917p02.html (accessed 23 February 2018).
[66] Steiner, *The Portal of Initiation*, pp. 28, 35.
[67] Steiner, *The Portal of Initiation*, p. 31.
[68] Rudolf Steiner, *The Soul's Probation* in *Four Mystery Dramas*, trans. Ruth and Hans Pusch (Great Barrington, MA: Steiner Books, 2007), p. 113.

> It is of the utmost interest to Ahriman that people should perfect themselves in all our illusory modern science, but without knowing that it is illusion. Ahriman has the greatest possible interest in instructing men in mathematics, but not in instructing them that mathematical-mechanistic concepts of the universe are merely illusions.[69]

In Johannes's vision, Lucifer entreats him to 'know yourself' as a way to 'experience me', that is, to celebrate the joys and pleasures within himself to come across the pride that Lucifer represents. Conversely, Ahriman invites Johnannes to 'know me', that is, to know the promise of scientific rationalism, as a way to 'experience yourself'.[70] For Steiner, the tension between the Luciferian and Ahrimanic forces was the core cause of European unrest during the early years of the twentieth century.

By the early scenes of *The Soul's Probation*, set several years after the events of *The Portal of Initiation*, Johannes has progressed into full mastery and control of his artistic skills, recognizing the legitimacy of Maria's conviction that 'forms, resembling thoughts, / can conquer matter'.[71] In *The Soul's Probation*, Lucifer entreats Johannes to 'conquer yourself' and 'redeem me' while Ahriman invites him to 'embolden yourself' and 'experience me'.[72] Here, the framing device of Sophia and Estella is now gone, having served its purpose of gradually inducing the audience to the world of the drama and setting up for them an array of possible responses to the plays themselves. In the final moments of the play, Maria makes her final, decisive retort to Lucifer: 'In human beings there are springs of love / to which your power cannot penetrate / … / [and] which fructify true human progress.'[73] In *The Guardian of the Threshold*, the kingdoms of Lucifer and Ahriman are finally revealed, demonstrating that the characters are now advanced enough in their occult study to visualize the source of the urges and tensions that run through humanity. Lucifer's kingdom is 'a space not enclosed by artificial walls but by plant- and animal-like shapes and other forms of fantasy'.[74] Ahriman's kingdom, conversely, is 'a dark gorge enclosed by mountains that tower up in fantastic forms out of black rock-masses'.[75] As Hutchins explains of Steiner's personification of these two archetypical forces,

---

[69] Rudolf Steiner, 'The Ahrimanic Deception', trans. M. Cotterell, 1919, http://wn.rsarchive.org/Lectures/AhrDec_index.html (accessed 23 February 2018).
[70] Steiner, *The Portal of Initiation*, pp. 78–9.
[71] Steiner, *The Soul's Probation*, p. 34.
[72] Steiner, *The Soul's Probation*, p. 61.
[73] Steiner, *The Soul's Probation*, p. 126.
[74] Rudolf Steiner, *The Guardian of the Threshold* in *Four Mystery Dramas*, trans. Ruth and Hans Pusch (Great Barrington, MA: Steiner Books, 2007), p. 47.
[75] Steiner, *The Guardian of the Threshold*, p. 98.

'Lucifer, when recognised, can inspire human begins with a love of beauty, but can no longer dominate men's souls. Ahriman can introduce those who approach him to the true value of the material work, but cannot chain the ones who have attained spiritual vision to a belief in its ultimate truth.'[76] It is clear that the advice of Lucifer and Ahriman cannot simultaneously exist, setting up the central conflict of the soul which Steiner's play investigates.

The Soul's Probation features at its centre a three-scene flashback to a twelfth-century mystic brotherhood, of which many of the present-day characters were members in previous incarnations. Although Hutchins reads the mystical order as a direct allusion to the Knights Templar, it seems apparent that Steiner is writing more broadly about an ahistorical order, generally Rosicrucian in nature, but predating both the Rosicrucian manifestos and the illusory life of Christian Rosenkreutz.[77] Steiner's mystery plays are not Rosicrucian in the literal sense of detailing the events of Father Christian Rosenkreutz and his company of wayfaring mendicants but speak more broadly about immanence along esoteric Christian lines and aim to present 'dramatic initiation that symbolically describes the inspired consciousness in order to initiate and facilitate the attainment of such a consciousness in the spectator itself'.[78] In his lecture series on *The Theosophy of the Rosicrucian*, Steiner takes the history of the Rosicrucian Brotherhood as outlined in the *Fama* at face value, or at least accepts its validity as symbolic formulation with continued relevance. For Steiner, the publication of the manifestos in 1614–17 was evidence of 'the mission of this Brotherhood to allow certain esoteric truths to flow, by spiritual ways, into the culture of Middle Europe'.[79] As Frances Yates points out in *The Rosicrucian Enlightenment* (1972):

> The meditative reader of the manifestos is struck by the contrast between the serious tone of their religious and philosophical message and the fantastic character of the framework in which the message is presented. A religious movement using alchemy to intensify its evangelical piety, and including a large programme of research and reform in the sciences, is surely an interesting phenomenon.[80]

---

[76] Eileen Hutchins, *Introduction to the Mystery Plays of Rudolf Steiner* (Forest Row: Rudolf Steiner Press, 2014), p. 28.
[77] Hutchins, p. 46.
[78] Clement, p. 137.
[79] Rudolf Steiner, *The Theosophy of the Rosicrucian* (1907; repr. London: Rudolf Steiner Press, 1966), p. 6.
[80] Frances Yates, *The Rosicrucian Enlightenment* (1972; repr. St Albans: Paladin, 1975), p. 80.

Steiner's interest in the Rosicrucian ideal inheres in its treatment of initiation into a secret order, and he takes the Rosicrucian fraternity of initiatory wisdom as a potent element of biblical exegesis. Steiner understood the story of Lazarus in the Gospel of John as evidence of an initiatory process (similar in implication but not outward appearance to the Brotherhood of the Rosy Cross), following which Lazarus became John the Apostle; 'only thus do we grasp the real meaning of this chapter', he summarily notes.[81] His reading of the *Gospel of John* portrays Jesus as an esoteric spiritual leader, confident in both his spiritual status and the validity of his message. For Steiner part of the initiatory process is meditation which commences from 'a combination of feeling and will', what he explains as the 'Christian-Rosicrucian method'.[82] For Steiner, the role of the occult teacher is to be one who has been through the process before and helps facilitate the passage of another emphasizing the direct communication of wisdom rather than allowing for the possibility of spontaneous illumination. Steiner's own approach to the *mysterium fidei* comes not through the portrayal of classical Christian allegory but the distinctively modern lives of characters who remain committed to modern spiritual training fortified by simple living, aesthetic cultivation and a communitarian power structure.

The Soul's Awakening has perhaps the most mundane plot of all four, centring its attention on a factory owner's plans to offer his buildings and workshops to the students of Benedictus to use as a place of spiritualized labour and rest, operating under the artistic direction of Johannes. 'Thus craftsmanship will be combined with art / and daily life imbued with taste', the factory owner explains.[83] Johannes, however, worries 'how can I guard my knowledge at all times' when involved in the mundane world.[84] Scenes seven and eight of *The Soul's Awakening* build up to the grand climax of the cycle as a whole, in an extended return to the characters' previous incarnation in ancient Egypt to witness an initiatory rite – 'the solemn rites of sacred wisdom'[85] – which offers the sharpest and most compelling thematic conclusion to Steiner's epic *Künstlerroman*. The figure of Johannes becomes the everyman of Steiner's anthroposophical world view, the prototypical artist-mystic whose aim is to find an artistic expression for the

---

[81] Rudolf Steiner, 'The Raising of Lazarus', in *The Essential Steiner*, ed. Robert McDermott (San Francisco, CA: Floris, 1996), pp. 234–54 (p. 240).
[82] Rudolf Steiner, 'Christian Initiation', in *The Essential Steiner*, ed. Robert McDermott (San Francisco, CA: Floris, 1996), pp. 255–65 (p. 261).
[83] Rudolf Steiner, *The Soul's Awakening* in *Four Mystery Dramas*, trans. Ruth and Hans Pusch (Great Barrington, MA: Steiner Books, 2007), p. 17.
[84] Steiner, *The Soul's Awakening*, p. 67.
[85] Steiner, *The Soul's Awakening*, p. 97.

increasingly transcendent attentiveness to the natural world surrounding him. 'All that Johannes gains', John O'Mara argues 'in the way of an outer content from his journey into himself is to be set down to a power that Steiner explains is the one that more and more must be tapped into, if we are indeed to have further success with the imaginative process'.[86] The opposing forces of Lucifer and Ahriman must first be resolved within his own perception of the world, offering a hopeful but incomplete elevation of artistic form and a divinization of the realms of the creative imagination.

What Farr and Steiner shared was belief in the transformative power of drama, that to see a course of spiritual life portrayed on stage could lead to a form of reverie as transcendent as religious experience. This experiential form and thematic aim echo the deep structures emerging from modernist developments in theatre which continued to underscore the spiritual embodiment of the New Drama. On 5 September 1937, several months before the essays which comprise *The Theatre and Its Double* were collected, Artaud wrote to André Breton from Galway with a magic spell with which he very sincerely intended to curse the Surrealist writer Lise Deharme. 'Madame X.'s grave responsibility lies in having said that there are no more Gods. That's the reason for my hatred of her', Artaud explained to Breton of Deharme. 'Because there are still Gods, even though God no longer exists. And ranged above gods there is the unconscious, criminal law of nature, and the gods and Us – this is, *We the Gods* – are collectively victims of that law.'[87] Artaud's apocalyptic visions while travelling in Ireland during 1937 are recorded in a manifesto, 'The New Revelations of Being' (1937), which has received limited critical attention but give rich insight into the ornate immanence of Artaudian theatre:

> I know how the dead have been revolving around their own dead bodies for the exact duration of thirty-three Centuries that my own Double never stopped turning.
>
> And, no longer existing, I see what exists.
>
> I truly identified with that Being, that Begin that ceased to exist.
>
> And that Being has revealed everything to me.[88]

---

[86] John O'Mara, *The New School of the Imagination: Rudolf Steiner's Mystery Plays in Literary Tradition* (Ottawa: Heart's Core, 2005), p. 23.
[87] Antonin Artaud, *Apocalypse*, trans. and ed. Stephen Barber (London: Infinity Land Press, 2018), p. 40.
[88] Antonin Artaud, 'The New Revelations of Being', in *Apocalypse*, trans. and ed. Stephen Barber (London: Infinity Land Press, 2018), pp. 12–14 (p. 14).

This vision of drama as a mode that surpassed the mimetic by tearing down and frustrating the soul to reveal its immortal 'Double' is entrenched in an unmistakably esoteric framework which has curiously underpinned many key innovations in modernist drama.

3

The modernist shadow: Psychoanalysis, occultism and the taming of the unconscious

In a 1935 lecture at the Tavistock Clinic in London, Carl Jung asserted that 'there is nothing mystical about the collective unconscious',[1] a sentiment he echoed two years later in a lecture at Yale University when he claimed that 'although I have often been called a philosopher, I am an empiricist and adhere as such to the phenomenological standpoint'.[2] Throughout his life, Jung resolutely insisted that he was, above all else, a man of medical science, and it was only during the final years of his career that his personal practice of astrology and the I Ching became widely known.[3] Jung's doctoral thesis, 'The Psychology and the Pathology of So-Called Occult Phenomena', was written at a time when the blurring of mesmerism, hypnotism and spiritualism was giving rise to a psychodynamic view of the mind (of such research, he would obliquely argue in 1937 that 'I trust that it does not conflict with the principles of scientific empiricism if one occasionally makes certain reflection which go beyond a mere accumulation and classification of experience'[4]), and, in spite of his claims to the scientific empiricism of his work, Jung's long-held interest in the occult contributed to the development of depth psychology in many crucial ways. Jung's occult interests

---

[1] C. G. Jung, *Analytical Psychology: Its Theory and Practice* (London: Routledge, 1982), pp. 44–5.
[2] C. G. Jung, *Psychology and Religion: West and East, Collected Works*, vol. 11, trans. Gerhard Adler and R. F. C. Hull (Princeton, NJ: Princeton University Press, 1969), para 2.
[3] While Jung undertook reading in the Kabbalah – still the fashionable mystic tradition of the time – it was the older and distinctly less stylish world of alchemy that provided to him ample material with which to understand what would come to be called the process of individuation and the repudiation of duality. Jung's interest in alchemy was largely symbolic, suggesting that the great labours of the alchemists were really metaphors for individuation, moving the soul through increasing stages of expansion and contraction to free the authentic soul. Similarly, astrology would be construed as an elaborate metaphor of interpretative archetypes as opposed to mere divination; Jung's views in this regard continue to influence the popular practice of astrology. On Jung and astrology, see Liz Greene, *Jung's Studies in Astrology: Prophecy, Magic, and the Qualities of Time* (Abingdon: Routledge, 2018); Liz Greene, *The Astrological World of Jung's Liber Novus: Daimons, Gods, and the Planetary Journey* (Abingdon: Routledge, 2018).
[4] Jung, *Psychology and Religion*, para 2.

began when he experienced hypnagogic visions before sleep from an early age, experiences which he connected to a series of seemingly paranormal occurrences. While Lionel Corbett remains generally equivocal on the occult nature of Jung's thinking, suggesting that 'perhaps the publication of *The Red Book* had to be delayed until the Judeo-Christian tradition had lost enough authority for the culture to be ready to assimilate Jung's insights',[5] Stephan Hoeller goes as far as to position Jung as a link in the chain of gnostic transmission which views the fruits of perennial knowledge as experiential and thus largely non-transferrable.[6] Taking an even stronger view, Richard Noll argues that Jung's work aimed to 'initiate [practitioners] into secret, "occult" knowledge'.[7] As Harold Coward describes, 'For Jung the basic psychic process involved in the mystical experience is clearly the replacing of the conscious ego with the more powerful, numinous, forces of the unconscious – called by the Western Christian "God."'[8] It is this process of self-inquiry which animates much of Jung's writing. Although Jung self-reflexively positioned himself throughout his career as a medical doctor trained in the rational epistemologies of scientific materialism, his most lasting contributions to psychoanalysis and to the study of human subjectivity come in his acute awareness of the direct connection humans have to divinity through the imaginative resources of the mind.

Early in his life, Jung recognized two aspects of himself (no. 1, the scientific rational self, and no. 2, the contemplative, mystical self) which he sought to draw out and understand through a form of contemplative internal dialogue. 'There are things in the psyche which I do not produce, but which produce themselves and have their own life', he explained in his autographical *Memories, Dreams, Reflections* (1962), and he would attempt to seize and understand these elements of his psyche through a process he called active imagination,[9] 'a method of consciously entering into a dialogue with the unconscious, which triggers the transcendent function, a vital *shift* in consciousness, brought about through the union of the conscious and unconscious minds'.[10] Beginning in October 1913 and continuing with ominous regularity through the spring of 1914, Jung had a

---

[5] Lionel Corbett, 'Jung's *The Red Book* Dialogues with the Soul: Herald of a New Religion?', *Jung Journal*, 5.3 (2011), 63–77 (p. 75).
[6] Stephan A. Hoeller, *The Gnostic Jung and the Seven Sermons to the Dead* (London: Theosophical Publishing House, 1982), p. 31.
[7] Richard Noll, *The Jung Cult: Origins of a Charismatic Movement* (London: Fontana Press, 1996), p. 46.
[8] Harold Coward, *Jung and Eastern Thought* (Albany: State University of New York Press, 1985), p. 129.
[9] C. G. Jung, *Memories, Dreams, Reflections* (London: Fontana, 1995), p. 207.
[10] Gary Lachman, *Jung the Mystic: The Esoteric Dimensions of Carl Jung's Life and Teachings* (New York: Tarcher, 2010), p. 117. In contemporary practice, this may take the form of, for instance, asking a psychotherapeutic client to speak to an imagined person with whom concerns exist or asking the client to talk through the dialogue of two opposing views of a topic. See John Rowan,

series of nightmares which showed him the obliteration of Western Europe. In the first of these terrifying dreams, he witnessed a 'terrible flood that covered all the northern and low-lying lands between the North Sea and Alps. ... I saw yellow waves, swimming rubble, and the death of countless thousands.'[11] In a dream several months later he saw himself fleeing from England after 'a terrible cold had fallen from space', making the country unsafe and uninhabitable; shortly after he would, indeed, have to quickly return to Switzerland while visiting the UK during the outbreak of the First World War.[12] Sigmund Freud – the mentor from whom Jung had split just over a year earlier, following his refusal to accept the centrality of the libido that Freud laid out in *Psychology of the Unconscious* (1912; English trans. 1916) – portrayed dreams as the messengers of suppressed trauma or the enactments of repressed desires, but Jung understood his unsettling dreams as the channel to transpersonal insight unavailable to the conscious ego. The personal journal in which he captured these dreams would grow over the course of sixteen years into a vast, delicately illuminated six hundred-page red-bound folio. It was never meant for public distribution; however, in 1984 facsimile editions were prepared for Jung's descendants and in 2009 the full text was publicly published with considerable fanfare.[13]

In the aptly named *Red Book*, Jung meditates on the characteristically gnostic image of a divine spark of wisdom that remains trapped within the physical body, and, in doing so, laid the foundations for one of the most influential traditions of psychoanalytic inquiry and analysis. *The Red Book* represents both a poetic representation of the psyche and a psychic attempt at poetry. hearn that the soul tensely except at the cost of the self.'thers strive.rsos. I cannot understand nor share these joye suffactBut Jung's personal and professional interest in the occult is by no means unusual in the history of modern approaches to the human mind. In his monumental history of psychoanalysis, Henri Ellenberger dates the emergence of dynamic psychiatry to a 1775 dispute between the exorcist Father Johann Joseph Gassner and the freethinking physician Franz Anton Mesmer, the founder of mesmerism.[14] From these earliest demonstrations of dynamic

---

'Dialogical Self and the Soul', in *Jungian and Dialogical Self Perspectives*, ed. Raya A. Jones and Masayoshi Morioka (Basingstoke: Palgrave Macmillan, 2011), pp. 152–66 (p. 156).

[11] C. G. Jung, *The Red Book: A Reader's Edition*, ed. Sonu Shamdasani, trans. Mark Kyburz, John Peck and Sonu Shamdasani (London: W. W. Norton, 2009), p. 123.

[12] Jung, *The Red Book*, p. 124.

[13] On the history and publication of the *Red Book*, see Sonu Shamdasani, 'Introduction' to Jung, *The Red Book*.

[14] Henri Ellenberger, *The Discovery of the Unconscious: The History and Evolution of Dynamic Psychology* (New York: Basic, 1970), p. 53; Antoine Faivre, *Western Esotericism: A Concise History*, trans. Christine Rhone (Albany: State University of New York Press, 2010), p. 63.

psychiatry emerged a close affinity between the domains of psychology and the occult that continued for at least a further century and a half. In *Literature, Technology and Magical Thinking, 1880–1920* (2001), Pamela Thurschwell describes the Society for Psychical Research as one of the key progenitors and promoters of psychoanalysis and, similarly, Leon Surette recognizes the curious points of commonality between psychoanalysis and the occult, both of which 'privilege the "inward gaze" over the outward look of empirical science'.[15] Practices such as hypnotism, automatic writing and active imagination were utilized in both psychoanalysis and occultism to gain access to modes of thought far removed from the testable realms of scientific materialism: association, fluidity, indirectness, misdirection, receptivity, metaphor and other forms of knowledge that seemed counterintuitive to the rational mind. Ira Progoff points out that 'one of the great expectations that the nineteenth century bequeathed to us was its confidence that the methods of the physical sciences would succeed equally well in the study of man. That hope, of course, has not materialized.'[16] The modern excavation of the unconscious was thus not a new discovery as much as it was a pathologization and professionalization of a series of often mystical epistemologies, and psychoanalysis mastered the mystical senses as a mean to uncover the unconscious, a method that had for millennia been the territory of the shaman, mystic and priest.[17] As Jung explained in *Modern Man in Search of a Soul* (1933):

> It is a fact that the beginnings of psychoanalysis were fundamentally nothing else than the scientific rediscovery of an ancient truth; even the name catharsis (or cleansing), which was given to the earliest method of treatment, comes from the Greek initiation rites. The early method of catharsis consisted in putting the patient, with or without hypnotic aid, in touch with the hinterland of the mind – that is to say, into that state which the Eastern *yoga* systems describe as meditation or contemplation. In contrast to the meditation found in *yoga* practice, the psychoanalytic aim is to observe the shadowy presentation – whether in the form of images or of feelings – that are spontaneously evolved in the unconscious psyche and appear without his bidding to the man who looks within.[18]

---

[15] Leon Surette, *The Birth of Modernism: Ezra Pound, T.S. Eliot, W.B. Yeats, and the Occult* (Quebec: McGill-Queen's University Press, 1993), p. 85.

[16] Ira Progoff, *Jung, Synchronicity, and Human Destiny: Noncausal Dimensions of Human Experience* (New York: Delta, 1973), p. 1.

[17] On the sustained points of influence between occultism and psychoanalysis, see John Boyle, 'Esoteric Traces in Contemporary Psychoanalysis', *American Imago*, 73.1 (2016), 95–119.

[18] Carl Jung, *Modern Man in Search of a Soul* (1933; repr. Abingdon: Routledge, 2001), p. 35.

The modern innovation of psychoanalysis presents a living tradition of tamed occult practices – neo-platonism, Paracelcesianism, Swedenborgianism and Mesmerism – and the psychoanalytic dynamic became contextualized, both in practice and in the literature of its time, as a form of gnostic return to source in which the individual could discover their innate selfhood.

This chapter considers the suggestive interface between occult practice and psychoanalytic thinking in Hermann Hesse's *Demian* (1919; trans. 1923) and Dion Fortune's collection of short stories *The Secrets of Doctor Taverner* (1926). Both Hesse and Fortune were deeply immersed in the emergent discipline of psychoanalysis – Hesse as a compliant patient of one of Jung's protégés and Fortune as a psychoanalyst at the Medico-Psychological Clinic of London – and would present their gnostic vision of immanence and human ascent to the divine in psychoanalytic terms. One of the most celebrated writers directly influenced by Jung's thinking was Hesse, whose work captures characters in search of Jungian individuation. In addition to offering a therapeutic model, psychoanalysis provides the framework for analysing the world and giving form to a belief that there is a small voice operating seemingly separately to the conscious self; it is precisely this affordance which inspires and animates Hesse's work. While Fortune ultimately understood the extraordinary value of psychoanalysis and the modern retrieval of the unconscious, she came to recognize that psychoanalysis provided only one of several possible routes into the inner workings of the human mind and would fuse her training in psychoanalysis with modern ceremonial magic to create one of the most influential and evocative initiatory frameworks of the modernist period. The challenges of drawing together psychoanalysis and occultism in this way are allegorized by Fortune in the form of Dr John Silence, a ceremonial magician and psychoanalyst who relies on the insights of both domains to solve impenetrable mysteries. Although the domains of literature and psychoanalysis have long been close and comfortable companions, this chapter intends to challenge pre-existing models of psychoanalytic literary criticism by proposing esoteric epistemology as a third crucial coordinate in the exploration of the relationship between the unconscious and literature.

Following a nervous breakdown during the early years of the First World War, a 39-year-old Hermann Hesse began analysis with Jung's acolyte J. B. Lang and would meet Jung himself shortly after. Hesse's fiction from this period onward traffics in the shadows of human experience and the constant tension between what is perceived as real and what is merely an illusion. As Joseph Mileck affirms, 'Hesse's art bears the indelible imprint of psychoanalysis, but only its imprint. … In his usual eclectic manner he borrowed from both analysts and from others whatever appealed to him and whatever he could use to advantage, and as usual, whatever he appropriated was modified to accord with his bent of thought and to suit his purposes.'[19] The classic expression of the modern unconscious comes in the pages of Hesse's *Steppenwolf*, where, through the interpenetrating frames of discursive account – first from an intrigued bystander, then from Harry Haller the 'Steppenwolf', then from a phantasmagorical version of the main character – he captures the enervated spirit of the age, an unconscious that has been washed clean of the ennobling symbols and archetypes of the past. To the initial narrator, Harry Haller 'gave the impression of having come out of an alien world, from another continent perhaps'.[20] He is 'ailing, ailing in the spirit' and 'a genius of suffering' who embodies psychical discontent in physical form.[21] Haller's existential trauma becomes emblematic of the modern world: as the narrator explains in the preface, 'Every age, every culture, every custom and tradition has its own characters, its own weakness and its own strength, its beauties and cruelties; it accepts certain sufferings as matters of course, puts up patiently with certainly evils.'[22] Patricia Merivale describes the model at work in *Steppenwolf* as a form of 'gothic pedagogy' which turns on 'the linkage between such a god-game and such a hero-quest: its inner artifacts are, so to speak, the strings by which the puppets are controlled'.[23] It is these 'inner artifacts' which inspire the *Bildung* of Hesse's text and lead its central anti-hero towards a fuller if antithetical understanding of the immortality of the soul.

A similar thematic programme is pursued in Hesse's *Demian*, originally published pseudonymously under the name of the central protagonist, the impressionable and impassioned Emil Sinclair. The text introduces a prototypically divided self whose potential for growth and self-possession is personified in the form of Demian, a wealthy widow's son who miraculously appears in Emil's life around the same time as a particularly shameful encounter with a local bully. Countering the sacred redemptive potential offered by Demian is the personification of Emil's shadow self in the form of bully Franz Kromer, who enters Emil's dreams 'torturing me, spitting and kneeling on me and, what was worse, leading me on to serious crimes'.[24] Kromer's sinister hold over the ethical dimensions of Emil's growth and development leads ultimately to the

---

[19] Joseph Mileck, *Hermann Hesse: Life and Art* (London: University of California Press, 1980), p. 100.
[20] Hermann Hesse, *Steppenwolf*, trans. David Horrocks (London: Penguin, 2012), p. 9.
[21] Hesse, *Steppenwolf*, p. 15.
[22] Hesse, *Steppenwolf*, p. 28.
[23] Patricia Merivale, 'Learning the Hard Way: Gothic Pedagogy in the Modern Romantic Question', *Comparative Literature*, 36.2 (1984), 146–61 (p. 146).
[24] Hermann Hesse, *Demian*, trans. W. J. Strachan (London: Penguin, 2017), p. 26.

earliest expression of separation and his awareness of 'some kind of lost paradise' of a unified psychosexual self.[25] Identified but unresolved, Emil's guilt leads to the splitting of self which, when matched by the equally pressing guilt brought on by sexual desires in his early puberty, gives rise to 'a double life of the child who is no longer a child. My conscious self lived in the homely and sanctioned, my conscious self denied the new world that was darkling round me.'[26] While the physical reality of Demian and Kromer within the world of the novel is clear, they stand equally as cyphers of the higher self and shadow which Emil must reconcile in order to work towards his own psychotherapeutic individuation:

> I realize that many people will be unable to credit a child not yet eleven years old with such feelings, but this story is not intended for them. I am recounting it to those who have a better understanding of human nature. The grown-up who has learnt to translate a part of his feelings into thoughts, misses these thoughts in the child and therefore finally denies even the experiences themselves. But I have rarely felt and suffered more deeply than at that time.[27]

As Emil continues to mature, he learns the significance of the 'mark of Cain' that Max Demian identified in him at an early age. 'What nature wants of man', Demian explains to him at university, 'is written in a few individuals, in you, in me. It was written in Christ, it was written in Nietzsche. Only for these important currents along – which can of course assume a different form every day – will there be a place when the communities of today collapse.'[28] Emil's journey of psychotherapeutic discovery and individuation is to recognize the significance of this nondual nature of reality which recognizes the divinity is contained within him. Max later explains to him:

> We who bore the 'sign' might rightly be considered odd by the world, even mad and dangerous. We were 'awake' or 'wakening' and our striving was directed at an ever-increasing wakefulness, whereas the striving and quest for happiness of the rest was aimed at identifying their thoughts, ideals, duties, their lives and fortunes more and more closely with that of the herd. That too was striving, that too was power and greatness. But whereas we, in our conception, represented the will of nature to renew itself, to individualize and march forward, the others lived in the desire for the perpetuation of things as they are. For them humanity – which they loved as we did – was something complete that must be

---

[25] Hesse, *Demian*, p. 27.
[26] Hesse, *Demian*, p. 38.
[27] Hesse, *Demian*, p. 28.
[28] Hesse, *Demian*, p. 111.

maintained and protected. For us humanity was a distant goal towards which we were marching, whose image no one yet knows, whose laws were nowhere written down.[29]

Demian's supersensible abilities – described to Emil simply as a form of 'thought-reading'[30] – take an increasingly central role in Emil's spiritual development and awareness. While Demian repeatedly argues this his abilities of perception, awareness and insight can be achieved by anyone, the recognition of his unorthodox and potentially blasphemous view of humanity and the divine becomes a simultaneously compulsive and repulsive lure. His classically gnostic interpretation of the curse of Cain as a sign of distinction initially horrifies and delights Emil, as he begins to see himself as part of a divinely inspired class alongside his daemon Max Demian and perhaps even alongside Cain himself.

Midway through the text, Demian mystically transports a message to Emil which communicates to him the name 'Abraxas', a deity who he shortly after learns in school 'symbolizes the reconciliation of the godly and the satanic'.[31] The gnostic figure of Abraxas had then recently returned to prominence in Jung's *The Seven Sermons to the Dead* (1916), which contained a series of discourses attributed by Jung to the second century CE Gnostic teacher Basilides (this work now appears in the final 'Scrutinies' section of *The Red Book*). As Jung describes through the prophetic voice of Basilides in 'The Second Sermon', 'There is a God about whom you know nothing, because men have forgotten him. We call him by his name: Abraxas. … Abraxas is activity; nothing can resist him but the unreal, and thus his active being freely unfolds. The unreal is not, and therefore cannot truly resist. Abraxas stands above the sun and above the devil.'[32] In *The Red Book*, Jung describes a number of spirits and guides with whom he has communicated, including a figure called Philemon who he initially identifies as his own higher self. As he writes, Philemon 'taught me psychic objectivity, the reality of the psyche … through conversations with Philemon, the distinction was clarified between myself and the object of my thought'.[33] 'Jung described a Gnostic revelation much like those of his ancient colleagues', Murray Stein argues, 'Analytical psychology, based as it is so strongly on Jung's own inner experiences, is a Gnostic-like psychology that sees beyond the ego dominants

---

[29] Hesse, *Demian*, p. 117.
[30] Hesse, *Demian*, p. 30.
[31] Hesse, *Demian*, p. 75.
[32] Carl Jung, *The Seven Sermons to the Dead*, in Hoeller, *Gnostic Jung and the Seven Sermons to the Dead*, p. 50.
[33] Jung, *Memories, Dreams, Reflections*, p. 207.

of the individual, the society, and the age to the deeper historical and archetypal layers.'[34] Seemingly both mystical and mundane, Emil's engagement with the equalizing energy of Abraxas underscores his psychological development and progress towards individuation. Indeed, the juxtapositioning of opposites has long been on Emil's mind and serves as one of the crucial ways in which divinity is made imminent which him and, subsequently, within the world of the novel. The dissolute local organist Pistorius continues Emil's education and invites him to explore the meaning of Abraxas by staring into the shifting patterns and images of a burning fire. As he explains of the ever-presence of this deity:

> All the gods and devils whether among the Greeks, Chinese or Zulus are all within us, existing as possibilities, wishes, outlets. If the human race dwindled to one single, half-developed child that had received no education, this child would rediscover the entire course of evolution, would be able to produce gods, devils, paradise, commandments and interdictions, the whole of the Old and New Testament, everything.[35]

For Emil, the encounter with Abraxas – who represents here the deep structures of human experience and the collective unconscious imagined by Jung – is a development in self-knowledge. Emil's full sense of abandonment and sin emerges more completely when he is sent away to boarding school, and the anxiety and worry that has arisen from his sense of being out of step with the methodical progress of his soul. A romantic attachment to a woman named Beatrice leads Emil to attempt to paint her portrait but he is only able to produce what appears to him as 'a kind of god-image or sacred mask, half male, half female, ageless, purposeful yet dreamy, frozen yet mysteriously alive'.[36] Only later does he realize that the image he painted is of Demian, his own tutelary divine wisdom. Emil's final incomplete reconciliation to Demian is transferred to an erotic attachment to Demian's mother who, in the final pages of the novel, becomes a figure of profound desire even while Emil recognizes that 'she existed as an outward symbol of my inner self and her sole purpose was to lead me more deeply into myself'.[37] The First World War breaks out, and Emil and Demian meet one final time in a military hospital where, with beds placed next to each other, Emil's soul returns to fullness in a psychodynamic integration: 'I find the

---

[34] Murray Stein, 'The Gnostic Critique, Past and Present', in *The Allure of Gnosticism: The Gnostic Experience in Jungian Psychology and Contemporary Culture*, ed. Robert A. Segal (Chicago: Open Court, 1995), pp. 39–53 (p. 43).
[35] Hesse, *Demian*, p. 85.
[36] Hesse, *Demian*, p. 66.
[37] Hesse, *Demian*, p. 122.

key and look deep down into myself where the images of destiny lie slumbering in the dark mirror, I only need to bend my head over the black mirror to see my own image which now wholly resembles him, my friend and leader.'[38]

If the modern development of psychoanalysis represented both the poignant return to mystical forms of knowledge and the taming and professionalization of occult practices, then the novelist, psychoanalyst and occult leader Dion Fortune stands out as a critical yet still underexplored contributor to the modern encounter with the unconscious. Born Violet Firth into a family of well-heeled steel manufacturers, Fortune was initiated into the Alpha et Omega lodge, a splinter group which hived off of the Hermetic Order of the Golden Dawn, and trained as a psychoanalyst at the Medico-Psychological Clinic of London where she practiced during the final years of the First World War. The Medico-Psychological Clinic of London was founded in 1913 at 14 Endsleigh Street just off of Tavistock Square, the home shared by Jessie Murray and her partner Julia Turner.[39] Founded in the same year as Ernest Jones's London Psycho-Analytical Society, the Medico-Psychological Clinic was, nevertheless, 'the only public clinic in Great Britain making use of psychoanalytical therapy as a psychological medicine' until the Tavistock Square Clinic was opened in 1920 (Fortune is often inaccurately presumed to have practiced at the Tavistock clinic).[40] Even in the mutable and sometimes eccentric world of early psychoanalysis, the work of the Medico-Psychological Clinic raised concerns as to the connection between its practices and the popular occultism that permeated the public consciousness, leading one of the founders to reaffirm in the *Lancet* that 'occultism is not only alien to the spirit of the proposed clinic; it is in direct contradiction of it'.[41] The Clinic's published Articles of Association indicated its objectives:

> I. – The treatment by medical and psychological means of functional nervous diseases and of functional disorders accompanying organic diseases.
>
> II. – The advancement of this brand of Medical Science.

---

[38] Hesse, *Demian*, p. 135.
[39] Suzanne Raitt, 'Early British Psychoanalysis and the Medico-Psychological Clinic', *History Workshop Journal*, 58 (2004), 62–85 (p. 68). The clinic moved into 30 Brunswick Square in July 1914, shortly before the outbreak of war, and then expanded into 33 and 34 Brunswick Square to provide residential annex for patients, initially those travelling to the clinic for treatment and then a more permanent care home. See Theophilus E. M. Boll, 'May Sinclair and the Medico-Psychological Clinic of London', *Proceedings of the American Philosophical Society*, 106 (1962), 310–26 (p. 312).
[40] Boll, pp. 310–26 (p. 312). Fortune never mentions by name the clinic at which she received her psychoanalytic training, and many scholars have subsequently misidentified it as the Tavistock Square Clinic, founded six years after the Medico-Psychological Clinic took up premises at nearby Brunswick Square.
[41] Charles Speakman, *Lancet*, 20 December 1913, p. 1, 803. Qtd. in Raitt, pp. 62–85 (p. 67).

III. – The extension in the community of a knowledge of the laws of Mental Hygiene.[42]

With its stated focus on treating functional disorders of the mind within the organizing precepts of 'Medical Science', the clinic presented outwardly as an orthodox follower of Freud, but Ernest Jones remained suspicious of the eclectic Jungian leanings of the Medico-Psychological Clinic, which he saw as a significant concern for preserving the integrity of a Freudian lineage in England.[43]

Considering that many of the patients of the Medico-Psychological Clinic would go on to become practitioners in the clinic, Suzanne Raitt reasonably imagines that 'the psychoanalytic therapy that was offered at the Clinic must also have been highly improvisational [and] there was no clear dividing line between the practice of qualified doctors and that of enterprising lay people'.[44] During her training at the Medico-Psychological Clinic, Fortune would have completed a three-year programme in 'Normal and Abnormal Psychology and Psychogenesis' alongside her own training analysis and supervised treatment of patients.[45] As she explains in an article published in *Inner Light Magazine* in 1936,

> I saw that although psychoanalysis could diagnose, it had no real remedy to offer, and in actual practice did not get results. It was in the quest for a solution to the problems of life and its pathologies that I came in touch with occultism, and found that the two methods, psychology and occultism, with their practical applications in psychoanalysis and initiation, fitted each other like key and lock. From this realisation everything else that I have done has followed.[46]

Susan Johnston Graf argues that 'it was her psychoanalytic practice that fostered her interest in the workings of the human psyche, and her conclusions led her to believe in reincarnation and to accept the possibility of occult phenomena'.[47] The outbreak of war meant that attentions were turned to treating cases of shell shock, and in 1915 a sister organization called the Society for the Study of Orthopsychics was founded to train analysts. Fortune would go on to lecture

---

[42] Boll, p. 314.
[43] Ken Robinson, 'A Brief History of the British Psychoanalytical Society', in *100 Years of the IPA: The Centenary History of the International Psychoanalytical Association, 1910-2010*, ed. Peter Loewenberg and Nellie L. Thompson (London: Routledge, 2011), pp. 196–230 (p. 201).
[44] Raitt, pp. 62–85 (pp. 68, 74).
[45] Raitt, p. 69.
[46] Dion Fortune, 'The Novels of Dion Fortune', repr. in Gareth Knight, *Dion Fortune's Rites of Isis and of Pan* (Cheltenham: Skylight, 2013), pp. 94–102 (p. 97).
[47] Susan Johnston Graf, 'The Occult Novels of Dion Fortune', *Journal of Gender Studies*, 16.1 (2007), 47–56 (p. 48).

for the Society with material that would be later published under her given name of Violet Firth as *The Machinery of the Mind* (1922). She later reflected that 'we students were soon struck by the fact that some cases were exceedingly exhausting to deal with. It was not that they were troublesome, but simply that they "took it out" of us, and left us feeling like limp rags at the end of treatment.'[48] Fortune ultimately left psychoanalysis in 1922 when she founded the Fraternity of the Inner Light, initially as an outer court training ground for the Alpha et Omega but later separating from its mother lodge once Fortune's teachings became more explicitly rooted in a Christological framework. In Fortune's view, her work and training at the Medico-Psychological Clinic presented only one fragment of the answers she sought:

> Psychology demonstrates the mechanism of the mind and can explain the mental processes whereby the ideas of the deranged assumed their ultimate form. It can show the connection between these ideas and the dreams of the normal mentality. What it cannot explain is the fundamental difference between these subjective states and the normal consciousness. It is here that the occultist can tell the psychologist something that it is worth his while to hear.[49]

Although Fortune's contributions are primarily in occultism rather than psychoanalysis, she is, nevertheless, and much like Jung, a thinker whose own training in and practice of dynamic psychology gave space to the full bourgeoning of her imaginative gift.

The Secrets of Doctor Taverner represents Fortune's most sustained treatment of her engagement with psychoanalysis. John Taverner, 'doctor of medicine, philosophy and science, master of arts and bachelor at law', is a classically Holmesian character aided in the psychical treatment of patients by his rational assistant Rhodes who quickly becomes fascinated with the 'peculiar art' with which Taverner 'used his trained intuition to explore the minds of his patients as another man might use a microscope to examine the tissues of their bodies'.[50] Fortune's Taverner stories represent an uncanny fusion of the medieval romance with Romantic sensibilities: there is a triumph of good over evil, even while the reader is invited to uncomfortably align with the unseemly evil inherent lurking out of sight. The Taverner stories detail the nefarious workings of a sinister 'Black Lodge' and the criminal aspects of occultism; on the side of good

---

[48] Dion Fortune, *Psychic Self-Defense* (1930; repr. San Francisco, CA: Red Wheel/Weiser, 2001), p. 42.
[49] Fortune, *Psychic Self-Defense*, p. 129.
[50] Dion Fortune, *The Secrets of Doctor Taverner* (San Francisco, CA: Red Wheel/Weiser, 2011), pp. 27, 40.

is Taverner, who belongs to his own quasi-Masonic occult lodge to which he pledges his sureties. As one of Taverner's clients explains, 'I have read something of occultism and something of psychology and heard how you work the two systems in combination' – what it ultimately means to use occultism and psychology 'in combination' is one of the most fundamental concerns of the text, which ultimately suggests that modern dynamic psychology is perhaps not as remote from the practices and principles of occult belief as the uninitiated would assume.[51] The cover of the 2011 Red Wheel/Weiser edition of *The Secrets of Doctor Taverner* by American artist Owen Smith shows a somewhat ironic pastiche of the mode: a figure who appears very much like Sigmund Freud is taking notes while his client, distinctly reminiscent of Bela Lugosi's Dracula, reclines on a tufted *chaise longue*, handheld faintingly to his forehead while blood dripping from his fangs. In spite of this somewhat flippant portrayal of a fusion of classical images of early psychoanalysis with equally well-remembered scenes from the Universal Classic Monsters universe, *The Secrets of Doctor Taverner* portrays a much more nuanced and intimately detailed account of what Fortune perceived to be the unmistakable correspondence between psychoanalytic and occult systems of knowledge. As she describes in *Psychic Self-Defence*, a text for magical practitioners which details the interface between psychological disturbance and occult phenomena:

> Nervous and mental disorders can stimulate a psychic attack, especially if the subject is familiar with the terminology of occultism. … We will not go into academic considerations, for these pages are not written for the orthodox professional psychologist, who has an abundance of textbooks at his disposal, but for the person whose interest is primarily in occult matters, and who comes to the study of the subject unequipped with the technicalities of psychology and psycho-physiology, two sciences of which at least a working knowledge is exceedingly necessary in the pursuit of practical occultism.[52]

Through the pages of *Psychic Self-Defence*, Fortune presents an occult explanation for neurosis that is curiously adjacent to Jung's, whose concept of a pool of shared cultural expression is reformulated by Fortune in the terms of reincarnation and implacable spirits of the unconscious which might enact their vengeance. As Miriam Wallraven argues, Fortune's use of psychoanalysis within her stories 'does not mean that psychoanalysis and the occult are interchangeable; on the contrary, it has to be stressed that with regard to the occult the language of

---

[51] Fortune, *Taverner*, p. 67.
[52] Fortune, *Psychic Self-Defense*, p. 121.

psychoanalysis is only used in order to describe it and legitimate it in "modern" and scientific terms'.[53] Fortune explains in the introduction to *The Secrets of Doctor Taverner* that the stories are 'studies in little-known aspects of psychology put in the form of fiction because, if published as a serious contribution to science they would have no chance of a hearing'.[54] While the concern faced in the detective fiction of Arthur Conan Doyle is the relationship between the individual and the fearsome otherness inherent in the rapidly expanding late Victorian metropolis, Fortune become much more concerned with the successful management of the relationship between the self and the spirit, something which is famously lacking in Sherlock Holmes.

Scholars including Jon Thompson point to the fact that Holmes is 'the quintessential empiricist'.[55] In Catherine Belsey's view, the Holmes canon works in direct opposition to the occult energies animating the final decades of the nineteenth century and aims 'to dispel magic and mystery, to make everything explicit, accountable, subject to scientific analysis':

> The stories are a plea for science not only in the sphere conventionally associated with detection (footprints, traces of hair or cloth, cigarette ends), where they have been deservedly influential in forensic practice, but in all areas. They reflect the widespread optimism characteristic of a period concerning the comprehensive power of positivist science.[56]

Ronald Thomas positions Holmes as the consummate 'scientific' detective, whose journeys through the environs of London did not merely echo the rise of forensic modes of policing but contributed, furthermore, to the invention of this very mythos. 'The exact "science" of detection and the technological apparatus for that enterprise he has assembled in his laboratory grant him the authority to tell a truth that is otherwise undiscoverable.'[57] However, Nils Clausson reads the Holmes canon as firmly rooted in the fin-de-siécle gothic, and, as such, the work 'questions and even subverts the aspirations of criminal science to subject crime and criminality to scientific analysis'.[58] The gothic interest in psychological

---

[53] Miriam Wallraven, *Women Writers and the Occult in Literature and Culture: Female Lucifers, Priestesses, and Witches* (Abingdon: Routledge, 2015), p. 101.
[54] Fortune, *Taverner*, p. xiii.
[55] Jon Thompson, *Fiction, Crime, and Empire* (Chicago: University of Illinois Press, 1993), p. 66.
[56] Catherine Belsey, *Critical Practice*, 2nd edn (London: Routledge, 2002), pp. 91, 93.
[57] Ronald R. Thomas, *Detective Fiction and the Rise of Forensic Science* (Cambridge: Cambridge University Press, 1999), pp. 1–2.
[58] Nils Clausson, 'Degeneration, Fin-de-Siécle Gothic, and the Science of Detection: Arthur Conan Doyle's *The Hound of the Baskervilles* and the Emergence of the Modern Detective Story', *Journal of Narrative Theory*, 35 (2005), 60–87 (p. 63).

interiority and the recesses of the subconscious become, in Clausson's reading, a site of significant and ultimately serious thematic engagement in Conan Doyle's writing and, it is clear, in Fortune's as well.

Fortune was not alone in recognizing the occult implications of the detective genre. Algernon Blackwood's Dr John Silence is a freelance detective and occult adept who draws equally upon his understanding of human nature and his ability to perceive the supersensible. In the world of Blackwood's Silence stories, outward forms of divination are merely tools for clearing away the chatter of the mind and reaching to the heart of the matter. The ability to do so does not rely specifically on any occult tools but merely on the prior rigorous training of the body and the mind which created Silence's profound mental control. In 'A Psychical Invasion', a writer of humorous stories inadvertently begins to write horror stories after taking an experimental dose of drugs which he had hoped would make him more humorous. In Silence's verdict, the drug opened the hapless Felix Pender up to the subtle energies that existed in his house, which had once belonged to a murderer. In 'Ancient Sorceries', a passive and downcast man living under the thumb of his unmarried sister imagines himself as the erotic counterpart to an ancient witch involved with devil worship, which, under further inspection by Silence, turns out to be a fantasy projection; in keeping with Blackwood's usual agenda, a supposedly occult phenomenon is finally revealed to have been caused by a deeply rooted psychological trauma. Aleister Crowley had his own occult detective in the form of Simon Iff, first introduced as a 'little old man, who was known as a mathematician of great eminence, with a touch of the crank'.[59] More forcefully didactic than Fortune's Taverner or Blackwood's Silence, the elderly mage is a mouthpiece of Crowley's Thelemic philosophy: '"Do what thou wilt shall be the whole of the Law." Failure to observe this precept is the root of all human error. It is our right and duty – the two are one, as Éliphas Lévi very nearly saw – to expand upon our own true centre, to pursue the exact orbit of our destiny.'[60] Thematically, the Simon Iff stories, which centre around a society of ill repute known as the Hemlock Club which had 'passed a rule that no man should be eligible for membership unless he had done something 'notorious and heretical', could not be further from the genteel, august narrative fabric of Fortune's occult detective stories.[61]

---

[59] Aleister Crowley, 'The Big Game', in *The Simon Iff Stories and Other Works* (Ware: Wordsworth, 2012), p. 37.
[60] Aleister Crowley, 'The Artistic Temperament', in *The Simon Iff Stories and Other Works* (Ware: Wordsworth, 2012), p. 52.
[61] Aleister Crowley, 'Outside the Bank's Routine', in *The Simon Iff Stories and Other Works* (Ware: Wordsworth, 2012), p. 38.

Writers of occult detective fiction like Fortune, Blackwood and Crowley would seek to silently replace Holmes's scientific method with the methods of the adept, all the while accepting that the vagaries of the unconscious mind almost certainly play a significant role in the meaning and importance of occult practice. The success of the narrative formula set out by Doyle comes with its 'open-ended, continuous form responsive to public fears, hopes, and anxieties'.[62] This story grammar offers an enduringly flexible model which offers an almost unlimited potential for villainy and the punctilious restitution of order. Indeed, this narrative elasticity has been crucial not merely to the propagation and widespread appeal of the genre but also to the curious and occasionally unexpected uses to which it is put in a display of parodic ecstasy in later fiction in the Holmes-implicated fiction by practicing occultists. In *The Secrets of Doctor Taverner* there is an unmistakable inversion of the Holmes method, in which deductions are made not through knowledge and reason but through intuition, which, in Taverner's case, has been developed to advanced degree through occult training. 'I have never been able to make up my mind whether Dr Taverner should be the hero or the villain of these histories', Rhodes confesses at the outset of 'Blood Lust'. 'That he was a man of the most selfless ideals could not be questioned, but in his methods of putting these ideals into practice he was absolutely unscrupulous.'[63] The nature of the crimes often remains indistinct, created, ultimately, by a psychic force beyond the precincts of the real world, and, for that reason, unobservable. David Lehman asserts the centrality of the *corpus delicti* to detective fiction,[64] a trope which, as Ronald Thomas explains, provides the narrative cause for action and a subject upon which the detective 'focuses his gaze and employs his unique interpretative powers' in order to explain the cause of events that created the current situation and to become the key 'body' of subjectivity upon which a display of analysis can be made.[65] Thomas accepts that the 'body of the crime' does not always exist in physical form – for instance, in Conan Doyle's 'A Scandal in Bohemia' the *absence* of the scandalous photograph presents the cause for action – but remains intent on how this body contains within it a code of meaning that must be determined. 'The Return of the Ritual' commences with Taverner emerging from a deep trance in which he has determined that 'there is a very curious affair afoot … which

---

[62] Thompson, p. 61.
[63] Fortune, *Taverner*, p. 1.
[64] David Lehman, *The Perfect Murder: A Study in Detection* (Ann Arbor: University of Michigan Press, 2000), p. 3.
[65] Thomas, p. 2.

I do not understand'.⁶⁶ It emerges that a ritual has been stolen which Taverner is able to detect is now being performed and thus, like the stolen photograph in 'A Scandal in Bohemia', it is the absence rather than the presence of something which identifies that a crime has been committed.

'Blood Lust', the first of the stories, signals Fortune's move from traditional psychotherapy to occult modalities, fictionalizing a complex case of shell shock she encountered at the Medico-Psychological Clinic. In the story, Captain Donald Craigie has returned from war with an insatiable thirst for blood, which Taverner diagnoses as a 'vitality hunger', a presumably vampiric tendency that emerged in the battlefield.⁶⁷ The horrors of the First World War played an unmistakable role in the development of psychoanalysis. Shortly after the signing of the Armistice of Compiégne brought an end to war, Freud began to revise his early theory of the pleasure principle, which, having been treating shell-shocked soldiers, now seemed to him to offer an incomplete account of the nature of the mind. The well-remembered *fort/da* sketch, which opens *Beyond the Pleasure Principle* (1920), centres on the young child's recognition that his father is at the front 'and was far from regretting his absence; on the contrary he made it quite clear that he had no desire to be disturbed in his sole possession of his mother'.⁶⁸ In addressing 'the dark and dismal subject of the traumatic neurosis' of wounded soldiers,⁶⁹ Freud explains:

> If we are to take it as a truth that knows no exception that everything living dies for *internal* reasons – becomes inorganic once again – then we shall be compelled to say that '*the aim of all life is death*' and, looking backwards, that 'inanimate things existed before living one'.⁷⁰

Freud's work with shell-shocked soldiers caused him to re-evaluate the role of both the libido and the pleasure principle in the organization of the unconscious.⁷¹ Fortune's response to the impacts of shell shock was markedly different. The challenges of treating some of the earliest recorded cases of shell shock are recorded in Fortune *Psychic Self-Defense* (1930), a curious amalgam of occultism and psychoanalysis woven into a pointillist memoir of rising through the ranks of both systems of arcane knowledge. In *Psychic Self-Defence*, she recounts at

---

⁶⁶ Fortune, *Taverner*, pp. 19–20.
⁶⁷ Fortune, *Taverner*, p. 7.
⁶⁸ Sigmund Freud, *Beyond the Pleasure Principle* in *Complete Psychological Works of Sigmund Freud*, vol. 18 (London: Vintage, 2001), p. 16.
⁶⁹ Freud, p. 14.
⁷⁰ Freud, p. 38.
⁷¹ Allan Johnson, *Masculine Identity in Modernist Literature: Castration, Narration, and a Sense of the Beginning, 1919–1945* (London: Palgrave Macmillan, 2017), pp. 109–10.

length the case of a shell shock patient who was accused of necrophilia on the front and, after family connections saved him from military prison, continued to be physically violent on his return to England. Fortune was in the process of training the analyst treating the patient and, unable to provide her own insight and answers, turned to her occult teacher Theodore Moriarty:

> His opinion concerning the case, though there was no means of obtaining independent confirmation of this, was that some Eastern European troops had been brought to the Western Front, and among these were individuals with the traditional knowledge of Black Magic for which South-Eastern Europe has always enjoyed a sinister reputation among occultists.[72]

In both cases, the treatment of symptoms offered the same opportunities for investigation as crime and detection – in some senses Holmes and Taverner are diagnosing as much as they are solving, and it is very often the case in Fortune's stories that once a diagnosis has been made (usually not revealed immediately to the reader), the psychic concerns will soon resolve themselves. After moving Cragie to his nursing home in Hindhead, Taverner and his assistant determined that Cragie, weakened by shell shock, has become the host of an undead spirit, who uses his body to ensure a supply of blood. Rhodes explains to the reader at the opening of 'Blood Lust' that

> Taverner's work began where ordinary medicine ended, and I have under my care cases such as the ordinary doctor would have referred to the safe keeping of an asylum, as being nothing else but mad. Yet Taverner, by his peculiar methods of work, laid bare causes operating both within the soul and in the shadowy realm where the soul has its dwelling, that threw an entirely new light upon the problem, and often enabled him to rescue a man from the dark influences that were closing in upon him.[73]

Psychoanalysis became a hermetic community of initiates required to have undergone their own painful and protracted analysis before subsequently initiating others in a similar manner, but the transformative aspects of this process were not left unnoticed by modernist writers concerned with capturing the vitality and reality of the human consciousness. Now more talked about than read following a peak of popularity during the counterculture revolution of the 1960s, Hesse's fiction provides a critical indication of the simultaneous lines of influence that connected psychoanalysis with magical ways of thinking

---

[72] Fortune, *Psychic Self-Defense*, p. 48.
[73] Fortune, *Taverner*, p. 3.

during the modernist period. Fortune's involvement in early psychoanalysis is captured in her largely unremarked-upon *The Secrets of Doctor Taverner* which features a Holmesian occult psychoanalyst who draws upon his occult training and knowledge of the unconscious to solve impenetrable whodunits. In doing so, Fortune offers a parodic recasting of the Holmesian formula in an occult milieu as a means by which to evaluate the challenging relationship between the spirit and the will, the endemic concern of the modern world. Even while figures including Carl Jung were resolutely defining themselves as medical doctors who were practicing a new but valid form of clinical therapy, the coveted lineages, revered masters, rarefied training and bitter feuds that outlined the early years of psychoanalysis bear a striking resemblance to the aims and operations of contemporaneous occult organizations.

4

The making of an overman: The superman and superwoman in modernist literature

The fin-de-siècle ferment of decadence, ceremonial magic and social transformation evidently struck Somerset Maugham as a marketable subject for a novel following a chance encounter in Paris with the infamous occultist Aleister Crowley. 'I took an immediate dislike to him', Maugham explained, 'but he interested and amused me. He was a great talker and he talked uncommonly well. ... He was a fake, but not entirely a fake.'[1] Trained as a doctor at St Thomas's, one of London's oldest and most prestigious training hospitals, Maugham was a writer of acute observation and rational curiosity whose early work cast a naturalist gaze on social and sexual propriety in the lives of commonplace London inhabitants. *The Magician* (1908), however, stretched his thematic palate with a captivated portrayal of ceremonial magic and the baleful magician Oliver Haddo, an intentional caricature of Crowley.[2] Haddo is a grotesque Svengali who lures art student Margaret Dauncey with 'that low voice of his that thrilled her with a curious magic' and 'enmeshed her [in a web] woven with skillful intricacy'.[3] She becomes a convenient sacrifice in Haddo's magical ritual to create new superhuman life, but it is really Margaret's fiancé, the surgeon Arthur Burdon, whom Haddo means to punish. 'Don't you remember that you hit him once, and kicked him unmercifully?' Margaret explains to Arthur midway through the text. 'He could have killed you, but he hated you too much. It pleased him a thousand times more to devise this torture for you and me.'[4] After Haddo is vanquished in a psychic battle, Arthur and his friend, the armchair occultist Dr Porhoët, travel to Haddo's magical laboratory to discover the abortive efforts of

---

[1] W. Somerset Maugham, *The Magician* (1908; repr. London: Vintage, 2000), p. vii.
[2] Nick Freeman draws attention to the influence of both Crowley and Oscar Wilde on Maugham's Haddo. See Nick Freeman, 'Wilde's Edwardian Afterlife: Somerset Maugham, Aleister Crowley, and *The Magician*, *Literature and History*, 16.2 (2007), 16–29.
[3] Maugham, pp. 113, 117.
[4] Maugham, p. 157.

the ritual which created 'a mass of flesh unlike that of any human being; and it pulsated regularly', an uncanny counterfeit of a human body.[5]

The Magician came to the literary scene seemingly a decade too late, with its central apprehension surrounding the possibility of a healthy, middle-class marriage being foiled by the supernatural faculties of an abject outsider now a well-worn trope redolent of George du Maurier, Henry James, Oscar Wilde and Bram Stoker, among others. What Maugham's fantasia on the theme ultimately offers, however, is an indication of how the appealing trimmings and frills of the nineteenth-century occult revival had been remembered, misremembered and reinterpreted as it moved into the twentieth century. Much of the occult philosophy portrayed through the expository sermons of Dr Porhoët was taken in large part from key texts of nineteenth-century occultism including Eliphas Levi's *Dogme et Rituel de la Haute Magie* (1854), translated by A. E. Waite in 1896. Although Maugham did not share a belief in magic, his gothic romance nevertheless implicitly understands the disquieting abilities of these so-called magicians and their nefarious aims; Crowley 'was a fake, but not entirely a fake', Maugham tellingly claimed.[6] In Crowley's review of *The Magician* in the 30 December 1908 issue of *Vanity Fair*, published brazenly under the pseudonym Oliver Haddo, he accuses Maugham of flagrant plagiarism and identifies passages taken indiscriminately from Samuel Liddell MacGregor Mathers's *Kabbalah Unveiled* (1887) and Franz Hartmann's *The Life of Paracelsus* (1891) as well as clear stylistic and thematic indebtedness to Mabel Collins's *The Blossom and the Fruit* (1890) and H. G. Wells's *The Island of Dr Moreau* (1896). Crowley was palpably riled by Maugham's unpleasant portrayal of him, suggesting that all it takes to write like Maugham is to 'get invited to [a well-educated man's] house – possibility some cosy vicarage – read in his library a few of the works dealing with our subject and copy them wholesale into our book; sometimes verbatim, sometimes altering words here and there'.[7]

The irony in Crowley's righteous repudiation is that several years later he would appropriate Maugham's thematic figurations in his own novel *Moonchild* (1917), which similarly centres on the erotic triangulation between two competing men and the woman who is intended to be sacrificed to create a powerful new life. Whatever Crowley's gifts may have been – and his systematizing intelligence and theological sense are unmistakable – his metier was not prose fiction. As Alan

---

[5] Maugham, p. 225.
[6] Maugham, p. vii.
[7] Aleister Crowley (writing as Oliver Haddo), 'How to Write a Novel! (After W. S. Maugham)', *Vanity Fair* (30 December 1908), pp. 838–40 (p. 838).

Richardson quite fairly acknowledges, 'Everyone approaches *Moonchild* for the first time with an air of excitement about the unusual subject matter, and most come away disappointed with the ineptness of style and banal characterisation.'[8] Somewhat more forgivingly, Dion Fortune admits that 'although Crowley's [fiction and poetry] are marred by the grossest ribaldry and the foulest personal abuse, they are the works of a man of genius and a writer of magnificent English'.[9] *Moonchild* is a chaotic airing of grievances against his earlier magical rivals including Samuel Liddell MacGregor Mathers and A. E. Waite, portrayed conspicuously as Count Macgregor of Glenlyon and Arthwait, initiates of a sinister magical lodge reminiscent (at least in its personnel) of the Hermetic Order of the Golden Dawn. Crowley himself is divided across two cyphers – the good magicians Cyril Grey and Simon Iff – and the text comes across as a particularly pitiable account of a wounded ego interspersed with meandering homilies on Thelemic philosophy. As Colin Wilson points out in *The Occult* (1979), 'Crowley's chief drawback as an "adept" was an intense self-preoccupation that was the opposite of what I mean by the "wide-angle lens". In this important sense, H. G. Wells or Albert Einstein were closer to "adeptship" than Crowley. In occultism, as in science, intellect and disinterestedness are the cardinal virtues.'[10] Both *The Magician* and *Moonchild* are charming yet fundamentally problematic novels. However, the primary interest in their comparison inheres in their metatextual knitting together of forged identities, imitation and ersatz biography, all put to the service of narratives about the magical affordances for creating new life. The trope of creating new superhuman life as an attempt to master the material world had been central to the nineteenth-century literary imagination since at least Mary Shelley's *Frankenstein* (1818), and, like their contextual predecessors, both *The Magician* and *Moonchild* reach devastating conclusions that underscore the hubris of such attempts. But Maugham's and Crowley's texts mark the closure of a distinctively nineteenth-century treatment of the superhuman trope and clear the way for a newly refocused modernist appreciation of what might occur if the suprarational and supernatural superman could live and survive as a salvational influence on modern life.

This chapter scans the emergence of the superman fable in three of its most characteristic modernist expressions. The first of these is A. R. Orage's iconic

---

[8] Alan Richardson, *Aleister Crowley and Dion Fortune: The Logos of the Aeon and the Shakti of the Age* (Woodbury, MN: Llewellyn, 2009), p. 72.
[9] Dion Fortune, 'Ceremonial Magic Unveiled', repr. in Gareth Knight, *Dion Fortune's Rites of Isis and of Pan* (Cheltenham: Skylight, 2013), pp. 82–93 (p. 91).
[10] Colin Wilson, *The Occult* (1979; repr. London: Watkins, 2003), p. 179.

little magazine *The New Age*, which, even before Orage committed fully to the occult philosophy of G. I. Gurdjieff and his 'Fourth Way', gave voice to a provocative correlation between plans for a modern England and the possibility that a Nietzschean overman could guide the way. Bernard Shaw was a founding contributor to *The New Age* and in both his dramatic writing and his public lectures promoted a Bergsonian notion of a 'life force' which could give rise to the obdurate but effective figures of providential change, represented within his drama by characters including John Tanner and Saint Joan. The work of Dion Fortune provides the third coordinate in this discussion. While Fortune's work is customarily seen to operate outside the thematic and aesthetic fabric of literary modernism, the ethical domain of her work, including, most notably, that portrayed within *The Sea Priestess* (1938), captures a prototypically modernist, and, in many ways problematical, handling of the image of wide-scale social redemption during a time when the upshots of social engineering and eugenics were about to be tragically revealed. Although much of literary modernism is concerned with the bliss of being ordinary, a suggestive undercurrent of writing – inspired by Nietzsche but a distinct product of the events and sympathies of the early twentieth century – simultaneously worked towards imaging a perfected *Übermensch* who channelled the redemptive and dynamic powers of divinity into an earthly force in a fable of radical social organization and progress.

The term *Übermensch* was first introduced by Nietzsche and then translated influentially but imperfectly into English as 'superman' by Bernard Shaw in his strange and wonderful *Man and Superman* (1903). As Nietzsche's Zarathustra – a figure, it must be noted, whose theological message bears little resemblance to his namesake Zoroaster – explains to his early followers, 'All creatures hitherto have created something beyond themselves: and do you want to me the ebb of this great tide, and return to the animals rather than overcome man? ... The Superman is the meaning of the earth. Let your will say: The Superman *shall be* the meaning of the earth!'[11] 'All gods are dead: now we want the Superman to live', Nietzsche writes, a poignant and deeply influential indication of the late Victorian recognition that humanity's future lies within the realm of the physical and mundane rather than the incorporeal depictions of the divinity of the Abrahamic religions.[12] Goethe's Faust was a superman whose ambitions were thwarted by the humanity which he was never able to relinquish, while

---

[11] Friedrich Nietzsche, *Thus Spoke Zarathustra*, trans. R. J. Hollingdale (London: Penguin, 2003), pp. 41–2.
[12] Nietzsche, p. 104.

Wagner's Siegfried presents the other great German example: as Colin Wilson writes of these examples, it is 'the drama of the rationalist suffocating in the dusty room of his personal consciousness, caught in the vicious circle of boredom and futility'.[13] Richard Noll points out that 'the doctrine of Nietzscheanism was seductive: it promised the release of creative powers of genius within the individual, the courage to freely express oneself and to reject authority and moral and social conventions. Through *deeds* one could truly be who one was, and perhaps even achieve symbolic immortality'.[14] Nietzsche's *Thus Spoke Zarathustra* is, in Michael Levenson's words, 'both a denunciation of the rabble and a hymn to individual preeminence'.[15] While the term *Übermensch* was Nietzsche's, the concept of an insurrectionary hero of humanity was being redeveloped and redeployed in the light of the growing urbanization, industrialization, internationalization and liberalism which defined the modern spirit. In his novel *Mafarka the Futurist* (1909), Marinetti images the birth of a mechanical son, a technological superman that represents 'the fruit of pure will, synthesis of all the laws that science is on the brink of discovering'.[16] For the modernists, there was perhaps no clearer manifestation of the notion of immanence than the figure of the *Übermensch*, which grounded progressive and occasionally radical social ideals in a messianic figure freed from religious dogma.

A. R. Orage was a schoolteacher with Theosophical interests and Fabian sympathies when Holbrook Jackson introduced him to *Thus Spoke Zarathustra* (1883, trans. 1896), a text which suggested to him the possibility of real-world application for his social and spiritual ideals.[17] Together Orage and Jackson founded the Leeds Arts Club in 1902, a discussion group that fused radical politics, progressive arts and Theosophy, and would remount a similar group in London in January 1907 under the new name of the Fabian Arts Group. W. B. Yeats was present at the first meeting which was chaired by Shaw, and both G. K. Chesterton and H. G. Wells would deliver lectures to the group over the next several months.[18] That same year, Shaw contributed £500 to purchase a foundering decade-old socialist magazine called *The New Age: A Weekly Record of Culture, Social Service, and Literary Life*, which would relaunch under the editorship of

---

[13] Wilson, p. xxv.
[14] Richard Noll, *The Jung Cult: Origins of a Charismatic Movement* (London: Fontana, 1996), p. 4.
[15] Michael Levenson, *Modernism* (London: Yale University Press, 2011), p. 6.
[16] F. T. Marinetti, 'Contempt for Women', in *Modernism: An Anthology*, ed. Lawrence Rainey, trans. Lawrence Rainey (1911; repr. Oxford: Blackwell, 2005), pp. 9–11 (p. 11).
[17] Wallace Martin, *The New Age under Orage: Chapters in English Cultural History* (Manchester: Manchester University Press, 1967), p. 18.
[18] Martin, p. 22.

Orage and, for a short time, Jackson. As Orage wrote in 1909, 'We are sometimes told by the old Socialist buccaneers that *The New Age* is too damned literary, or too damned aesthetic, or too damned something or other. But the fact is that Socialism in *The New Age* is losing its bony statistical aspect and putting on the colours of vivid life.'[19] It was both a political weekly and a literary review and covered a wide gamut of subjects including literature, politics, economics and philosophy, at a time when other serial publications were refining their offerings for increasingly segmented readerships. *The New Age* was, in this regard, the iconoclastically modernist little magazine which sought to reimagine the shards of human experience fusing into form, uniting highbrow socialism, literary and social experimentation and an opening up of spiritual boundaries. 'The *New Age* could not be said to be an organ of the public opinion of today', Orage buoyantly observed, 'but of the public opinion of tomorrow'.[20] Wallace Martin portrays Orage as one of the most influential editors of his time for his ability 'to make *The New Age* a presentative periodical which would mediate between specialized fields of knowledge and public understanding, and encourage a vital relationship between literary experimentation and the literary tradition'.[21] This balance between experimentation and tradition continued through to Orage's emergent spiritual nous and his understanding of the relevance of a Nietzschean superman to heal the abrasions and upsets of the rapidization of modern life. Orage's first book, published at the Christ-like age of thirty-three, describes Nietzsche not merely as a philosopher but also as 'the greatest European event since Goethe'.[22] In one of his most perceptive passages, Orage recognizes that

> in the absence of any positive knowledge of the nature or even the existence of any future life, it is folly, Nietzsche declared, to train a race by morality, religion, and all the other instruments of education for a future of which we can know nothing. For what we do know, we may, however, make ourselves responsible. And the certain thing is, that humanity lives, has lived, and will continue to live on the earth. Hence the problem is, in Nietzsche's words, to determine what type of man we are to cultivate, to will, as the more valuable, and the more worthy of life, and certain of the future, here upon the earth.[23]

The philosophy of Nietzsche and Bergson was comfortably at home in the pages of *The New Age*, and while neither was occult in aims or objectives, the philosophy

---

[19] A. R. Orage, *The New Age*, IV (28 January 1909), p. 280.
[20] A. R. Orage, *On Love and Psychological Exercises* (York Beach, ME: Samuel Weiser, 1998), p. 31.
[21] Martin, p. 3.
[22] A.R. Orage, *Friedrich Nietzsche: The Dionysian Spirit of the Age* (London: T.N. Foulis, 1906), p. 11.
[23] Orage, *Friedrich Nietzsche*, pp. 67–8.

of both Bergson and Nietzsche nevertheless bespoke a subtle repudiation of the scientific materialism which had become the seemingly most enduring social framework in the years leading to the outbreak of war. By the time of *The New Age*'s closure in 1922 when Orage had committed himself full-time to teaching and studying the occult philosophy of Gurdjieff, the journal had published work by Crowley, Shaw, Wells, Chesterton, Hilaire Belloc, Max Beerbohm, Ambrose Bierce, Edward Carpenter, H. D., Frank Harris, Augustus John, Robert Ross, Siegfried Sassoon, Sidney Webb, Arnold Bennett, F. S. Flint, Ezra Pound, T. E. Hulme, Katherine Mansfield, Wyndham Lewis and Richard Aldington, among many others whose contribution to the modernist moment proved to be more fleeting.

A largely forgotten contributor to *The New Age* was the actress, producer, playwright, journalist and Golden Dawn initiate Florence Farr, whose articles for the magazine on women's rights and suffrage were gathered together in *Modern Woman: Her Intentions*, published by Frank Palmer in 1910. After a lecture tour of America in 1907, she returned to England looking for work. She was never broken on the wheel of poverty but was acutely aware that her £50 yearly inheritance provided financial security but also needed to be supplemented by additional income; her friend Shaw introduced her to Orage and *The New Age* with this objective in mind.[24] The collected articles demonstrate Farr's vision for not merely a New Woman but also a *superwoman* whose superior economic, intellectual and reproductive proficiency was required for the betterment of all humanity. Farr's argument centres on a captivating argument that enfranchisement affords the most compelling economic future for the country; however, her vision for the superwoman is troubling to twenty-first-century eyes: her palpable classism – consistent with mainline Fabian views that working-class people are too enfeebled by labour to productively engage in political discourse and action – impugns the ambitions of marginalized women and she optimistically supports sterilization, which she describes as 'a newly discovered and harmless operation which can be performed without making the slightest difference to an individual's happiness'.[25] But *Modern Woman: Her Intentions* also offers bold illustration of the fact that marriage is a social construct which is not suitably aligned with the needs of the individual, and

---

[24] Josephine Johnson, *Florence Farr: Bernard Shaw's New Woman* (Gerrards Cross: Colin Smythe, 1975), p. 13.
[25] Florence Farr, *Modern Woman: Her Intentions* (London: Frank Palmer, 1910), p. 65.

especially not with the needs of women whose task is to be of service to society at large:

> Women can look upon love as a physical act which enables them to become mothers. They can look upon it as a sanctification or a means of enjoyment. They can look upon it as a subject of scientific curiosity, in which mood they logically compare facts and come to sage conclusions. They can consider their own temperaments and peculiarities, and take into account their personal bias and characters, philosophically.[26]

In the pages of *The New Age*, Farr advocated for decisive action, for a committed feminism which acknowledged the social, financial, religious, educational and professional equality of women. As Lucy Delap demonstrates, the term 'superwoman' was equally in currency during the Edwardian period and represented a distinct form of contemplative feminism correlated to the traditionally masculine notion of 'genius'.[27] Near the conclusion to *Modern Woman: Her Intentions*, Farr instructs that 'I want the women who read this book not to dwell upon the past, but to look forward to the great century that is waiting for their alchemy, to transmute its life by giving it a more intent purpose'.[28] For writers such as Farr, suffrage suggested an unmistakably necessary route to the creation of both supermen and superwomen as well as a resuscitated social order.

Although Orage was a member of the Theosophical Society, he publicly espoused a rational agnosticism in the pages of *The New Age* until after the end of the First World War. By this time *The New Age* had become both the indisputable tastemaker and journal of record for modern liberal thinking, and when European spiritual teachers shaken loose after the war were attempting to find a foothold in a new country, *The New Age* was where they turned upon their arrival. Orage had first met Gurdjieff's disciple P. D. Ouspensky in 1914, but it was only when Ouspensky came to London in 1920 with a view to introducing Gurdjieffian thought to England that Orage became fully absorbed in his spiritual practice. The principal aim of Gurdjieff's method was the achievement of what he called 'self-remembering', the connection to an embodied physical presence that identified to the individual the spark of innate divinity. The influential publisher C. S. Nott recounts a first-hand conversation during which Orage explained to him that

---

[26] Farr, *Modern Woman*, p. 78.
[27] Lucy Delap, 'The Superwoman: Theories of Gender and Genius in Edwardian Britain', *Historical Journal*, 47.1 (2004), 101–26.
[28] Farr, *Modern Woman*, p. 92.

> I [Orage] was already beginning to be disillusioned with the purely literary and cultural life when I met Ouspensky, who came to see me before 1914. It was becoming more and more difficult for me to force myself to write the notes of the week in the *New Age*. It had been a profound disappointment to me to realize that my intellectual life, with which was associated all that was highest and best in Western culture, was leading me nowhere.[29]

Although *The New Age* was thus well-positioned to become an official publishing organ for the Gurdjieff method and was well equipped to reach out to a readership of potential converts, Orage would ultimately sell the magazine to undertake a period of teaching Gurdjieffian philosophy in New York before settling at Gurdjieff's Institute for the Harmonious Development of Man near Fontainebleau, France. During this time, he produced commentaries on Gurdjieff's *Beelzebub's Tales to His Grandson*, translated *Meetings with Remarkable Men* and encouraged Katherine Mansfield to travel to the Institute, where she died in 1923. 'The real reason, and the only reason, that led Katherine Mansfield to the Gurdjieff Institute', Orage explains, 'was less dissatisfaction with her craftsmanship than dissatisfaction with herself; less dissatisfaction with her stories than with the attitude toward life implied in them; less dissatisfaction with her own and contemporary literature than with literature'.[30] Nott records a conversation shortly before her death in which Mansfield disclosed to him that

> if I [Mansfield] had gone away from the Prieuré and lived the old life ... I should have died very soon of boredom. Here, at any rate, I am alive inside, and the people around me are alive. And I am not Katherine Mansfield the writer, but Mrs Murry, a sick woman, looked after without fuss or sentimentality. Another thing – here at last I see what I have always wanted to see; people who are themselves, and not playing a part behind a mask.[31]

Orage had been a close friend and mentor since Mansfield's arrival in London and would spend a great deal of time with her at Fountainbleu in the days and months leading up to her death. In Mansfield, Orage saw a writer of extraordinary ability and sensitivity whose fine technique could be improved further only through 'the adoption of an entirely new means', namely the spiritual work of Gurdjieff.[32]

---

[29] C. S. Nott, *Teachings of Gurdjieff: The Journal of a Pupil* (London: Routledge & Kegan Paul, 1961), p. 27.
[30] Orage, *On Love and Psychological Exercises*, p. 38.
[31] Nott, p. 47.
[32] Orage, *On Love and Psychological Exercises*, p. 39.

'A man cannot remember himself', Gurdjieff is reported to have said, 'because he tries to do so with his mind – at least, in the beginning. Self-remembering begins with self-sensing. It must be done through the instinctive-moving centre and the emotional centre. Mind alone does not constitute a human being any more than the driver is the whole equipage.'[33] Gurdjieff's system, broadly theosophical in cosmology but richly influenced in both style and sentiment by Middle Eastern mysticism, caught in the minds of an interwar intelligentsia looking for a new approach to the sacred. It is often believed that Gurdjieff's complex occult system and practices are best described in the work of Ouspensky; however, Orage's account of his time with Gurdjieff remains a valuable and largely unrecognized source in the history of occult philosophy. Orage presented a palatable and idiomatic introduction to the system for his students, casting his net wide in the hopes of gathering new followers and donors. It was in New York that Jean Toomer, Herbert Croly (editor of the *New Republic*) and John O'Hara Cosgrave (editor of the Sunday magazine of the *New York World*) encountered Gurdjieffian thought.[34] Orage's 'Aphorisms', which emerged from his teaching in New York from 1924 to 1930, offer a lucid summary of Gurdjieff's doctrine and precepts:

> A normal man is one who has not only actualized his potentialities but has freed himself from his subjectivity.[35]
>
> Ordinary man is at the mercy of his organism: of the instinctive centre – impressions received by the senses, or appetites, inertia, disease; of the feelings – associations connected with people and places past and present, likes and dislikes, fear and anxiety; of the mind – imagination, day-dreaming, suggestibility.[36]
>
> Mere intellectualism, mere philosophy, produces monsters.[37]
>
> Unless we can 'remember' ourselves, we are completely mechanical. Self-observation is possible only through self-remembering. These are the first steps in self-consciousness.[38]

Orage speaks of 'blank gramophone records upon which, from the first day or first hours [after birth], impressions of both the inner and outer world become inscribed'.[39] These inscriptions like a gramophone record create an

---

[33] Nott, p. 37.
[34] Rudolph P. Byrd, *Jean Toomer's Years with Gurdjieff: Portrait of an Artist, 1923–1936* (Athens: University of Georgia Press, 1990); Nott, p. 88.
[35] Orage, *On Love and Psychological Exercises*, p. 47.
[36] Orage, *On Love and Psychological Exercises*, p. 47.
[37] Orage, *On Love and Psychological Exercises*, p. 52.
[38] Orage, *On Love and Psychological Exercises*, p. 54.
[39] Nott, p. 4.

outward-facing mask, and 'only when the mask has been destroyed can we study and observe the man himself, that is, his real type'.[40] Gurdjieff's occult philosophy attempted to wake followers from the somnambulant state of modernity to create a confederacy of spiritually and intellectually evolved supermen, just as Orage's *New Age* had intended to inspire radical, just change and stimulate a new generation of super-evolved thinkers and advocates.

Bernard Shaw, original backer and regular contributor to *The New Age*, was at the same time developing his own idiosyncratic understanding of the possibility of a super-evolved overman as a redemptive force for society. In his classic biography of Shaw, Michael Holroyd summarizes the key ethical positions of Shaw's philosophy with the wit, candour and efficiency of G. B. S. himself:

> Act, though in a sensible way, selfishly (that is, with self-control) and do not be peevishly self-sacrificing; arm yourself with politeness which is a mark of superiority over unpleasant people; cultivate hypocrisy with others for kindness' sake, but never with yourself; read anything except what bores you; leave religion alone until you've grown up; get into mischief, but do not look for pity; neither ask anything as a favour, nor expect more than you've deserved by your conduct.[41]

While it is true that this type of positivism defined much of Shaw's ethical stance, his writing evinces a cosmopolitan heterodoxy and a sustained interest in ways of knowing the self which emerged from modernist occultism. Although in no way practically engaged in occult practice, Shaw did attend meetings of the Society for Psychical Research and formed erotic friendships with the prominent occultists Annie Besant and Florence Farr, key leaders in the Theosophical Society and the Hermetic Order of the Golden Dawn, the iconically late Victorian organizations that renewed interest in occultism and the hidden traditions of both East and West. Captain Shotover's frequent mysterious allusions to the 'seventh degree of concentration' in *Heartbreak House* (1919) are perhaps a knowingly humorous commentary on this occult milieu.[42] Shaw likely first met Farr around 1890, at a time when she was quickly rising both through the theatrical world of late Victorian London and the equally vibrant occult circles of the capital.[43] He had also formed an equally significant collaborative relationship with Besant, who

---

[40] Nott, p. 6.
[41] Michael Holroyd, *Bernard Shaw: Volume 1, 1856–1898: The Search for Love* (London: Penguin, 1988), p. 72.
[42] Bernard Shaw, *Heartbreak House: A Fantasia in the Russian Manner on English Themes* (1919; repr. London: Penguin, 2000), p. 52.
[43] Margot Peters, *Bernard Shaw and the Actresses* (New York: Doubleday, 1980), p. 69.

was well connected to the London literary beau monde through the Dialectical Society, the Fabian Society and, shortly after, the Theosophical Society. She edited the magazine *Our Corner* from 1883 to 1888, during which time Shaw was a regular contributor to the Arts Corner section. Standard biographies of both Besant and Shaw identify Besant as a clear source behind the central female figures in the *Plays Pleasant* – Raina Petkoff in *Arms and the Man* (1894), Candida Morell in *Candida* (1894) and Mrs Clandon in *You Never Can Tell* (1897). As the stage directions describe Mrs Clandon, she

> belongs to the forefront of her own period (say 1860–1880) in a jealously assertive attitude of character and intellect, and in being a woman of cultivated interests rather than passionately developed personal affections. Her voice and ways are entirely kindly and humane; … but displays of personal sentiment secretly embarrass her; passion in her is humanitarian rather than human; she feels strongly about social questions and principles, not about persons.[44]

The play later indicates that Mrs Clandon had first met Finch M'Comas at the Dialectical Society, as did Besant and Shaw, where, on 21 January 1885, she asked him to nominate her for the Fabian Society. Besant had already commissioned 'The Irrational Knot' from Shaw for *Our Corner* several days before, but it was there at his talk on socialism that she first properly judged his intellect. Shaw's caustic but undeniably esteeming treatment of Mrs Clandon undoubtedly reflects some of his own complex feelings towards Besant following her conversion to Theosophy.[45]

Shaw would chastise Farr for her 'love of miracles and moonshees' and would subsequently transmute his mother's Spiritualism into a kind of stoic distress.[46] But he was a self-confessed mystic with a world view circumscribed by his faith in the advancement of humanity and the 'Life Force' that sped such progress. Shaw's early drama bears the unmistakable personal influence of two of the leading occultists of the day; however, Shaw's own mystical views developed along very different lines. Indeed, in the pages of *The New Age* Farr would take a dim view of Shaw's treatment of orthogenesis in *Man and Superman*:

> Mr. Orage's mind is equipped by nature and subtle Eastern practices to give us a far clearer idea of Superhuman of Aristocratic Consciousness than we gather from the songs of Nietzsche or from Shaw's great classic, 'Man and Superman',

---

[44] Bernard Shaw, *Plays Pleasant* (1898; repr. London: Penguin, 2003), p. 220.
[45] Sally Peters, *The Ascent of the Superman* (London: Yale University Press, 1996), pp. 130–1.
[46] Clifford Bax (ed.), *Letters: Florence Farr, Bernard Shaw, W. B. Yeats* (London: Home & Van Thal, 1946), p. 12.

with its preface, notes, and appendix. Mr. Orage is more intimately in touch with Greek and Brahmic traditions than Mr. Shaw; he has the knack of entering into such phases of existence and holding them up to our view, warm and throbbing with their own ecstasies; whereas Mr. Shaw has such an antipathy to vivisection in any form that he often loses these qualities of lifelike representation, and examines the dead forms of things with a critical distaste quite alien to Mr. Orage's instincts.[47]

To Farr's mind, *Man and Superman* falls short of achieving its ultimate aim by capturing the spirit rather than the truth of what she viewed as the inherently mystical premise of creative evolution. But *Man and Superman*, more than any of Shaw's other work, relies on the explicit development of ideas which form naturally into their own antithesis: the play is as equivocal as it is dialectical, undermining its own conceptual framework in that same way that Tanner aims to 'shatter creeds and demolish idols'.[48]

As the Reverend James Mavor Morell of *Candida* (1898) explains, 'I well know that it is in the poet that the holy spirit of man – the god within him – is most godlike', and, in spite of what Farr perceived, Shaw's ever-evolving beliefs surrounding the relationship between humanity and the divine bear subtle yet consistent traces of theosophical, hermetic and gnostic influence.[49] Orthogenesis was typically gnostic belief, seized upon by Shaw from the work of Bergson and Francis Galton, and a late Victorian attempt to reconcile the scientific premise of evolution with an animistic and often mystical belief that biological evolution provides evidence of divinity. 'Evolution is a vital part of the New Theology', Shaw professed in 1907, and for him this New Theology had the capacity to supplant the hierarchies of, in particular, nineteenth-century muscular Christian orthodoxy to imagine the world as being built up from the lowest creature to the highest, as humanity involved in the process of creating their own god.[50] This is a standard position in early Gnosticism, and one that Shaw himself explicitly described:

> We are all experiments in the direction of making God. What God is doing is making himself, getting from being a mere powerless will or force. This force has implanted into our minds the ideal of God. We are not very successful attempts at God so far, but I believe that if we can drive into the heads of men the full

---

[47] Florence Farr, 'Superman Consciousness', *The New Age*, 1.6 (6 June 1907), 92.
[48] Bernard Shaw, *Man and Superman* (1903; repr. London: Penguin, 1946), p. 74.
[49] Shaw, *Plays Pleasant*, p. 116.
[50] Bernard Shaw, 'New Theology', in *The Religious Speeches of Bernard Shaw*, ed. Warren Sylvester Smith (University Park, PA: Penn State University Press, 1963), p. 14.

consciousness of moral responsibility that comes to men with the knowledge that there never will be a God unless we make one – that we are the instruments through which that ideal is trying to make itself a reality – we can work towards that ideal until we get to be supermen, and then super-supermen, and then a world of organisms who have achieved and realized God.[51]

Four years earlier Shaw expressed a similar point: 'If I were God, I should try to create something higher than myself, and then something higher than that, so that, beginning with a God the highest thing in creation, I should end with a God the lowest thing in creation.'[52] What Shaw had called the Life Force, Bergson would later call the *élan vital* in the pages of *Creative Evolution*, published four years after *Man and Superman* and translated into English eight years after John Tanner sermonized on the topic. In *Creative Evolution* (1907, trans. 1911), Bergson refers to the *élan vital*, 'the explosive force – due to an unstable balance of tendencies'.[53] The notion of the 'life force' or 'vitalism' suggests a naturally gnostic teleology in which the organism is constantly working towards creating greater and greater versions of itself; post-Darwinian evolutionary theory, against which Bergson and others resisted, suggests that the organism that is produced just happens to be so because it presents the strongest example of its species. The central establishing symbol in Bergson's sustained consideration of social organization was duration, the measurement of time against a standard of utility (this idea would be partly echoed and brought into the domain of literature in Gérard Genette's *Narrative Discourse* (1980) with the treatment of duration as the sequence between event and narration and influence Deleuze and Guattari's thinking on becoming and unfolding).[54] Bergson pointed out that while time had become the quintessential form of measurement in the industrialized world, the notion of time was a construct to ascertain the relationship between cause and effect, between discrete moments of being that form into a linear pattern of progression that emerges only in a retrospective account and not during the always-past moment of being.

Although Shaw would come to Bergson only later, a useful comparison here indicates evidence of wider spheres of cultural knowledge into which Shaw

---

[51] Bernard Shaw, 'The Religion of the Future', in *The Religious Speeches of Bernard Shaw*, ed. Warren Sylvester Smith (University Park, PA: Penn State University Press, 1963), p. 35.
[52] Shaw, 'New Theology', p. 17.
[53] Henri Bergson, *Creative Evolution*, trans. Arthur Mitchell (1907; repr. New York: Henry Holt, 1911), p. 98.
[54] See Daniel Colucciello Barber, *Deleuze and the Naming of God: Post-Secularism and the Future of Immanence* (Edinburgh: Edinburgh University Press, 2015); Tamsin Lorraine, *Deleuze and Guattari's Immanence Ethics* (Albany: State University of New York Press, 2011).

and Bergson separately tapped. In spite of being remembered as one of the most iconoclastically modernist philosophers, Bergson, like Shaw, was deeply invested in the richness of mystical belief. Bergson's doctoral thesis, *Time and Free Will*, draws its notion of 'duration' from fourteenth-century apophatic theology and the mystical devotional works of the anonymous *The Cloud of Unknowing*, among others.[55] And as he argues in *Creative Evolution*, his later, fuller development of this theme:

> The line of evolution that ends in man is not the only one. On other paths, divergent from it, other forms of consciousness have been developed, which have not been able to free themselves from external constraints or to regain control over themselves, as the human intellect has done, but which, none the less, also express something that is immanent and essential in the evolutionary movement.[56]

Shaw's notion of the superman and creative evolution were not his own, but, as Warren Sylvester Smith argues, 'the patches supplied by Shaw make the doctrine of creative evolution and the search for social and economic justice into a unified garment. It is the synthesis that is original.'[57] Shaw's mysticism and belief in what he referred to as the 'Life Force' was predicated on rational self-interest but a form of self-interest whose ultimate aim was the advancement of society. It was deeply pragmatic and practical in its emphasis on the inherent divinity of the individual and runs unmistakably through his dramatic writing. Shaw's notion of the life force permeates all of his work:

> You have many names for it, but at any rate here is a particular thing that is working this miracle of life, that has produced this evolution and is going on producing it, and it is by looking back over the long evolution and seeing that in spite of all vagaries and errant wanderings one way or another that still the line as it goes up and up seems to be always driving at more power and more knowledge, you begin to get a sort of idea.[58]

While Shaw's typical reaction to the question of faith was the repudiation of organized religion, his work equally expresses an unmistakably well-focused mystical motivation which sought to wrest the power of religious experience

---

[55] Allan Johnson, *Masculine Identity in Modernist Literature: Castration, Narration, and a Sense of the Beginning, 1919–1945* (London: Palgrave Macmillan, 2017), pp. 51–3.
[56] Bergson, *Creative Evolution*, p. xii.
[57] Warren Sylvester Smith, *Bishop of Everywhere: Bernard Shaw and the Life Force* (London: Pennsylvania State University Press, 1982), p. 35.
[58] Bernard Shaw, 'Modern Religion II' (1919), in *The Religious Speeches of Bernard Shaw*, ed. Warren Sylvester Smith (University Park, PA: Penn State University Press, 1963), p. 77.

from the church and return it to the *genius*, or tutelary spirit, of the individual. An individual's capacity to produce original, unalloyed content – the 'messages of God' that so confound those surrounding the Maid of Orléans – remains a key topic of concern throughout his body of work.[59] The imagination has been a topic of significant interest to philosophers since late antiquity, and the history of Western thinking can be traced through the shifting understanding of the divine or mundane sources of imagination, and, furthermore, what the imagination may tell us about the relationship between humanity and the divine. Aristotle and Plato were both unconvinced that the imagination was a form of heavenly intervention but were unable to put forward a more convincing theory for its existence; however, several centuries later the Neo-Platonists were more willing to accept the ineffable godhead as the source of innovative thought. The fourteenth-century mystics and monastic mendicants invested in apophatic theology believed that the immateriality of god meant that the imagination was the only way to approach the divine, while Romantic philosophers broadly understood imagination as the conduit between the senses and the self.[60] Closer to our own time, Freud would famously and influentially define the imagination as a storehouse of latent images. In *The Future of an Illusion* (1927), Freud argued that mystical experience is merely an infantile throwback, and it would be this staunch repudiation of the spirit in favour of sexual instinct which would contribute to Jung's break from Freud. Both agreed that a rich symbolic framework lay behind all expressions of human civilization and subjectivity, but Freud saw this as the earliest stages of development that needs to be necessarily transcended while Jung saw it as a valuable fount of knowledge that had sustained humanity and could continue to do so into the future. For Freud, the unconscious that was awakened in dreams was the derelict storehouse of urges and desires that had been repressed, initially, through the socialization of primary narcissism from birth to early childhood, and later through the compulsive repetition of subsumed desires; for Jung this material exists already in a collective unconscious, and if it were to be repressed by an individual it would rear its head elsewhere in society.

Shaw innovated in form as well as theme. In building his drama on equivocation rather than action, he did away with the conventional format of

---

[59] Bernard Shaw, *Saint Joan* (1923; repr. London: Penguin, 2003), p. 68.
[60] See, in particular, John Cocking, *Imagination: A Study in the History of Ideas* (Abingdon: Routledge, 1991); James Engell, *The Creative Imagination: Enlightenment to Romanticism* (New York: Harvard University Press, 1981); Paul Gavrilyuk and Sarah Coakley (eds), *The Spiritual Senses: Perceiving God in Western Christianity* (Cambridge: Cambridge University Press, 2011).

the 'well-made play' favoured by his contemporaries, and Christopher Innes argues that 'the artistic ethos [Shaw] promoted was antithetical to that of the European *avant-garde* [and] it is largely due to Shaw that British drama in the twentieth century is distinct from the European tradition, rather than being the effect of cultural, or even linguistic differences'.[61] More specifically, it was Shaw's matter-of-factness that showed the inerrable effects of society on the individual (and how society, in turn, must respond to such influences) alongside a potent Gnosticism that viewed the deified individual as able to improve, if not their own lives, then the lives of subsequent generations. Shaw writes in the preface to *Plays Pleasant* that in the year leading up to the writing of *Arms and the Man* and *Candida* 'religion was alive again, coming back upon men, even upon clergymen, with such power that not the Church of England itself could keep it out'.[62] But this return was not a reoccurrence as much as it was a renewal of something rather quite different. The material of most interest in *Arms and the Man* – that is, the congruent hypocrisies of love, class and war which, as the play contends, have never been fully or convincingly untangled – reverberates across all of the *Plays Pleasant*. Both *Arms and the Man* and *Candida* deal, at their core, with ways of knowing and understanding various forms of romantic and erotic attachment. In both, a naïve young person has been misled by the forces of society to view marriage as a personal aim rather than a mechanism for the collective advancement of society. And both end with an ironic auction at which men offer up what they see as their most valuable possessions in order to seek the favour of a woman: in *Arms and the Man* Bluntschli is able to admit, following the death of his hotelier father, to owning nearly countless houses, horses and carriages, and in *Candida* it is a betting of masculine morals which Marchbanks and Morell undertake, ultimately being pitifully undercut by the ruthlessly feminine Candida. *Candida* is, as Michael Holroyd wryly points out, an ironic response to Ibsen's *A Doll's House* which 'reveals the doll in the house to be the man'.[63]

By the time Shaw had moved to Ayot St Lawrence in 1906 (where he would become again a regular churchgoer at the parish church), he had evolved his own faith system centred around the life force. Although Shaw would be the

---

[61] Christopher Innes, *Modern British Drama: 1890–1990* (Cambridge: Cambridge University Press, 1992), p. 2.
[62] Shaw, *Plays Pleasant*, p. 8.
[63] Michael Holroyd, 'George Bernard Shaw: Women and the Body Politic', *Critical Inquiry*, 6.1 (1979), 17–32 (p. 18).

first to admit that 'I do not profess to be a Christian',[64] he also recognized that 'if anything is to be done to get our civilization out of the horrible mess in which it now is, it must be done by men who have got a religion'.[65] In a 1911 lecture on 'The Religion of the Future', Shaw proclaimed that 'I am, and always have been a mystic. I believe that the universe is being driven by a force that we might call the life-force'.[66] Leon Hugo describes Shaw as a 'practical mystic',[67] and Robert Whitman points out that

> Shaw considered himself a mystic, but only so far as mysticism would be consistent with thorough-going realism. He dreamed of the superman, but experience told him that if salvation was to be in this world and not in the next, it would have to be for everyone, not just the few, and that human progress toward that salvation came in infinitesimal increments.[68]

Echoing these views, Sally Peters's more recent biography portrays Shaw as inspired by a 'self-appointed mission as prophet and deliverer of mankind'.[69] However, what Shaw meant by his assertion that 'I am, and always have been a mystic' is best understood in the context of the renewed interest in mystical experience in the years surrounding the turn of the twentieth century.

In *The Varieties of Religious Experience* (1902), William James defined four key characteristics of the mystical experience: 'ineffability', in the sense that the experience remains ultimately indescribable; 'noetic', in the sense that the experience brings with it some real sense of new knowledge; 'transiency', in that the experience necessarily and unceremoniously passes; and 'passivity', in that the mystic is a figure acted upon rather than an active contributor. Any insight derived from mystical experience, James contended, 'resembles the knowledge given to us in sensations more than that given by conceptual thought'.[70] Mystics 'have been "there," and know', he concludes enigmatically, and James's taxonomy of mystical experience would eventually influence both the language and sentiment of Ralph W. Hood's influential 1975 Mysticism Scale.[71] Evelyn

---

[64] Bernard Shaw, 'Christianity and Equality', in *The Religious Speeches of Bernard Shaw*, ed. Warren Sylvester Smith (University Park, PA: Penn State University Press, 1963), p. 54.
[65] Bernard Shaw, 'Modern Religion I', in *The Religious Speeches of Bernard Shaw*, ed. Warren Sylvester Smith (University Park, PA: Penn State University Press, 1963), p. 38.
[66] Shaw, 'Religion of the Future', p. 33.
[67] Leon Hugo, *Bernard Shaw: Playwright and Preacher* (London: Methuen, 1971), p. 53.
[68] Robert Whitman, *Shaw and the Play of Ideas* (London: Cornell University Press, 1977), p. 48.
[69] Peters, *Ascent*, p. 3.
[70] William James, *The Varieties of Religious Experience* (1902; repr. London: Penguin, 1982), p. 405.
[71] James, p. 423. See also Ralph W. Hood, 'The Construction and Preliminary Validation of a Measure of Reported Mystical Experience', *Journal for the Scientific Study of Religion*, 14.1 (1975), 29–41.

Underhill's *Mysticism* (1911) furthered James's view that religious embodiment is the goal of organized religion, but one often inefficiently or incompletely met:

> Possessed like other men of powers of feeling, thought, and will, it is essential that his love and his determination, even more than his thought, should be set upon Transcendent Reality. He must feel a strong emotional attraction toward the supersensual object of his quest: that love which scholastic philosophy defined as the force or power which causes every creative to follow out the trend of its own nature.[72]

Underhill is concerned not merely with mysticism as a form of experiential knowledge but as an experience curiously consonant with the contemporaneous philosophical work of Bergson, Nietzsche and Eucken whose 'focal point is not Being but Becoming'.[73] The mystic, she explained, is 'a type which refuses to be satisfied with that which other men call experience, and is inclined, in the words of its enemies, to "deny the world in order that it may find reality"'.[74] Within the context of the then widely read work of James and Underhill, Shaw's identification as a mystic indicates his sense that inspiration came from beyond himself, creating a form of embodied knowledge, understanding and insight in the form of 'genius', Shaw's more frequently used term for immanence and mystical gnosis. It is this term which he uses in the preface to *Saint Joan* to describe the experiential knowledge gained through mystical experience:

> A genius is a person who, seeing farther and probing deeper than other people, has a different set of ethical valuations from theirs, and has energy enough to give effect to this extra vision and its valuations in whatever manner best suits his or her specific talents.[75]

In an attempt to encourage Farr to acknowledge her own prodigious gifts of originality, Shaw explained into a letter to her on 28 January 1892 that 'there are two sorts of genius in this world':

> One is produced by the breed throwing forward to the godlike man, exactly as it sometimes throws backward to the apelike. The other is the mere monster produced by an accidental excess of some faculty – musical, muscular, sexual even.[76]

---

[72] Evelyn Underhill, *Mysticism* (London: Methuen, 1911), p. 49.
[73] Underhill, p. 28.
[74] Underhill, p. 3.
[75] Shaw, *Saint Joan*, p. 7.
[76] Bax, p. 7.

As he explained later in 'The Religion of the Future', 'the man of genius finds it difficult to make people understand him. I know this, for I am by profession a man of genius.'[77] This comment was met by laughter and applause from those gathered at the Victoria Assembly Rooms, Cambridge, and it was the anxiety-inducing effect of genius, or embodied wisdom, which Shaw would portray through characters including Eugene Marchbanks, John Tanner and the newly canonized Saint Joan.

In *Man and Superman* Shaw's own sense of the possible outcomes for Tanner, Tavy, Ann and, more broadly, the society which they metonymically represent is necessarily rooted in his sense of the faulty lenses through which the idle middle classes perceive their vision of reality. Tanner's first extended speech is on the topic of shame, and through the course of the play he philosophizes on topics including education, labour, domestic service, class, hypocrisy, ageing and the artist. However, his central message throughout *Man and Superman* remains unwaveringly that of the relation between men and women in its connection to orthogenesis and sexual selection. 'They accuse us of treating them as mere means to our pleasure', he explains to Tavy early in the play, 'but how can so feeble and transient a folly as a man's selfish pleasure enslave a woman as the whole purpose of Nature embodied in a woman can enslave a man?'[78] To Tanner, women enable men not merely in their mundane lives but in their social call to action, stimulating men's generative instincts through the display of women's constitutional superiority:

> TANNER: The true artist will let his wife starve, his children go barefoot, his mother drudge for his living at seventy, sooner than work at anything but his art. To woman he is half vivisector, half vampire. He gets into intimate relations with them to study them, to strop the mask of convention from them, to surprise their inmost secrets, knowing that they have the power to rouse his deepest creative energies, to rescue him from his cold reason to make him see visions and dream dreams, to inspire him as he calls it.[79]

In Shaw's explication of creative evolution in *Man and Superman*, 'women are not treated as objects of men's desire but as imperfect contrivances employed by the Life Force in its trail-and-error experiments for improving the future'.[80] While donning his fantasia disguise as Don Juan, Tanner states:

---

[77] Shaw, 'Religion of the Future', p. 31.
[78] Shaw, *Man and Superman*, p. 61.
[79] Shaw, *Man and Superman*, p. 61.
[80] Holroyd, 'George Bernard Shaw', 17–32 (p. 18).

> To Life, the force behind the Man, intellect is a necessity, because without it he blunders into death. Just as Life, after ages of struggle, evolved that wonderful bodily organ the eye, so that the living organism could see where it was going and what was coming to help or threaten it, and thus avoid a thousand dangers that formerly slew it, so it is evolving today a mind's eye that shall see, not the physical world, but the purpose of Life, and thereby enable the individual to work for that purpose instead of thwarting and baffling it by setting up shortsighted personal aims as at present.[81]

The information withheld from Tanner is that Ann is chasing him rather than Tavy, and it is typical of Shaw's ironical mode that Tanner's mordant analysis of the world emerges only midway through Act One, while Ann still appears to the audience as a meek and retiring figure still most ideally suited to Tavy. As Tanner explains:

> You think that you are Ann's suitor; that you are the pursuer and she the pursued; that it is your part to woo, to persuade, to prevail, to overcome. Fool: it is you who are the pursued, the marked down quarry, the destined prey. You need not sit looking longingly at the bait through the wires of the trap: the door is open, and will remain so until it shuts behind you forever.[82]

Through its trenchant account of sexual selection and the convoluted courtship of Tanner and Ann, *Man and Superman* depicts the circumstances required for Shavian progress rather than a fulfilled superman in action. The ultimate message of the play is perhaps most clearly expressed by Tanner: 'The only man who behaved sensibly was my tailor: he took my measure anew every time he saw me, whilst all the rest went on with their old measurements and expected them to fit me.'[83] In spite of his vitality, potency and high ideals, Tanner remains always a comic shadow of the true *Übermensch*, emblematic of the potential of humanity rather than indicative of its highest achievements.

While *Man and Superman* details Shaw's own recapitulation of the pursuit of love of an ideologue fixated on the potential affordances of orthogenesis, his later *Saint Joan* represents his mature struggle to comprehend the implications of his own 'genius', the tutelary spirit of gnosis. E. M. Butler includes Joan of Arc in her historical account of the figure of the magus, stretching back to Moses and Zoroaster and forward to Helena Blavatsky and Rasputin. Butler accepts Margaret Murray's argument in *The Witch-Cult in Western Europe*

---

[81] Shaw, *Man and Superman*, p. 151.
[82] Shaw, *Man and Superman*, p. 91.
[83] Shaw, *Man and Superman*, p. 75.

(1921) that witches are a continuation of an underground, semi-organized religion stretching from distant antiquity of which Joan of Arc was presumably aligned: 'Joan of Arc, as mysterious today as she was during her short and tragic life, was perhaps the heroic prototype of all those unfortunates called witches among whom she was finally classed, and who in their hundreds and thousands suffered torture and death for their god and their faith.'[84] Shaw's play questions issues of legitimacy in the triad of power of medieval Europe – the state, the church and the people – and its titular character, as Shaw describes in the preface, is 'the queerest fish among the eccentric worthies of the Middle Ages [and] was in fact one of the first Protestant martyrs'.[85] When Shaw describes the Maid of Orléans as a 'Protestant' he is not provoking debate on Irish Nationalism but suggesting that Joan's own unmediated sense of truth, devotion and honour – itself a form of protest against the politically and ethically deflated figureheads of the play – removes the interceding role of the church. Shaw would argue in 1919 that 'a genuine Protestant knows no Church and knows no priest. Practically, he believes in the direct communion between himself and the spirit that rules the universe.'[86] (Ironically gesturing towards Shaw's anachronistic use of the term 'Protestant', the Chaplain states at the end of Scene 4 that 'I do not understand what your lordships mean by Protestant and Nationalist: you are too learned and subtle for a poor clerk like myself'.[87])

Shaw was probably in sympathy with the Archbishop who warns the Maid that 'there is no harm in [being in love with religion]. But there is danger' and he almost certainly sensed a curious correlation of faith and belief between the 1920s and 1420s in so much as, as the Archbishop remarks, 'there is a new spirit rising in men: we are at the dawning of a wider epoch'.[88] It is also the Archbishop who defines miracles in a way that patently captures Shaw's own treatment of the theme in the preface:

> THE ARCHBISHOP: A miracle, my friend, is an event which creates faith. That is the purpose and nature of miracles. They may seem very wonderful to the people who witness them, and very simple to those who perform them. That does not matter: if they confirm or create faith they are true miracles.
>
> LA TRÉMOUILLE: Even when they are frauds, do you mean?

---

[84] E. M. Butler, *The Myth of the Magus* (Cambridge: Cambridge University Press, 1948), p. 117.
[85] Shaw, *Saint Joan*, p. 3.
[86] Shaw, 'Modern Religion II', p. 63.
[87] Shaw, *Saint Joan*, p. 108.
[88] Shaw, *Saint Joan*, pp. 80, 82.

THE ARCHBISHOP: Frauds deceive. An event which creates faith does not deceive: therefore it is not a fraud, but a miracle.[89]

Shaw is keen to allow for the viability of Joan's miracles if, of course, one accepts that the ultimate yield of a miracle is theurgic faith rather than physical conjuration. 'If [an historian] is Rationalist enough to deny that saints exist', Shaw writes in the play's preface, 'and to hold that new ideas cannot come otherwise than by conscious ratiocination, he will never catch Joan's likeness'.[90] Pushing strongly against Weber's notion of modernity as a period of great societal disenchantment, Shaw is particularly interested in accentuating the symbolic value of spiritual revelation precisely because it is 'modern science [that] is making short work of the hallucination without regard to the vital importance of the things they symbolize'.[91] Throughout both the preface and the playtext itself, this mystical power is inspected though the channel of visionary capacity, which, as Shaw suggests in the preface, comes to 'exceptionally imaginative persons, especially those practicing certain appropriate austerities':[92]

> [Saint Joan] saw imaginary saints just as some other people see imaginary diagrams and landscapes with numbers dotted about them, and are thereby able to perform feats of memory and arithmetic impossible to non-visualizers. Visualizers will understand this at once. Non-visualizers who have never read Galton will be puzzled and incredulous.[93]

Shaw's turn to Galton is curious, and this influence remains an underappreciated component of the creation of *Saint Joan*. Involved in disciplines as varied as statistics, anthropology and geography, Galton produced an expansive body of work which presented a new approach to the notion of the Romantic genius through its attempt to contextualize the performance of genius along positivistic lines. But this body of knowledge led to more harmful conclusions: it was Galton who coined the term 'eugenics'. For Galton, the capacity for visualization was a tangible marker of genius, and as he argues in *Inquires into Human Faculty and Its Development* (1883), the development of visualization is a key factor in the development of societies: 'There are some who visualise well, and who also are seers of visions, who declare that the vision is not a vivid visualisation, but

---

[89] Shaw, *Saint Joan*, p. 79.
[90] Shaw, *Saint Joan*, p. 8.
[91] Shaw, *Saint Joan*, p. 15.
[92] Shaw, *Saint Joan*, p. 15.
[93] Shaw, *Saint Joan*, p. 18.

altogether a different phenomenon.'⁹⁴ Anxieties surrounding the deceleration of cultural advancement were widespread in the final two decades of the nineteenth century in works such as Edwin Ray Lankester's *Degeneration: A Chapter in Darwinism* (1880), Eugene S. Talbot's *Degeneracy: Its Causes, Signs, and Results* (1898) and, most famously, Max Nordau's *Degeneration* (1892). Nordau codified a view held by other staunch social conservatives of the time that the breaking down of traditional values – particularly those surrounding issues of gender and the body – was contributing to the cumulative weakening of society. If the concept of degeneration saw society moving increasingly towards a downward spiral, the concept of creative evolution saw society moving in an upward direction. 'No less than Nordau', Sally Peters argues, 'Shaw presented totalizing categories: degenerate or artists, crucifer or crucified, reactionary or pioneer. By definition, the superman was the ultimate outsider.'⁹⁵

By Scene 4, Joan is recognized as a sorceress by Warwick and those around him, a perception buttressed by Cauchon's recognition that 'she acts as if she herself were The Church. She brings the message of God to Charles; and The Church must stand aside.'⁹⁶ In Shaw's portrayal, it is Joan's refusal to accept the instructions of the Church above her own experiential mysticism which is the cause of concern. Shaw's ultimate approval of Joan comes in the recognition that she 'must be judged a sane woman in spite of her voices because they never gave her any advice that might not have come to her from her mother wit'.⁹⁷ 'That the voices and visions were illusory, and their wisdom all Joan's own, is shewn by the occasions on which they failed her, notably during her trial, when they assured her that she would be rescued.'⁹⁸ Joan is celebrated by Shaw's play not because of her decisiveness or military action but because she is a 'superwoman' with the genius that society requires. And Shaw's play is concerned not with the theorization of genius of gnostic revelation but an exploration of its pragmatic immediacy, showing Joan to be the superwoman whom the world has most unfairly misunderstood. Cauchon asks, 'Must then a Christ perish in torment in every age to save those that have no imagination?'⁹⁹ Joan's final lines are a resonant indication of the play's thematic programme: 'O God that madest this

---

⁹⁴ Francis Galton, *Inquires into Human Faculty and Its Development* (1883; repr. London: J. M. Dent & Sons, 1919), p. 118.
⁹⁵ Peters, *Ascent*, p. 194.
⁹⁶ Shaw, *Saint Joan*, p. 103.
⁹⁷ Shaw, *Saint Joan*, p. 12.
⁹⁸ Shaw, *Saint Joan*, p. 17.
⁹⁹ Shaw, *Saint Joan*, p. 159.

beautiful earth, when will it be ready to receive Thy saints? How long, O Lord, how long?'[100]

Did Shaw feel a personal affinity towards this character whose innate genius – her ability to receive wisdom from a source seemingly outside of herself – was misunderstood and feared by her orthodox surroundings? It seems almost certain that he did. Shaw's dramatic writing and religious speeches show a cosmopolitan heterodoxy spirituality and a clear intellectual engagement with the modernist resurgence of spiritual practice. From his early collaborative relationships with the prominent occultists Florence Farr and Annie Besant to his late masterpiece in which the visionary brilliance of a gifted young woman becomes the source of canonization, Shaw remained deeply connected to a wide array of occult and esoteric influences that swirled through modern London. But, as always, Shaw remained an inscrutable iconoclast who would not simply replace the orthodoxy of Christian belief with blind faith in faddish movements. Instead, Shaw's dramatic writing and religious speeches capture a complex understanding of the ever-shifting relationship between humanity and the divine and an unerring faith in the ability of the individual to find their own gnostic genius.

By the time that Joan of Arc was canonized in 1920, the world really was in need of new heroes. While the century had begun with fanciful literary reckonings of homunculi and mechanical children, there was a sense among other writers that, with the scars of war not even yet beginning to heal, a very significant and serious breed of super-evolved heroes was needed to create providential change in the physical world. Like Shaw, Dion Fortune understood that the orthogenesis can be achieved only through the careful mating of men and women, what Fortune referred to in occult terms as a 'circuit of force' of sexuality. Fortune remains one of the most influential occultists of the twentieth century, in no small part due to her egalitarian approach to spiritual training and a belief in opening up the hermetic secrets both through her fiction and through the widely popular correspondence course run by her Fraternity of the Inner Light. Her fiction played an equally significant role in this public curriculum. In her four major occult novels (the first three published in the late 1930s, and the final published posthumously in 1956), she details the search for new meaning and a superman role for both men and women. Each of these texts centres on an emasculated man who has been cast aside by the forces of modernity but discovers curative redemption through an electrically charged entanglement with a woman whose inborn magical sensibilities enable him to

---

[100] Shaw, *Saint Joan*, p. 164.

connect with a vast, nationally bounded history of enchantment. In *The Winged Bull* (1935), 33-year-old Ted Murchison is still struggling to return to civilian life after his experiences as a junior officer in the First World War when he meets the flamboyant magician Colonel Brangwyn, whose half-sister Ursula inducts him into an ardent circuit of force; in *The Goat-Foot God* (1936), following the motoring death of his unfaithful wife, Hugo Paston joins with the intuitive bohemian designer Mona Wilton to conjure the mystical retentions of a former abbey before happily marrying in the end; in *Moon Magic* (posthumous, 1956), the dejected and disaffected medical doctor Rupert Malcolm is visited by a primeval priestess whose magical tutelage enables him to move beyond the unbearable despondency caused by his ailing wife and failing marriage.

Of her four major occult novels, Fortune's *The Sea Priestess* (1938) offers the most resounding and influential treatment of the healing of society through its portrayal of the fantastical arrival of the ancient priestess Miss Le Fay Morgan and her transformation of a local estate agent into what Fortune perceived as the ideal of masculine decisiveness and empathy. Fortune's occult cosmology as reflected through her fiction, Andrew Radford notes, 'intersects with, and is complicit in the refinement of, eugenic tropes and discriminatory notions of heredity and ethnicity'.[101] In each of these cases, the numinous forces that emerge between the two main characters offer not merely a way out for the fallen man but become suggestive of a wider possible potential for the cultivation of similarly super-evolved overmen and overwomen who could bring about the necessary rebuilding of society. Susan Johnston Graf writes:

> Dion Fortune believed that her occult work would promote human evolution and the eventual betterment of humankind. She thought that she and fellow occultists were the vanguard that would usher in the Aquarian Age, which she defined as a more enlightened stage of human spiritual evolution than the current Piscean Age, now in its eclipse. A magical world view – belief in an objective supernatural reality – would be the norm. Humans would develop latent spiritual powers. As Fortune envisioned it, the Aquarian Age would be dominated by neither a patriarchy nor a matriarchy. The Goddess would re-emerge, assuming equal power with the God; Isis would be just as valid as Jehovah.[102]

---

[101] Andrew Radford, 'Anxieties of Mystical Influence: Dion Fortune's *The Winged Bull* and Aleister Crowley', in *The Occult Imagination in Britain, 1875–1947*, ed. Christine Ferguson and Andrew Radford (Abingdon: Routledge, 2018), pp. 165–180 (p. 167).

[102] Susan Johnston Graf, 'The Occult Novels of Dion Fortune', *Journal of Gender Studies*, 16.1 (2007), 47–56 (p. 50).

The salvational aim of Fortune's work is unmistakable, and Fortune's fiction demands that society change pace and recognize the potential that lies within. Speaking of Fortune as a modernist seems initially unexpected: her work appears on to the surface to be invested in late Victorian decadence while simultaneously resisting the modernists' stylistic innovations of elision, fragmentation and stream of consciousness. As Miriam Wallraven points out, Fortune's customary exclusion from literary modernism stems not merely from such recognition of formal and thematic difference but from the 'double marginalisation' experienced by women who write occult literature.[103] Yet Fortune's treatment of psychological interiority as expressed through ritual enactment and put to the service of a wider thematic interest in the possibilities of a renewed superman to ease the social traumas of war situates her work distinctly in the modernist landscape, and her fiction is more categorically modernist than often imagined.

Henpecked by his sister, committed against his will to the monotonous drudgery of life as a rural estate agent and hampered by myopia and debilitating asthma, the first-person narrator of *The Sea Priestess* opens the text at some unspecified, unseen point in the future when he is looking back to his powerfully transformative relationship with Le Fay Morgan, or, as he later simply calls her, Morgan Le Fay. 'The keeping of a diary is usually reckoned a vice in one's contemporaries, though a virtue in one's ancestors', Wilfred begins:

> These old journals, volume upon volume of them, lie in a tin trunk in the attic. I have dipped into them occasionally, but they are dreading reading; all the pleasure lay in the writing of them. They are an objective chronicle of things seen through the eyes of a provincial business man. ... I record it for what it is worth. I am the last person to be able to assess its value. It appears to me to be a curious chapter in the history of the mind, and as such, to be of interest as data if not as literature. If I learn as much from the reliving of it as I learnt from the living of it, I shall be well repaid.[104]

The retrospective turn that opens this novel is a crucial to the thematic underpinning of the work, and the multicursal piecing together of diary fragments offers an obvious allusion to Bram Stoker's *Dracula* (1897), which is similarly built as a narrative of evidential fragments, edited and compiled by Mina Harker as the only means by which to defeat the ancient menace. It is also perhaps not incidental that Wilfred is, like Jonathan Harker, involved in the sale

---

[103] Miriam Wallraven, *Women Writers and the Occult in Literature and Culture: Female Lucifers, Priestesses, and Witches* (Abingdon: Routledge, 2015), p. 21.
[104] Dion Fortune, *The Sea Priestess* (1938; repr. York Beach, ME: Red Wheel/Weiser, 2003), pp. 1–2.

of property to a mysterious outsider. Wilfred's severe recurrent asthma attacks offer an early indication of the text's later fetishization of human sacrifice in a watery grave, and patently gives presence to the claustrophobia that Wilfred faces in his current life before a mythical call to action thrusts him into a magical encounter. And it is during one of these early attacks, when medicated with morphine, that he gains his first supersensible approach to the world of Miss Morgan. 'I gradually learnt the knack of day-dreaming', he explains, 'and although I could not obtain the same reality as I got when I was doped, I got quite a bit, and every now and again a day-dream would carry over into a night-dream and I got something really worth while'.[105] As Wallraven notes, 'It is Wilfred's liminal experiences that stimulate his subconscious and initiate a development towards occult perceptions and techniques, and these are explains as "normal" psychological abilities, i.e. scientifically explainable processes of the human mind.'[106] In the world of Fortune's fiction, the door to the occult is open to all through mundane routes – the British Museum in *The Winged Bull*, a dusty bookshop in *The Goat-Foot God* and Wilfred's asthma drugs in *The Sea Priestess* – but, as her fiction demonstrates, rigour and discipline are needed on the part of the seeker once their journey has begun. As Fortune explained in an article for the January 1933 issue of *The Occult Review*:

> There is no legitimate reason that I have ever been able to see for keeping these things secret. ... The only reason of which I am aware, and one which I suspect of being a weight one with those who have so long sat resolutely upon the lid of occult secrecy, is that for purpose of priestcraft and prestige a secret system is a useful weapon. A weight reason, this, human nature being what it is, but not a justification in the eyes of those who have the welfare of humanity at heart.[107]

After dreaming of a ghostly ship helmed by an enchanted Atlantean priestess, Wilfred is startled to meet this priestess in the waking world. Le Fay Morgan explains that her unique name is partly because she is 'part Breton, part Welsh' and partly because of a codicil in a complex inheritance agreement, but it is not an entirely satisfactory explanation and seems largely a contrivance for giving her the name of an Arthurian witch (it is with similar shamelessness which Fortune christens the heroine of *The Winged Bull*, Ursula Brangwyn, after D. H. Lawrence's famous character).[108] For Wilfred, 'getting in touch with the Unseen

---

[105] Fortune, *The Sea Priestess*, p. 13.
[106] Wallraven, p. 97.
[107] Fortune, 'Ceremonial Magic Unveiled', pp. 82–93 (p. 84).
[108] Fortune, *The Sea Priestess*, p. 34.

is like taking to drink – once you get started you can't leave it alone', but when employed by Miss Morgan to secure a derelict fort for the creation of a temple, he worries that she might be 'a liar and a vamp and a general adventuress' even while remaining conscious of the prescience of his dream and of the curious effect that her presence has on him.[109] She flatters his artistic sensibility and awakens in him a new curiosity in living, instigating Fortune's central thematic figuration of a non-sexual, although unmistakably erotic 'circuit of force' between male and female polarity has the unmistakable effect of reviving masculine identity and healing the wound of the Fisher King that had settled upon British society during the interwar period.

Beginning seven months before the outbreak of the Second World War and continuing until August 1940, Fortune published a series of essays in *The Inner Light Magazine* which detailed her beliefs in how sexual energy could be channelled and, most crucially, transmuted for the production of a redemptive future. Fortune's articles in this direction, gathered by Gareth Knight as *The Circuit of Force*, represent both one of her most cogent and comprehensively established précises of spiritual development as well as one that was most urgently wrought: ritual, she explained, 'can provide dietary supplements that will enable the undernourished to keep alive, but it will not give the bounding energy of real health'.[110] If ceremonial magic had any value at all, she contends, then now is the time for it to be demonstrated, ideally in well-constituted magical lodges

> wherein each member of the ritual team works with true magical power, knowing the meaning of the symbols employed, and that the personal forces of each officiant have to act syphon-like for the bringing through of the corresponding cosmic forces. This being achieved with genuine power and understanding by those working the ritual, the onlookers can participate each according to his need if they have the necessary knowledge.[111]

To be thusly trained in the requisite symbolic knowledge, concentration and personal command requires an intimate connection to the ability to first supersensibly acknowledge and then manipulate subtle energies centred on key vortexes that overlap in both the Eastern chakra system and the Western Kabbalah tree of life glyph. These energies, when suitably developed, can lead to a form of magnetism: 'The subtle magnetism of a living creature is a very curious

---

[109] Fortune, *The Sea Priestess*, pp. 43, 89.
[110] Dion Fortune and Gareth Knight, *The Circuit of Force: Occult Dynamics of the Etheric Vehicle* (Loughborough: Thoth, 1998), p. 22.
[111] Fortune, *The Circuit of Force*, p. 22.

thing, and in human beings it is quite as much mental as physical.'[112] In *The Sea Priestess* when work begins in earnest on both restoring the derelict fort and on his magical training, Wilfred realizes that 'I was living in a kind of dream-world, and the only things that were real to me were Morgan Le Fay and the fort. But by way of compensation something else was becoming real to me – the curious kingdom of the moon and the sea.'[113] It is this 'curious kingdom' that contributes to Wilfred's growth and development:

> 'The next step', she said, staring into the fire and not looking at me, 'is to complete my own training'.
> 'That being – ?' said I.
> 'To make the magical image of myself as a sea-priestess.'
> I asked her if I were to do the carving, and if so, how? For I could no more do figures then I could fly.
> She shook her head. 'A magical image does not exist upon this plane at all', she said. 'It is another dimension, and we make it with the imagination. And for that', said she, 'I need help, for I cannot do it alone. If I could I would have done it long ago.'
> 'Are you counting on me for that?' said I.
> 'Yes', she said.[114]

Following the production of this magical image of Le Fay as the embodiment of all goddesses, Wilfred will soon come to realize 'why Troy was burnt for a woman. For this woman was not one woman, but all women; and I, who mated with her, was not one man, but all men, but these things were part of the lore of the priesthood, and it is not lawful to speak of them.'[115] Le Fay later confirms this recognition:

> Do you not know the Mystery saying that all the gods are one god, and all the goddesses are one goddess, and there is one initiator? Do you not know that at the dawn of manifestation the gods wove the web of creation between the poles of the pairs of opposites, active and passive, positive and negative, and that all things are these two things in different ways and upon different levels, even priests and priestesses, Wilfred?[116]

---

[112] Fortune, *The Circuit of Force*, p. 106.
[113] Fortune, *The Sea Priestess*, p. 89.
[114] Fortune, *The Sea Priestess*, p. 109.
[115] Fortune, *The Sea Priestess*, p. 116.
[116] Fortune, *The Sea Priestess*, p. 124.

Yet for all of her commentary on sex magic and the possibility of revitalizing humanity, Fortune remained unmistakably prudish in her accounts of sexuality and physical desire. As she explains in *The Problem of Purity* (1928),

> I suggest that we should deal with sex, not from the standpoint of its wickedness, nor of its commonplaceness, but of its sacred-ness. We should realise its tremendous potency on the mental as well as on the physical plane; we should regard it as the direct expression of the Divine Life through the channel of our organisms; it does not belong to us, to be used for our personal pleasure, for we are trustees for the race, and unborn generations are beneficiaries under this Divine Trust. This is the essence of sex life and the secret of right use of the sex force it is not ours, it belongs to the race. The fact that it gives us pleasure in its use is incidental to its real object, and is simply a provision of Nature to secure that object.[117]

Rather than portraying her call to abstinence as a restrictive and repressive injunction, she knowingly represents it as a flourishing and refinement in innate human motivations because 'those who have sublimated the life-forces into the service of the race will have little need to complain of a lonely life; love will flow to them from all sides and their companionship will be sought by all because they are radiating something that is as vitalising as sunlight'.[118] Like Samael Auer Weor, the mid-twentieth-century Colombian occultist whose teachings on practical Gnosticism have a small yet committed following today, Fortune advocates for the prevention of orgasm as a means by which to cultivate valuable spiritual energy that could be transmuted into more significant although less gratifying endeavours: wearing clothes that are too tight, being too warm in bed or having a full bladder can trigger sexual urges and must be avoided in order to maintain spiritual potency.[119] Averting the sexual act, she writes, will 'vitalise the whole personality in a most extraordinary way and give it that peculiar magnetic quality so rarely seen and so noticeable when present'.[120] Describing this in more directly occult terms in *The Circuit of Force*, she contends that

> this does not mean that every magical act must culminate in orgasm. Far from it. Orgasm is the earthing of the force; its expenditure like a flash of lightning. … A magical rite, properly worked, leaves the operates in the same harmonised state that follows coitus, and magic can be used as a most effectual and satisfying

---

[117] Dion Fortune (as Violet M. Firth), *The Problem of Purity* (New York: Samuel Weiser, 1985), p. 18.
[118] Fortune, *The Problem of Purity*, pp. 65–6.
[119] Fortune, *The Problem of Purity*, p. 41.
[120] Fortune, *The Problem of Purity*, p. 65.

form of sublimation, not because it deteriorates into orgy, but because it rises on the planes.[121]

Fortune's cosmology, which would inspire various traditions of Goddess worship and female-centred spirituality, including Wicca, during the 1970s and beyond, imagines a single creative force beyond approachability, which divides into the polar formation of goddess and god, with each goddess representing all goddesses and so on. As Alan Richardson points out, 'What the Wiccans got from Dion Fortune was a *tone*.'[122] The resolution to the novel comes when Wilfred is able to put his erotic circuity into force with a mortal woman and 'took Molly in my arms in a way I had never done before, and something suddenly flowed between us like warm light; it encircled us in a single aura so that our lives mingled and interchanged and stimulated each other and then flowed back to us, and I was reminded of the flow and interchange of force that had taken place in the rite I had worked with Morgan'.[123] In the same way that Shaw's *Man and Superman* offers up the ghostly outline of a possible but as-yet unachieved *Übermensch*, the magical thought experiments that the two conduct here is creating the image of the godly and goddessly archetypes.

---

[121] Fortune, *The Circuit of Force*, p. 162.
[122] Richardson, p. 24.
[123] Fortune, *The Sea Priestess*, p. 218.

5

The other East: The *Philosophia Perennis* and the modern pilgrim

In August 1902 the official publishing arm of the Theosophical Society drew censorious attention to the Buddhist initiation in Burma of a 29-year-old Englishman, one Allan Macgregor. Macgregor was ordained as a novice on 12 December 1901 and then received higher ordination on 21 May 1902, when, following a brief thirty-minute ceremony, he took the new name A'nanda Metteyya.[1] 'One can't help remarking', Henry Steel Olcott wrote in *The Theosophist*, 'that the priestly name – A'nanda Metteyya (Maitriya) – conferred upon the young Englishman, was rather pretentious, for Maitriya is the name of the Buddha who is to come at the end of the Yuga and lead mankind into the full knowledge of the Arya Dharma, and into the peace which will result'.[2] Although Olcott and Helena Blavatsky, co-founders in 1875 of the Theosophical Society, had been the first two American citizens to convert to Buddhism in Asia, the elevation of a Westerner to the priesthood – and, particularly, a Westerner who had clear intentions to introduce his Buddhist tradition to the world – was clearly a matter of a different order. 'Well, let the young man dream his dreams in peace', Olcott concluded of Macgregor's plans for bringing Buddhism to Europe, 'and let us all hope that when his day of disillusionment comes, as it has to all of us his predecessors, he may have the pluck and perseverance to stand alone and fight his fight and, if it need be, die at his post, courageous and undaunted'.[3]

Olcott had similarly hoped to bring Buddhism to the West, and while his *Buddhist Catechism* (1881) remains in use today, his dream of a global ecumenical council for Buddhists was never fully realized.[4] His dismissive account of

---

[1] Elizabeth J.Harris, *Theravada Buddhism and the British Encounter* (London: Routledge, 2006), p. 150.
[2] Henry Steel Olcott, 'The Ordination of Allan Macgregor', *The Theosophist*, 23.11 (1902), 683–8 (p. 687).
[3] Olcott, p. 688.
[4] Stephen Prothero, 'Henry Steel Olcott and "Protestant Buddhism"', *Journal of the American Academy of Religion*, 63.2 (1995), 281–330 (p. 285).

Allan Macgregor's initiation perhaps becomes better understandable once one recognizes that 'Macgregor' was a pseudonym. The man in question was in fact Allan Bennett, a leading member of the Hermetic Order of the Golden Dawn and one of Aleister Crowley's most influential mentors, an effort which Crowley repaid by portraying him as Mahatera Phang in his conspicuously uneven novel *Moonchild* (1917). Suffering from asthma which had plagued him since childhood, Bennett travelled to Asia in 1899 where he began to spuriously claim he had been adopted by a 'Mr McGregor'.[5] The prominent travel writer Paul Brunton knew Bennett and was led to believe that he had been adopted by Samuel Liddell MacGregor Mathers, one of the three founders of the Golden Dawn, but there is little evidence to support this and the name (given both as McGregor and Macgregor) was almost certainly an affectation.[6] Bennett had a varied and enthusiastic association with contemporary occult movements, joining the Brixton Lodge of the Theosophical Society in 1893 and then the Golden Dawn a year later in 1894. While during the early years of the Theosophical Society Olcott and Blavatsky had been occupied with taming American Spiritualism into a coherent system of mystical insight, their attention turned by 1878 to the sacred traditions of the East as the purported source of the *philosophia perennis*, the occult knowledge believed to connect all faith systems.[7] Their work confronted one of the most challenging tasks facing the fusion of Eastern and Western spirituality, namely the overlapping of an Eastern cyclical progression of humanity with a Western providential and linear progression of humanity. The Buddhism arriving in the West became increasingly esoteric in its practice and philosophy – a simulacra of the perennial philosophy envisaged through the lens of Western occultism – and since Bennett's brand Buddhism ran counter to the vision of the Theosophical Society, they sourly distanced themselves from him.[8]

Yet whether by the name Allan Bennett, Allan M(a)cGregor or A'nanda Metteyya, it is certain that he played a key role in the introduction of Buddhism to the West during the early years of the twentieth century. In 1903, shortly after his initiation in Burma, Bennett founded *Buddhism: An Illustrated Quarterly Review* and set out his plans for *Buddhasasana Samagama*, the International

---

[5] Elizabeth J. Harris, 'Ananda Metteyya: Controversial Networker, Passionate Critic', *Contemporary Buddhism: An Interdisciplinary Journal*, 14.1 (2013), 81.
[6] Paul Brunton, 'A Pioneer Western Buddhist', *Ceylon Daily News, Vesak Number* (1941), n.p.
[7] Stephen Prothero, 'From Spiritualism to Theosophy: "Uplifting" a Democratic Tradition', *Religion and American Culture: A Journal of Interpretation*, 3.2 (1993), 197–216 (pp. 198–9).
[8] Thomas A. Tweed, 'Toward a Translocative History of Occult Buddhism: Flows and Confluences, 1881–1912', *History of Religions*, 54.4 (2015), 423–33; Harris, 'Ananda Metteyya', 77–92 (p. 80).

Buddhist Society, which aimed to bring the authentic spiritual teachings of the Buddha to Western devotees.[9] Brunton, who would later become a noteworthy commentator on Eastern spiritual traditions in his own right, assisted Bennett on the publication of *Buddhism* but sensed himself playing a somewhat complex role in the publication because he could 'never bring [himself] either then or now to wear a doctrinal label',[10] a knowing position to take at a time when Buddhism was still viewed through Western eyes as 'nihilistic, exotically romantic or esoteric'.[11] For others, though, Buddhism presented a model of spiritual thought and practice that, although not inherently scientific, offered a seemingly more tangible and testable advance towards the divine. Blavatsky's baggy and boisterous *Isis Unveiled* (1877) emerged shortly before other, more historically sound Orientalists began drawing attention to the spiritual record of Asia.[12] Edwin Arnold's 1879 *The Light of Asia* was widely influential, as was *Sacred Books of the East*, a fifty-volume edition of English translations edited by Max Müller for Oxford University Press between 1879 and 1910. As Alex Owen points out, Blavatsky's Theosophy 'emerged at a time when discussion of the world's major religions and exposure to Eastern sacred texts were part of educated Victorian cultural life'.[13] It was a period in which a new a 'global Buddhism' became divorced from any particular regional expression and began to take on a new facet as a product of the growth of transnational collaboration and travel.[14]

While earlier chapters in this book concerned themselves with the modernist intention to draw down the divine in order to ennoble an enervated interwar Europe, this final chapter turns attention to the modernists working outside the customary geographical remit of literary modernism, those pilgrims and explorers who, like Bennett, sought to distil the *philosophia perennis* of India and Tibet in textual form. Alexandra David-Neel's *Magic and Mystery in Tibet* (1932) and Paul Brunton's *A Search in Secret India* (1934) represent the fruits of audacious pilgrimages to the spiritual heart of Tibet and India. Indeed, this final chapter examines the most radical form of immanence of all: traditions

---

[9] Harris, *Theravada Buddhism*, p. 150.
[10] Brunton, 'A Pioneer Western Buddhist', n.p.
[11] Harris, 'Ananda Metteyya', p. 79.
[12] On syncretism in the Theosophical Society, see, in particular, Siv Ellen Kraft, '"To Mix or Not to Mix": Syncretism/Anti-Syncretism in the History of Theosophy', *Numen*, 49.2 (2002), 142–77.
[13] Alex Owen, *The Place of Enchantment: British Occultism and the Culture of the Modern* (London: University of Chicago Press, 2004), p. 30.
[14] Alicia Turner, Laurence Cox and Brian Bocking, 'A Buddhist Crossroads: Pioneer European Buddhists and Globalizing Asian Networks 1860–1960', *Contemporary Buddhism: An Interdisciplinary Journal*, 14.1 (2013), 1–16 (p. 2).

which centre on moving away from the world of division and seek recognition of divine union. Both David-Neel and Brunton came of age in the post-Blavatsky Theosophical Society (the latter joined the Theosophical Society under his given name of Raphael Hurst in 1920 and two years later co-founded the famous occult bookshop Atlantis in London) and would both travel to the Society's international headquarters in Adyar, India, during their extensive journeys. James Hilton's *Lost Horizon* (1933) and Somerset Maugham's *The Razor's Edge* (1944) – both now better remembered than David-Neel's and Brunton's travelogues – offer fictional reflections of the possibility that the sacred traditions of India and Tibet could heal the incurable wounds of the First World War. While Maugham's text is inspired by his own momentous meeting with the guru Bhagavan Sri Ramana Maharshi at Arunachala in 1936, Hilton's entirely fictional text invents the Tibetan lamasery of Shangri-La, a sort of doomsday vault of European art and culture.

In each of these texts, the spiritual traditions of India and Tibet invest the individual with gnostic wisdom which, providentially and problematically, can never be perfectly rendered in the linear constructions of narrative language. David-Neel, Brunton and Maugham all experienced moments of staggering spiritual transcendence during their travels in India and Tibet that they would attempt to transfigure into prose as a means by which to both substantiate their ineffable experiences and to root their own sense of subjectivity in a newly enhanced vision of the divine. Zygmunt Bauman understands that

> identity as such is a modern invention. To say that modernity led to the 'disembedding' of identity, or that it rendered the identity 'unencumbered', is to assert a pleonasm, since at no time did identity 'become' a problem; it was a 'problem' from its birth – was *born as a problem* (that is, as something one needs to do something about – as a task), could exist only as a problem; it was a problem, and thus ready to be born, precisely because of that experience of under-determination and free-floatingness which came to be articulated *ex post facto* as 'disembeddedment'.[15]

The pilgrim is, Bauman continues, 'the most fitting metaphor for a modern life strategy preoccupied with the daunting task of identity-building'.[16] For Bauman, modern models of subjectivity led to a renewed interest in the narrative of the pilgrimage, a trope which, it must be said, appears with unerring regularity in

---

[15] Zygmunt Bauman, 'From Pilgrim to Tourist – or a Short History of Identity', in *Questions of Cultural Identity*, ed. Stuart Hall and Paul du Gay (London: Sage, 1996), pp. 18–36 (pp. 18–19).
[16] Bauman, p. 26.

modernist literature: Forster's Leonard Bast goes on a night walk in an attempt to find meaning but recognizes his own failure when he can extract much less from his experience than the self-assured and expressive Schlegel sisters; Leopold Bloom's day-long pilgrimage through his home city is more outwardly eventful than J. Alfred Prufrock's, but both roam the spaces around them as pilgrims rather than flâneurs; Clarissa Dalloway's halting pilgrimage of middle-class domesticity is mutated by its end into a transcendent opening that invites her into the realms of what Bauman would describe as that of 'inner-worldly pilgrims'.[17] Elsewhere in modernist literature, similar 'inner-worldly pilgrims' in search of a salve to the vulgarity and disunion of modern life make pilgrimages to sites such as Lhasa, Arunachala and the fictional Shangri-La, and it is these particular journeys which this chapter scrutinizes.

Although the phrase 'Western esotericism' has gained currency in academic circles due to the pioneering efforts of historians Antoine Faivre, Nicholas Goodrick-Clarke and Wouter Hanegraaff, the fact remains that much of what constitutes 'Western' esotericism has always necessarily implied and drawn its substance from a connection with the spiritual traditions of Asia and the Middle East.[18] But the lines of influence flow in both directions. What the work of David-Neel, Brunton and Maugham ultimately details is a potentially problematic sense of spiritual identity wrested free from national confines, the notion that a *philosophia perennis* exists which transcends the constructedness of national, cultural and even religious identity. Published in the immediate aftermath of the Second World War, Aldous Huxley's *The Perennial Philosophy* (1945) brought to a wider audience the notion of a singular body of divine wisdom connecting all spiritual traditions, an idea that had been circulating in small circles since at least the time of Marsilio Ficino and had gained traction with the Theosophical Society and through the work of later Traditionalists such as René Guénon and Frithjof Schuon. Huxley's book stands midway between the intrepid writers of the 1920s and 1930s such as David-Neel and Brunton who had experienced Eastern spiritual practices first-hand and the spiritual New Age of the 1960s and 1970s in which the East became increasingly accessible and commodified through Transcendental Meditation, yoga, bhakti and the I Ching, devotional practices

---

[17] Bauman, p. 21.
[18] Kennet Granholm, 'Locating the West: Problematizing the Western in Western Esotericism and Occultism', in *Occultism in a Global Perspective*, ed. Henrik Bogdan and Gordan Djurdjevic (London: Routledge, 2013), pp. 17–36; Aren Roukema and Allan Kilner-Johnson, 'Time to Drop the "Western"', *Correspondences*, 6.2 (2018), 109–15.

which could be freely combined in heterodox and deeply individualistic ways.[19] In this view, the three major monotheistic traditions of the Near Middle East were latter-days facsimiles of a truer or more authentic spiritual expression which found its home in South Asia. Leon Surette deliberately aligns his definition of occultism with Aldous Huxley's *The Perennial Philosophy* (1945): 'Both Perennial Philosophy and the occult claim for themselves whatever enlightenment is thought to be contained in Gnosticism, Neoplatonism, Hermeticism, or any other mystical, illuminated, pneumatic, or visionary tradition whatsoever.'[20] Drawing a similar conclusion through different means, René Guénon held that the project of modernity commenced when humanity has entered its fourth and most degenerate state of development, the point at which the *philosophia perennis* has been irrevocably lost. Trained by Gérard Encausse (Encausse was a Golden Dawn initiate, founder of the Martinist Order, occult advisor to Tsar Nicholas II and prolific occult writer under the penname Papus), Guénon argues in *The Crisis of the Modern World*:

> It will doubtless be asked if cyclic development must proceed in this manner, in a downward direction, from higher to lower, a course that will at once be perceived to be a complete antithesis to the idea of progress as the moderns understand it. The reason is that the development of any manifestation necessarily implies a gradually increasing distance from the principle from which it proceeds; starting from the highest point, it tends necessarily downward, and, as with heavy bodies, the speed of its motion increases continuously until finally it reaches a point at which it is stopped.[21]

Refusing an Enlightenment faith in the persistent onward progression of civilization, Guénon felt that the history of culture is one of constant decline, punctuated by the occasional return of an authentic spiritual voice. This 'progressive materialization', Guénon argues, has been mistakenly read as progress and teleological redemption is an unfulfilling and unfulfilled invention of the modern world.[22]

Jung played a key role in returning attention to the spiritual traditions of Asia, a process which had been ignited by Helena Blavatsky's vast body of writing

---

[19] See, in particular, Wouter J. Hanegraaff, *New Age Religion and Western Culture: Esotericism in the Mirror of Secular Thought* (Albany: State University of New York Press, 1998).
[20] Leon Surette, *The Birth of Modernism: Ezra Pound, T. S. Eliot, W. B. Yeats, and the Occult* (Montreal: McGill-Queen's University Press, 1993), p. 11.
[21] René Guénon, *The Crisis of the Modern World*, trans. Marco Pallis, Arthur Osborne Richard C. Nicholson (1942; repr. Hillsdale, NY: Sophia Perennis, 2004), p. 7.
[22] Guénon, p. 8.

and the system of belief that grew around it. Jung supported, particularly in his commentary on *The Secret of the Golden Flower* and introduction to the *I Ching*, an openness to the spiritual traditions of Asia, a gesture that had somewhat fallen into abeyance since the Theosophical Society, with many Western occult leaders such as Rudolf Steiner and Dion Fortune explicitly rejecting this transnational legacy. As David McMahan notices, 'Although all historical religious traditions in their encounters with modernity have had to reinterpret doctrines in light of the dominance and symbolic capital of scientific thinking', the cultural and ideological exchange of the past two hundred years has led to uniquely hybridized forms of Buddhism which integrate the scientific logic of the West 'or, in a stronger version of the claim, was scientific in some sense from the beginning'.[23] Cultural exchange predicated on a willing absorption of foreign traditions is in itself a modern expression: Arjun Appadurai perceptively explains that 'the two main forces for sustained cultural interaction before this century have been warfare (and the large-scale political systems sometimes generated by it) and religions of conversion'.[24]

Undoubtedly the most significant and enduringly influential commentator on the fraught exchanges of cultural expression is Edward Said. Said's heavily interrogated thesis is that the Oriental Other was constructed by the Occident as a shadow version of itself, forming an imprecise copy which was then reflected back on to the Occident as a means by which to define itself. As he writes, 'The Orient was Orientalized not only because it was discovered to be "Oriental" in all those ways considered common-place by an average nineteenth-century European, but also because it *could be* – that is, submitted to being – *made* Oriental.'[25] Scholars questioning this thesis tend not to take issue with its essential premise but, rather, highlight the fact that Said's view of history bears little resemblance to the historical record of European engagements with the East. In his sharp critique of Said, Robert Irwin indicates that Said had constrained and modified the historical record in order to suit his polemical aims:

> Although at times Said finds it convenient to ... present Orientalism as a discursive formation that cannot be escaped, at other times he wants to blame Orientalists for embracing the evil discourse, or even for actively engaging in fabricating that discourse. They are both victims and villains. ... Said, having

---

[23] David L. McMahan, 'Modernity and the Early Discourse of Scientific Buddhism', *Journal of the American Academy of Religion*, 72.4 (2004), 897–933 (p. 898).

[24] Arjun Appadurai, *Modernity at Large: Cultural Dimensions of Globalization* (London: University of Minnesota Press, 1996), p. 27.

[25] Edward W. Said, *Orientalism* (New York: Vintage, 1979), p. 6.

read Foucault and Gramsci, was unable to decide whether the discourse of Orientalism constrains Orientalists and makes them the victims of an archive from which they are powerless to escape, or whether, on the other hand, the Orientalists are the willing and conscious collaborators in the fabrication of a hegemonic discourse which they employ to subjugate others.[26]

In its most basic form, Said's argument provides a valuable demonstration of subject/object differentiation and how the core and periphery of a social construct can both inform and deny the other. But, as scholars have pointed out, this is a faulty construct multiple times over, and one which only partially engages the historical developments of East-West exchange. In his well-known *New York Review of Books* review, Bernard Lewis highlights the 'very arbitrary decisions' of time and geography that Said relied upon to make his case: 'By eliminating Turkish and Persian studies on the one hand and Semitic studies on the other, he isolates Arabic studies from both their historical and philological contexts.'[27] Lewis's concern is that the quality of scholarship has been reduced for a purely polemical purpose: 'The reader's anxiety is not allayed by the frequent occurrence of stronger synonyms such as "appropriate," "accumulate," "wrench," "ransack," and even "rape" to describe the growth of knowledge in the West about the East.'[28] As both Irwin and Lewis unambiguously indicate, Said avoids the Orientalists and Sinologists who had committed themselves to the possibility of a richer and more authentic understanding of cultural exchange. In *Unexpected Affinities* (2007), Zhang Longxi refers to the 'incommensurability argument', the belief that the art and culture of East and West can only be appreciated by the aesthetic ideals which produced it:

> Such an emphasis on cultural difference not only provides a seemingly attractive symmetry of thinking (not to mention the attractiveness of hierarchy), but also gives comfort in a sort of mental economy that makes it so easy to assert the self vis-a-vis the other and saves one the trouble of careful investigations of individual cases and meticulous inquiries into the equivalence, convergence, or overlapping of ideas, images, themes, and expressions.[29]

As Longxi reminds, 'The incommensurability argument is itself common to both East and West; therefore the commonality of that argument becomes its own

---

[26] Robert Irwin, *For Lust of Knowing: The Orientalists and Their Enemies* (London: Penguin, 2007), pp. 289–90.
[27] Bernard Lewis, 'The Question of Orientalism', *New York Review of Books*, 24 June 1982.
[28] Lewis, 'The Question of Orientalism'.
[29] Zhang Longxi, *Unexpected Affinities: Reading across Culture* (London: University of Toronto Press, 2007), p. x.

refutation',[30] and, as critics of Said such as Irwin and Lewis have demonstrated, the insinuations and inferences of cultural exchange can never be rooted in either individual point of exchange.

These interfaces between Eastern and Western conceptions of unmediated knowledge of the sacred play out in Hermann Hesse's *Siddhartha*, where the refined and haunting portrayal of youthful movement away from the material and towards the immortal stands in as a cypher for the interwar trauma and malaise faced by Western Europe. The son of a Brahmin, Siddhartha recognizes that the religious practices afforded to him and his class leave an 'insatiable thirst' for divine insight and, although materially rooted within his own comfortable world, they do not offer a true approach to the self or to the divine.[31] Siddhartha begins on a lifelong expedition to remember his purpose and to wrest free his unconscious from the material world surrounding him. Although Hesse's best remembered novel was translated to English only in 1951 and would come to prominence in England and America during the 1960s, the text's fifth century BCE setting offers a commanding reminder that the retreat of the unconscious into the tempting and tangible world of the material is not a modernist development but a steady state of being that has driven humanity for thousands of years. Siddhartha's metaphysical rebellion can thus become the rebellion of all readers. After living the life of an ascetic for three years, Siddhartha encounters the historical Buddha who, in the world of the narrative, has recently become a spiritual teacher of note. The middle path taught by the Buddha reminds Siddhartha that the harsh privations of the ascetics relentlessly return focus to the body, creating merely 'a flight from the Self [and] a temporary escape from the torment of Self'.[32] But the challenge he finds in the Buddha's teachings is that the wisdom 'was not teachable, that it was inexpressible and incommunicable', and part of a shared spiritual understanding that already existed with him.[33] It was ultimately through the process of living, striving, suffering and giving that he recognized the immeasurable value of 'a moderate life, pleasure in thinking, hours of meditation'.[34] His ultimate realization that begins his final stage of development is that 'no teacher could have brought him salvation' and that the progress of his life was dependent, in succession, on his time as a Brahmin, an ascetic, a playboy and, finally, a simple ferryman.[35]

---

[30] Longxi, p. 7.
[31] Hermann Hesse, *Siddhartha*, trans. Hilda Rosner (New York: New Directions, 1951), p. 5.
[32] Hesse, *Siddhartha*, p. 13.
[33] Hesse, *Siddhartha*, p. 39.
[34] Hesse, *Siddhartha*, p. 61.
[35] Hesse, *Siddhartha*, p. 81.

In a similar vein is Hesse's *In Search of the East* (1932; trans. 1956), which allegorizes the 'East' not as a physical location but as a constant direction of progress for a group of Rosicrucian-like initiates known as the League. Within the world of Hesse's narrative, the East provides an object of unobtainable glory and a possible remedy for the wounded mind of a returned First World War soldier set alongside accounts of the search for spiritual apotheosis. During 'the troubled, confused, yet so fruitful period following the Great War' when 'the beliefs of the conquered nations were in an extraordinary state of unreality', Hesse's narrator, H. H., joins the League in order to undertake a journey for diverse spiritual riches.[36] The diffuse nature of the League is one of its most curious features and an indication that Hesse's novel is primarily an allegory of psychic disarray. His fellow journeymen include Zoroaster, Lao Tse, Plato, Pythagoras, Albertus Magnus, Don Quixote, Tristram Shandy, Paul Klee, Wagner's Parsifal, Goldmund (from Hesse's *Narcissus and Goldmund* (1930; trans. 1932)) and Vasudeva (from Hesse's *Siddharatha*). One seeks the Tao, another seeks Kundalini, but the mystical aim of H. H. is to gain the love of Princess Fatima, a spiritualized love which seems to gesture towards the Islamic figure of Fatimah. Like Joyce's young Stephen Dedalus, H. H. collapses his erotic and romantic desires into a deeply spiritualized vision of the divine feminine. But the ideal form of Fatimah is only an allegory because, as he recognizes during his journey, 'the East was not only a country and something geographical, but it was the home and youth of the soul, it was everywhere and nowhere, it was the union of all times'.[37] Not permitted to use 'mechanical contrivances such as railways, watches and the like' (railways and watches representing in the text the human taming of distance and sidereal duration), the League journey randomly through time and space. 'Numerous groups were simultaneously on the move, each following their own leaders and their own stars, each one always ready to merge into a greater unit and belong to it for a time, but equally prepared to move on again separately.'[38] Thus freed not only from the limits of time and space (as suggested to be created by the modern technologies of trains and watches), the League is also free from doctrine apart from their commitment to fully engage with spiritual practice along their journeys – they represent the great perennial tradition. But he worries that 'instead of a fabric, I hold in my hands a bundle of a thousand knotted threads which would occupy hundreds of hands for years

---

[36] Hermann Hesse, *The Journey to the East*, trans. Hilda Rosner (London: Peter Owen, 2001), pp. 5, 7.
[37] Hesse, *The Journey to the East*, p. 24.
[38] Hesse, *The Journey to the East*, p. 20.

to disentangle and straighten out, even if every thread did not become terribly brittle and break between the fingers as soon as it is handled and gently teased out'.[39] When H. H. meets his childhood friend Lukas, a fellow First World War veteran, they discuss the difficulties that Lukas had transforming his experience of war into literary form:

> When I sat at my writing-desk, on a chair, by a table, the razed villages and woods, the earth tremors caused by heavy bombardment, the conglomeration of filth and greatness, of fear and heroism, of mangled stomachs and heads, of fear of death and grim humour, were all immeasurably remote, only a dream, were not related to anything and could not really be conceived.[40]

H. H. is ultimately held to account by the League not simply for his attempt to write the hidden secrets of their fraternity but his inability to do so and, therefore, his incomplete understanding of his own value and purpose, leaving him as merely 'the survivor and chronicler of a concluded and forgotten tale'.[41]

James Hilton's *Lost Horizon* (1933) is a somewhat more problematic example of modern portrayals of the East for the ease with which it traffics in Orientalist tropes, here in the form of a curiously Anglicized Tibetan lamasery which holds on to the aesthetic inheritance of Western Europe. One of the most popular and widely read interwar treatments of spiritual exploration in Asia (in this case, entirely fictional), *Lost Horizon* has been dismissed as irrepressibly middlebrow since its release, while contemporary critics are inclined to view it as a somewhat problematic return to the scene of the late imperial romance.[42] The text appeared a year after David-Neel's pivotal account of her journey to Lhasa in *Magic and Mystery in Tibet* and, owing to a number of identical details (monks wrapping themselves in wet sheets and then drying them with their bodies as a sign of spiritual perfection seems a detail that Hilton would not likely have come by himself), it seems clear that David-Neel's work provided much of the anthropological content that would inspire Hilton's fantasia. The novel recounts the arrival at the fictional Tibetan lamasery at Shangri-La of Hugh Conway, an aging golden boy whose charm and erudition were rocked by his experiences in the First World War. Like Maugham's *The Razor's Edge* (another narrative of a First World War soldier who travels to the East to find redemption), the

---

[39] Hesse, *The Journey to the East*, p. 38.
[40] Hesse, *The Journey to the East*, p. 45.
[41] Hesse, *The Journey to the East*, p. 78.
[42] On the popular and critical reception of the text, see Jeff Mather, 'Captivating Readers: Middlebrow Aesthetics and James Hilton's *Lost Horizon*', *CEA Critic*, 79.2 (2017), 231–43.

story is explicated through a multiplicity of disorientating narrative frames: it is a physical text read by an unnamed narrator, which was written by Rutherford, to whom it was described by Conway. The story thus comes at multiple levels of removal which not merely draws into question the veracity of the report but also underscores the other-worldly breathlessness and inscrutability of the environs of Shangri-La.

'We want to return to civilisation as soon as possible', pleads HM Vice Counsel Mallison early in *Lost Horizon*. 'And are you so very certain that you are away from it?' is their host's reply.[43] At a time when the possibility of a complete devastation of Western culture was acutely felt, this remote lamasery provided the perfect solution in the form of a fallout shelter to protect the treasures of Western civilization. The lamas are seemingly more interested in Mozart, Chopin and the Brontës than anything related to esoteric Buddhist practices: in their vast library, 'Plato in Greek touched Omar in English; Nietzsche partnered Newton; Thomas More was there, and also Hannah More, Thomas Moore, George Moore, and even Old Moore'.[44] Here enlightenment comes through study of art, literature and music, intellectual endeavours which the vastness of time afforded by immorality encourages. The lamasery benefits from both enormous stores of gold and local flora that enables extremely long life, and, in order to protect their gold, great care has been taken to secure the community from the outside world. Although there are the trappings of a Tibetan lamasery, there is negligible consideration of any spiritual beliefs – Conway is merely informed that this training will begin after their fifth year in Shangri-La, five years being considered enough time for new denizens to adjust to the endless future. The central guiding principle of the community is simply gentle moderation of all things, including a moderation of moderation itself. Whether or not these lamas are practicing anything in the manner of Buddhist ritual seems immaterial to Hilton, in that the possibility of a lost country where powers of clairvoyance and immortality have been developed through curious spiritual means is what is ultimately required for his text. The great turn of the novel, one which Conway glimpses seconds before the reader, is that the High Lama is an eighteenth-century Christian priest named Father Perrault who first arrived in the verdant mountain pass hundreds of years earlier.

The devastations of war had been foretold by Father Perrault early in his life: 'He foresaw a time when men, exultant in the technique of homicide, would

---

[43] James Hilton, *Lost Horizon* (1933; repr. Chichester: Summersdale, 2005), p. 58.
[44] Hilton, p. 107.

rage so hotly over the world that every precious thing would be in danger, every book and picture and harmony, every treasure garnered through two millennia, the small, the delicate, the defenceless – all would be lost like the lost books of Livy, or wrecked as the English wrecked the Summer Palace in Pekin.'⁴⁵ 'I don't know whether you classify the people who come here', Conway tells the High Lama, 'but if so, you can label me "1914–1918" '.⁴⁶ Only the mystical mountains of Tibet, the narrative suggests, can provide protection from the devastating events of 1914 to 1918. If, as Stephen Arata has influentially argued, the late Victorian anxieties of reverse colonization arose as a response to a growing sense of declining British influence,⁴⁷which was wasthe modern world', all of which appear unmistkably er than merely decentred culture. id-Neel'd harmony, every trea then Hilton's deployment of the imperial gothic allows for a mannered gesture towards the fearsome possibility of a future in which Western culture may be utterly destroyed rather than merely decentred.

Not all accounts of journeys to the East were entirely fictional, although there are some that certainly test the boundaries of plausibility. Both A. P. Sinnett's *Incidents in the Life of Madame Blavatsky* (1886) and William Kingsland's *The Real H. P. Blavatsky* (1928) recount the alluring but apocryphal story of a young aristocratic divorcée travelling independently through Europe before casting her sights on the more exotic locales of Mexico, India and Tibet. Kingsland suggests that 'it is more than likely that during this period Mme. Blavatsky was undergoing an occult training and initiation when out of her body, at night, as well as during her mysterious illness. There was a sort of tradition in the early days of the Theosophical Movement that she had spent seven years in Tibet with the Masters.'⁴⁸ In 1928, Kingsland was unwilling to accept Blavatsky's literal journey to Tibet as a certain fact but did recognize the indisputable significance of this 'sort of tradition' to the foundation and growth of the Theosophical Society. Throughout her writing, teaching and public appearances, Blavatsky drew her authority from her purported connection to the 'Ascended Masters' or 'Mahatmas' she had encountered on her journey to Tibet, perfected *Übermensch* who had passed from the body but maintained communication to the world as a means by which to support its future development.

---

⁴⁵ Hilton, p. 152.
⁴⁶ Hilton, p. 150.
⁴⁷ Stephen Arata, 'The Occidental Tourist: *Dracula* and the Anxiety of Reverse Colonization', *Victorian Studies*, 33.4 (1990), 621–45.
⁴⁸ William Kingsland, *The Real H. P. Blavatsky: A Study in Theosophy, and a Memoir of a Great Soul*, 2nd edn (London: Theosophical Publishing House, 1985), p. 50.

Blavatsky's Mahatmas were understood to be initiates of what was described as the 'Great White Lodge', an abstruse construction which fused the Rosicrucian example of a secret all-seeing fraternity with a notion of disincarnate yet animated sainthood far more redolent of Mahayana Buddhism than Western spiritual traditions. Additional influences in this heterodox mélange include the 'Unknown Superiors' of the eighteen-century Masonic Rite of Strict Observance (a tradition with which Blavatsky was acquainted) and Edward Bulwer-Lytton's occult novels *Zanoni* (1842) and *A Strange Story* (1862).[49] Several decades later, the theme would be reprised in the Secret Chiefs of the Hermetic Order of the Golden Dawn and G. I. Gurdjieff's Sarmoung Brotherhood. For a religious philosopher as cosmopolitan and well read as Blavatsky, Tibet would have been understood to have been the most likely site of a community of ascended spiritual masters, and, as late as 1937, an equally cosmopolitan Brunton could confidently report that 'the Hindus, like the Tibetans, firmly believe that the Himalayas are the secret abode of the gods, as well as of those spiritual supermen whom they call the Rishees, who today are supposed to dwell there in invisible etheric bodies'.[50] The wisdom that Blavatsky purported to have received from her Tibetan Masters is contained in her magnum opus *The Secret Doctrine* (1888). The content, she claims, is drawn from a text known as the *Book of Dzyan* written in the lost language of Senzar and given to her during her journey through Tibet. As she explains in the first volume, the secrets contained within 'are offered through an agency, incessantly discredited before the world by all those who hate unwelcome truths, or have some special hobby of their own to defend'.[51] Needless to say, no further evidence of the *Book of Dzyan* or the Senzar language has ever been discovered.[52]

The most confounding intervention of Blavatsky's Masters would come when, on 15 October 1880, they appeared to have entered into direct correspondence with A. P. Sinnett, committed theosophist and editor of *The Pioneer*, an English-language newspaper in India. The letters would continue to appear over the

---

[49] K. Paul Johnson, *The Masters Revealed: Madame Blavatsky and the Myth of the Great White Lodge* (Albany: State University of New York Press, 1994), p. 20; Nicholas Goodrick-Clarke, *Helena Blavatsky: Western Esoteric Masters* (Berkeley: North Atlantic Books, 2004), p. 6; John L. Crow, 'Taming the Astral Body: The Theosophical Society's Ongoing Problem of Emotion and Control', *Journal of the American Academy of Religion*, 80.3 (2012), 691–717 (p. 694).

[50] Paul Bruton, *A Hermit in the Himalayas: The Journal of a Lonely Exile* (1937; repr. Bombay: B. I. Publications, 1974), pp. 30–1

[51] H. P. Blavatsky, *The Secret Doctrine: The Synthesis of Science, Religion and Philosophy*, vol. 1 (London: Theosophical Publishing Company, 1888), p. xxxvii.

[52] On the production and reception of *The Secret Doctrine*, see, in particular, Mark Sedgwick, *Against the Modern World: Traditionalism and the Secret Intellectual History of the Twentieth Century* (Oxford: Oxford University Press, 2004), pp. 44–5.

course of the next three years, and Sinnett would distil them in *Esoteric Buddhism* (1883) in an effort to, as he explains at the outset, bring 'to my readers knowledge which I have obtained by favour rather than by effort'.[53] The Mahatma Letters were undoubtedly produced by Blavatsky, and in *The Key to Theosophy* (1889) she would curiously distance herself from Sinnett's interpretation of the letters, which, she contends, commences from a misunderstanding of the distinction between 'esoteric Buddhism' and 'esoteric budhism':

> The mistake has arisen from a misunderstanding of the real meaning of the title of Mr. Sinnett's excellent work, 'Esoteric Buddhism', which last word ought to have been spelt *with one, instead of two, d's*, as then *Budhism* would have meant what it was intended for, merely 'Wisdom*ism*' (Bodha, bodhi, 'intelligence', 'wisdom') instead of *Buddhism*, Gautama's religious philosophy. Theosophy, as already said, is the WISDOM-RELIGION.[54]

Rather differently, Sinnett, who wholly accepted the authenticity of the letters, described the purpose of *Esoteric Buddhism* as an

> inquiry as to the real inner meaning of the definite and specific religion called Buddhism. ... The cosmic conceptions, and the knowledge of Nature on which Buddhism not merely rests, but which constitute esoteric Buddhism, equally constitute esoteric Brahminism. And the esoteric doctrine is thus regarded by those of all creeds who are 'enlightened' (in the Buddhist sense) as the absolute truth concerning Nature, Man, the origin of the Universe, and the destines toward which its inhabitants are tending.[55]

Blavatsky's rebuff of *Esoteric Buddhism* came notably after she permanently left India following an investigation by the Society for Psychical Research in 1885 in which a representative was sent to scrutinize the creation and delivery of the miraculous Mahatma Letters. The report prepared by Richard Hodgson, then well-recognized as the exposer of several high-profile fraudulent mediums and psychics, concluded that Blavatsky was nothing more than a skilled charlatan. The Mahatma Letters were later transcribed by A. T. Baker for the publishing house T. Fisher Unwin in 1923, and the titles *The Mahatma Letters to A. P. Sinnett* and *The Letters of H. P. Blavatsky to A. P. Sinnett* have been used in various later editions, indicating divergent views on their potentially miraculous or mundane source.

---

[53] A. P. Sinnett, *Esoteric Buddhism* (London: Truber, 1883), p. 1.
[54] H. P. Blavatsky, *The Key to Theosophy* (1889; repr. Los Angeles: Theosophy Company, 1987), pp. 12–13.
[55] Sinnett, pp. vii–viii.

While there is little doubt that Blavatsky's journey to Tibet and meetings with these remarkable Mahatmas should be read as allegorical at best and blatantly fraudulent at worse, K. Paul Johnson offers a compelling proposition that a large number of real-life teachers and mentors were formed in the creative imagination of Blavatsky into the ranks of Mahatmas: 'HPB's life provided continual encounters with spiritual teachers of various traditions and nationalities. Her pilgrimage took her from Masonic Masters to Sufi sheikhs, from Kabbalah to Vedanta, from Spiritualism to Buddhism in no particular order.'[56] For followers of Theosophy, the pages of Blavatsky's work could provide an enchanted glimpse into physical realms they would never see for themselves, capturing luminously the grand Victorian preoccupations of physical expansion and temporal contraction. There is perhaps some truth in this sense that Blavatsky did have ascended masters, if only in her own richly fertile mind. 'To call the occultist view of the Masters a myth is not to deny its value or validity', Johnson concludes, 'but rather to characterize its function for those who accept it.'[57]

In his 1988 study of the arrival of Buddhism in England, Philip Almond frankly acknowledges that 'I have not dealt with the Esoteric Buddhism of Madame Blavatsky and her English disciple, Alfred Sinnett. Esoteric it may have been. Buddhist it certainly was not.'[58] And, indeed, Blavatsky's brand of Eastern spirituality might have had more traces of Western influence than she imagined. When a devotee asked Ramana Maharshi why members of the Theosophical Society 'mediate in order to seek masters to guide them', Maharshi replied:

> The master is within; meditation is meant to remove the ignorant idea that he is only external. If he were some stranger whom you awaited, he would be bound oi disappear also. What would be the use of a transient being like that? But as long as you think you are separate or that you are the body, so long is the outer master also necessary and He will appear as if with a body. When the wrong identification of yourself with the body ceases, the master will be found to be none other than the Self.[59]

While it seems certain that Blavatsky's pilgrimage to Tibet was merely emblematical, Alexandra David-Neel's *Magic and Mystery in Tibet* (1932) tells a richly detailed account of her own real travels through Tibet between 1916

---

[56] Johnson, p. 8.
[57] Johnson, p. 8.
[58] Philip Almond, *The British Discovery of Buddhism* (Cambridge: Cambridge University Press, 1988), p. 147 n. 10.
[59] Ramana Maharshi, *The Teachings of Ramana Maharshi*, ed. Arthur Osborne (1962; repr. London: Rider, 2014), p. 95.

and 1924, culminating in her incognito entrance to the forbidden city of Lhasa, then closed off to foreigners. Through David-Neel's eyes, Tibet becomes 'a country of wizards and magicians … enclosed between formidable mountain ranges and immense deserts'.[60] Aware of her status as an outsider, she recognizes with measured awe that she is one of the 'very few strangers [who] have ever approached the monk-king hidden in his sacred city, in the Land of Snows'.[61] The constantly shifting verb tense of the text captures the dreamy high altitudes of her journey – it is not a rigidly narrative account by any means but an immersive explication of place and sensibility set apart from the logic of Western teleology. *Magic and Mystery in Tibet* weaves first-hand account of these 'wizards and magicians' with more spectacular stories reported to her into an extended meditation on the meaning of initiation and death and the possibilities of finding a connection to the root of spiritual wisdom. David-Neel ultimately disregards widespread conventions of travel writing as a means through which to convey an expressionist, initiatory account of the magic of Tibet.

David-Neel was trained as an opera singer in Brussels and worked for a time as a professional singer under the name of Alexandra Myrial. Shortly after her arrival in London in the late 1880s, she joined the Theosophical Society, where she would eventually lecture on Buddhism in the early years of the twentieth century. During her travels she walked the rough terrain of Tibet and northern India, often in the company of her adopted son Lama Yongden, and, according to some estimates, travelled over 30,000 kilometres on foot.[62] In *Alexandra David-Neel au Tibet* (1972), David-Neel's former librarian Jeanne Denys would vigorously refute the possibility that David-Neel actually entered Lhasa in 1924, an argument which Sara Mills reads alongside a persistent trend to read the travel narratives of women as inherently less authoritative than those of men which 'have greater pretensions to scientificity and adhere to the conventions of travel writing in general'.[63] It perhaps goes without saying that the esoteric Buddhism that David-Neel found in Tibet bore no resemblance to the material produced by Blavatsky in *The Secret Doctrine*, and although David-Neel would curiously admit that 'regarding my own experience, I am certain that I did receive on

---

[60] Alexandra David-Neel, *Magic and Mystery in Tibet* (1932; repr. London: Souvenir Press, 2007), pp. 233–4.
[61] David-Neel, *Magic and Mystery in Tibet*, p. 2.
[62] Barbara Foster and Michael Foster, *The Secret Lives of Alexandra David-Neel* (New York: Overlook Press, 1998).
[63] Sara Mills, *Discourses of Difference: An Analysis of Women's Travel Writing and Colonialism* (London: Routledge, 1991), p. 128.

several occasions telepathic messages from lamas under whom I had practised mental or psychic training', it is undoubted that hers is the authentic record.[64]

In her writing, David-Neel does not position Tibetan Buddhism as the *philosophia perennis* but centres attention instead on how this supposedly primeval expression of spiritual transcendence is the product of a long and slow-moving history of syncretization. 'In every Lamist monastery', she notes, 'there exists a temple or a room reserved as a dwelling-place for the ancient deities of the aborigines or those imported from India'.[65] As she explains in the later *The Secret Oral Teachings in Tibetan Buddhist Sects* (1967), 'This Buddhism of a Tibetan elite is genuinely of Buddhist inspiration and dates from the most brilliant period of Buddhist philosophy. Its teachings are considered to be traditional having been handed down from Master to disciple in an uninterrupted line.'[66] As she points out, there are legends in Tibet that this esoteric wisdom originated in the 'lands of the north', but considerable dispute among Tibetans as to whether this refers to northern India or territories further north of Tibet.[67] Historically speaking, it is certain that it was India which gave rise to these traditions, but David-Neel believes that the 'repugnant mysticism' that runs through Tibetan Buddhism finds its origin in the syncretic fusion of 'Tantric Hinduism and the doctrines of the ancient *Bonpo* shamanists'.[68]

In a particularly poignant moment in *Magic and Mystery in Tibet*, David-Neel recounts witnessing two monks who were intoning sacred syllables with the aim to separate the immoral spirit from a corpse:

> This extraction of the spirit is produced by the ritualistic cry of *Hik!* followed by *Phat!* Before uttering the cry, the lama must concentrate his thoughts and identify himself with the man who has just died. He must make the effort which the man himself ought to have made, to cause the spirit to ascend to the summit of the skull with sufficient force to produce the fissure through which it can escape.[69]

So vigorous was the procedure that one of the monks began to spit blood, which she observes with an equal measure of horror and fascination. David-Neel reports the belief that monks must be careful when practicing these sacred

---

[64] David-Neel, *Magic and Mystery in Tibet*, p. 190.
[65] David-Neel, *Magic and Mystery in Tibet*, p. 41.
[66] Alexandra David-Neel and Lama Yongden, *The Secret Oral Teachings in Tibetan Buddhist Sects* (San Francisco, CA: City Lights Books, 1967), p. 12.
[67] David-Neel and Yongden, *The Secret Oral Teachings*, p. 84.
[68] David-Neel, *Magic and Mystery in Tibet*, p. 106.
[69] David-Neel, *Magic and Mystery in Tibet*, p. 21.

syllables because of the possibility that they will cause their own death, but 'this danger does not exist when he is officiating [at a funeral], because he acts by proxy, in place of the dead – lending him his voice, so that the effect of the magic words is felt by the dead man, not the lama'.[70] It is this movement from life to death which most concerns David-Neel's full narrative and serves as one of its most consistent motifs. Later she meets a *ngagspa* ('wizard') who recounts performing a rite that involves biting off the tongue of a corpse and then drying it as a magical weapon; he even shows her the results. 'A true initiate in the Tibetan secret lore, however, would scoff at the sorcerer and his repugnant practices. The power of the magic weapon does not, he thinks, depend on the substance of which it is made but is communicated to it by the magician himself.'[71] Her treatment of magic and death builds towards a complex ritual to satiate Shinjed, the Lord of Death, and bring him 'under the control of the lama-magician and to extort from him a promise, on his oath, to give up the slaughter of human beings for 12 years'.[72] While some of the most widely recognized aspects of Eastern religion are the precepts reincarnation and metempsychosis, David-Neel points out that this is a misunderstanding by Western audiences: 'Buddhism teaches that the energy produced by the mental and physical activities of a being brings about the apparition of new mental and physical phenomena when once this being has been dissolved by death.'[73]

David-Neel would reveal more of the secrets gleaned from the lamas in her 1967 *The Secret Oral Teachings in Tibetan Buddhist Sects*, a text which philosopher Alan Watts described as his '"I-told-you-so-book," because it has often been implied that I have invented my explanations of Buddhism out of thin air, thus falsifying its authentic teaching'.[74] As Watts continues, the title is 'reminiscent of the fantasies of H. P. Blavatsky' but very much rooted in an anthropological understanding of the spiritual practices of Tibet.[75] *The Secret Oral Teachings* opens with an account of David-Neel conversing with a lama who warns her against revealing the secrets because the audience would not understand their meaning and import: 'If you speak to them of profound Truths they yawn', he explains, 'and, if they dare, they leave you, but if you tell them absurd fables they are all eyes and ears'.[76] Given the specificity with which David-Neel usually

[70] David-Neel, *Magic and Mystery in Tibet*, p. 11.
[71] David-Neel, *Magic and Mystery in Tibet*, p. 111.
[72] David-Neel, *Magic and Mystery in Tibet*, p. 166.
[73] David-Neel, *Magic and Mystery in Tibet*, p. 19.
[74] Alan Watts, 'Foreword', in *The Secret Oral Teachings in Tibetan Buddhist Sects* (San Francisco, CA: City Lights Books, 1967), p. i.
[75] Watts, p. i.
[76] David-Neel, *The Secret Oral Teachings*, p. 1.

speaks, it seems likely that this 'Master' is not a real person at all but more likely an amalgam of several teachers that she has encountered. The principle admonition that she receives from this figure is the struggle of communicating spiritual wisdom: 'It is not only the Master that the "secret" depends but on the hearer. A Master can only be he who opens the door: it is for the disciple to be capable of seeing what lies beyond.'[77] The Tibetans call this *lhang tong*, or what David-Neel translates as 'transcendent insight', the gnostic immanence for which so many explorers have ventured to Asia, either on a physical journey like David-Neel or the less critical yet still spiritual journey one might encounter when reading such a book from the comfort of their home.[78]

Dion Fortune admitted that David-Neel was a significant influence and one of her key sources on Eastern spiritual practices, a surprising reflection given that Fortune was one among several occult teachers of the time (including also her student W. E. Butler) to position herself in opposition to the Eastern traditions supported by the Theosophical Society.[79] At least partly a gesture to differentiate the Fraternity of the Inner Light from other occult orders, she reiterated to her followers in a 1939 article in *The Inner Light Magazine* that 'it is frequently said that yoga as taught in the East is impractical in the West because the Western conditions of life are utterly unsuited to it, and the western attitude utterly unsympathetic. I can only repeat this standard advice yet again.'[80] However, her articles collected in *Circuit of Force* present her Christian mysticism through the lens and language of Eastern spiritual practices, offering curious evidence of how the supposedly ancient traditions of Western esotericism become reinterpreted and recast with the aid of the Asian occult. The 'Tibetan Buddhist Sects' indicated by the title of David-Neel's 1967 book refers to the Madhyamika school of Mahayana Buddhism, founded by the Indian philosopher Nagarjuna around the first century CE before being transmitted to Tibet some seven centuries later, which had provided much of the inspiration for the earlier *Magic and Mystery in Tibet*.[81] As David-Neel explains, Madhyamika 'leans neither toward affirmation nor toward negation because these only exist relatively to each other, and so, in consequence, neither one nor the other has any independent reality of its own.'[82]

---

[77] David-Neel, *The Secret Oral Teachings*, p. 3.
[78] David-Neel, *The Secret Oral Teachings*, p. 7.
[79] Dion Fortune and Gareth Knight, *The Circuit of Force: Occult Dynamics of the Etheric Vehicle* (Loughborough: Thoth, 1998), p. 67.
[80] Fortune, *The Circuit of Force*, p. 13.
[81] Karl Brunnhölzl, *Center of the Sunlight Sky: Madhyamaka in the Kagyu Tradition* (Ithaca, NY: Snow Lion, 2004), pp. 47–51.
[82] David-Neel, *The Secret Oral Teachings*, p. 79.

In the words of her biographers Barbara Foster and Michael Foster, *The Secret Oral Teachings in Tibetan Buddhist Sects* is 'not arcane but a reflection of the long rational conversations she had with the Gomchen while the buttered tea simmered and the wind howled outside'.[83]

The explorer Paul Brunton travelled similar terrain during a journey he describes in *A Hermit in the Himalayas* (1937). As he explains, he undertook the expedition neither as an 'explorer nor as researcher, but simply to cease my external activities and to tranquillize my mind to the point of utter placidity'.[84] *A Hermit in the Himalayas* is deeply redolent of the placid transcendentalism of *Walden* (1854): 'I am to seek no outer adventures, nor even any inner ones', Brunton writes, 'I am to take Nature as my tutor, to merge my spirit into the absolute silence of her surroundings, and to let every thought lapse away into mere nothingness'.[85] Brunton's first major spiritual journey is recounted in his *A Search of Secret India* (1934), an travelogue of the mystical practices of India in the years shortly after David-Neel would reveal the hidden traditions of India's north-eastern neighbour. One of the most significant features of Brunton's text is its introduction of yoga, then a largely unknown quantity in Europe (as he explains to the mystified reader, it is 'pronounced *Yogh*. Its spelling is unphonetic').[86] Brunton dissolves into the page of his text, leaving the reader as the interlocutor with the sages he encounters and at first his narrative self is deeply and uncomfortably self-conscious. 'I am indeed glad that Europe is sufficiently far away for none of my friends to notice this odd sight and laugh at me!' he exclaims when given a garland of marigolds to wear around his neck.[87] *A Search for Secret India* is as much a physical and spiritual quest as it is a textual quest, and the narrating Brunton explicitly recognizes the seeming unfeasibility of translating the embodied transcendent wisdom he seeks into the language of the everyday. Indeed, his first struggle to channel the divine into language comes when he futilely attempts to give a name to that for which he is searching: finding a yogi in possession of true esoteric knowledge is unlikely because, as a local man explains to him, 'there are thousands of wandering beggars who pass by this name. They swarm through the villages and attend the periodic religious fares in droves. Many are only lazy tramps and other vicious ones, while most are totally illiterate men, unaware of the history and doctrines

---

[83] Foster and Foster, p. 129.
[84] Paul Brunton, *A Hermit in the Himalayas: The Journal of a Lonely Exile* (1937; repr. Bombay: B. I. Publications, 1974), p. 23.
[85] Brunton, *A Hermit in the Himalayas*, p. 23.
[86] Paul Brunton, *A Search in Secret India* (1934; repr. York Beach, ME: Samuel Weiser, 1997), p. 15.
[87] Brunton, *A Search in Secret India*, p. 87.

of the science of Yoga, under whose shelter they masquerade.'[88] Undeterred by the requisite retreat from language, Brunton undertakes a journey in which he meets beggars, conjurors and self-professed messiahs, none of whom hold the key to the *philosophia perennis*.

By the text's conclusion he does meet someone whom he perceives to be an unequalled and unquestionably genuine mystical teacher, Ramana Maharshi. As Brunton ardently reports, Maharshi 'avoids the dark and debatable waters of wizardry, in which so many promising voyages have ended in shipwreck. He simply puts forward a way of self-analysis, which can be practised irrespective of any ancient or modern theories and beliefs which one may hold, a way that will finally lead man to true self-understanding.'[89] His narrative focus on Maharshi is penetrating and pungent – nine pages are devoted to the story of the guru, which he collected 'bit by bit, from his own reluctant lips and from those of his disciples'[90] – but the great challenge that he reports as a writer is that, in the presence of 'one of the last of India's spiritual supermen', words no longer convey meaning.[91] The influence of Maharshi comes through 'this unobtrusive, silent and steady outpouring of healing vibrations into troubled souls, this mysterious telepathic process for which science will one day be required to account'.[92] Brunton finally gives up his desire to account and name, and 'the power to think, which has hitherto been a matter for merely ordinary pride, now becomes a thing from which to escape, for I perceive with startling clarity that I have been its unconscious captive'.[93] In the final pages of the text, Brunton recounts a transcendent moment of connection, meaning and insight:

> I find myself outside the rim of world consciousness. The planet which has so far harboured me, disappears. I am in the midst of an ocean of blazing light. The latter, I feel rather than think, is the primeval stuff out of which worlds are created, the first state of matter. It stretches away into untellable infinite space, incredibly *alive*.[94]

What follows this journey to 'the rim of world consciousness' is an extended manifesto of the fruits of his mystical experience, an apophatic expression of absolute unity and fullness in which he understands that 'man is grandly related

---

[88] Brunton, *A Search in Secret India*, p. 28.
[89] Brunton, *A Search in Secret India*, p. 302.
[90] Brunton, *A Search in Secret India*, p. 281.
[91] Brunton, *A Search in Secret India*, p. 301.
[92] Brunton, *A Search in Secret India*, p. 290.
[93] Brunton, *A Search in Secret India*, p. 304.
[94] Brunton, *A Search in Secret India*, p. 305.

and a greater Being suckled him than his mother'.[95] The irony is that this act of translation is one that is beyond words themselves, as the narrative as a whole captures Brunton's increasingly frustrated attempt to see beyond words and to experience for himself the stories that he has merely heard about.

Somerset Maugham was similarly gripped by his meeting with Maharshi in 1936, an experience he describes in 'The Saint', published in his 1958 collection of essays *Points of View*. The meeting with Maharshi acted firmly upon Maugham's mind and gave him the primary material for one of his most suggestive and successful works of fiction, *The Razor's Edge* (1944). Maugham allegorizes his meeting with Maharshi, giving the experience to the character Larry Darrell and writing himself into the text as a fictionalized observer who is committing to paper the spiritual shudders of an interwar America and Europe. 'I have taken the liberty that historians have taken from the time of Herodotus', the fictionalized Maugham explains to the reader at the beginning of the text, 'to put into the mouths of the persons of my narrative speeches that I did not myself hear and could not possibly have heard'.[96] Maugham takes great pains to maintain his fictionalized presence in the narrative, as the events recorded become more and more remote from the narrator's own gaze and less directly implicating the narrator in the action. Wayne C. Booth famously described the dramatized narrator as an actor playing a role through the action of narration: 'The most important unacknowledged narrators in modern fiction', Booth argues, 'are the third-person "centers of consciousness" through whom authors have filtered their narratives'.[97] Modernist literature is, to a great extent, an extended experiment with narrative centres of consciousness; the fictional veneer between the reader and text directs and supports all knowledge available to the reader. In Maugham's text, the historicizing narrator increasingly dissolves into the background, floating through the text merely as a narrative omniscience rather than a narrator proper. Although Maugham self-consciously places himself in the text as the passive observer, and suggests initially that the snobbish dandy Elliott Templeton will be the main focus of interest, his narrative control finally releases its grasp, leaving Larry as an ersatz narrator and Maugham's surrogate. In order to maintain this technique, Maugham manipulates both language and sequence. While his narrator only hears about Larry's work in the coal mine long after the events, he conveys the information at its proper point in the plot

---

[95] Brunton, *A Search in Secret India*, p. 305.
[96] W. Somerset Maugham, *The Razor's Edge* (1944; repr. London: Vintage, 2000), p. 2.
[97] Wayne C. Booth, *The Rhetoric of Fiction*, 2nd edn (1960; repr. Harmondsworth: Penguin, 1987), p. 153.

'because it is more convenient to place events as far as I can in chronological order'.[98] But it is not convenience as much as it is essential to detailing Larry's mystical learning and development. What Maugham's narrative form ultimately presents the reader with is the cognate process of spiritual discipleship portrayed in literal terms elsewhere in the text: as a reader one has access only through the mediating mind of someone closer to the point of origin.

Early reviewers were eager to know the source for Larry Darrell, suggesting most often that Larry was perhaps a fictionalized Christopher Isherwood (that Maugham himself could be the source of the spiritual awakening narrative seemed then implausible, especially since Maugham writes himself into the text as a pragmatic novelist who is more concerned with collecting character types than searching for secret India). The narrating Maugham insists in the perfunctory opening chapters that the character is not based on anyone with notoriety, and that is perhaps precisely part of the point. Although the fictional Larry came from a prosperous background, his parents died early in his life and he was raised by a guardian, and it is the precarity of this social position within the fabric of American late Gilded Age society that initially fascinates the narrator, who becomes even more confounded when he sees Larry reading William James's *Principles of Psychology* undisturbed for almost an entire day. Larry is the everyman of modern enlightenment – both in life (if we are to accept the truthfulness of the account) and in his deployment within the text – and the greatest interest within the text emerges from Maugham's remarkably subtle treatment of the social decay created by the First World War and how the promise of money and growth became the new religion of America in the years immediately after the war, to be undercut abruptly by the stock market crash. The figure of Larry is as much Maugham – viewing as a passive observer the greed, pride and snobbery around him through a clear plate of glass, providing no direct commentary or disdain – as it is any real person.

The narrative is punctuated by accounts of the mundane experiences of life, of courtship, marriage, children and death, but remains constantly pushed forward with the narrative of Larry's spiritual development and what the narrator comes to recognize by the narrative's final lines of 'the radiance of such a rare creature'.[99] The modern world is about appearance, but Larry's spiritual gifts are internal and invisible, meaning that, after his enlightenment, he simply blends back into to surface, not because of his failure to understand what he had received but

---

[98] Maugham, p. 103.
[99] Maugham, p. 340.

precisely because he did; he learns that the modern push of the individual to the surface – of their performances of identity and purpose – was eroding the inner life of true connection to divinity. From its outset, *The Razor's Edge* is concerned with the decisive implications of nation and national identity, ultimately setting Larry Darrell up as an emblem of spiritually enervated American culture:

> It is very difficult to know people and I don't think one can ever really know any but one's own countrymen. For men and women are not only themselves; they are also the region in which they were born, the city apartment or the farm in which they learnt to walk, the games they played as children, the old wives' tales they overheard, the food they ate, the schools they attended, the sports they followed, the poets they read, and the God they believed in.[100]

There is otherwise nothing distinctive about Larry. He is 'neither handsome nor plain, rather shy and in no way remarkable'.[101] But, as a pilot during the First World War, Larry comes to represent the spiritual loss of the interwar era and the profound need for a spiritual revival to mend the broken pieces of modern life. His leave-taking from his engagement with Isabel and the life of upper-middle-class respectability that it would afford comes from his metaphysical question: 'I want to make up my mind whether God is or God is not. I want to find out why evil exists. I want to know whether I have an immortal soul or whether when I die it's the end.'[102]

Larry becomes what Bauman would describes as 'masterless': 'Being masterless (out of control, out of frame, on the loose)', he continues, 'was one condition modernity could not bear'.[103] The narrator makes a curiously resonant statement early in the text that will ultimately play a significant role later: 'You learn a lot more quickly under the guidance of experienced teachers. You waste a lot of time going down blind alleys if you have no one to lead you.'[104] The notion of leadership and social models is suggestive throughout this text, as Larry leaves the world of a richly endowed America, where 'everyone'll get richer and richer', for the possibility of spiritual transformation in the East.[105] Maugham's text recognizes modernity's erasure of the boundaries of the individual and the transmutation of the self into a swelling mass whose affiliates are easily replaced: an alternative fiancé for Isabel is even waiting in the wings like a replacement cog

---

[100] Maugham, pp. 2–3.
[101] Maugham, p. 19.
[102] Maugham, p. 73.
[103] Bauman, p. 28.
[104] Maugham, p. 34.
[105] Maugham, p. 50.

in a deterministic machine. Isabel's uncle Elliott believes that 'the resources of America are inexhaustible' and that the prosperity experienced during the first half of the novel 'isn't a boom, it's just the natural development of a great country'.[106] But the dull recognition of truth comes when, as the narrator grimly reports, 'on October the 23rd, 1929, the New York market broke'.[107] Financial ruin as both a counterpoint and an encouragement to spiritual development is a resonant trope that had appeared earlier in Hilton's *Lost Horizon*: there Bryant is a New York financier who loss of fortune led to warrants for his arrest in several countries – he ultimately decides to stay in Shangri-La, where the immortal life of art and culture that the lamasery provides is enough to remedy even the most scandalous of fiduciary crimes.

It is against this backdrop of financial ruin and spiritual poverty that Larry slips away to India following several decisive encounters with other spiritually minded travellers in Europe. While the action observed and reported by the narrator Maugham continues, Larry's pilgrimage is only revealed long after the fact:

> I feel it right to warn the reader that he can very well skip this chapter without losing the thread of such story as I have to tell … I should add, however, that except for this conversation I should perhaps not have thought it worthwhile to write this book.[108]

What follows in Larry's story is almost an anti-travel narrative in that he admittedly has 'no descriptive talent, I don't know the world to paint a picture; I can't tell you, so as to make you see it'.[109] As in Brunton's *In Search of Search India*, the experiences portrayed exist beyond words and meaning, and the meeting with a fictionalized Maharshi (or, more properly, an entirely fictional guru inspired by Maharshi) begins to break down the affordances of narrative language. The extended account of Larry's story in Part Six which begins over breakfast in Paris draws upon the classical religious mode of the dialogic interview, with Maugham frequently interjecting to show his ignorance of spiritual matters and the need for Larry to provide the answers that he too seeks: 'I'm afraid I don't quite understand' is the narrator's frequent sentiment.[110] The entire novel is leading up to this moment when the narrator Maugham

---

[106] Maugham, p. 126.
[107] Maugham, p. 135.
[108] Maugham, p. 261.
[109] Maugham, p. 298.
[110] Maugham, p. 282.

hears the account and, through the process of narration, becomes an initiate himself.

What Larry ultimately reveals to the narrator is his answer to his question of the meaning of evil. 'Has it occurred to you', he explains to the narrator, 'that transmigration is at once an explanation and a justification of the evil of the world?'[111] The ultimate aim – both the cause of evil and its solution – is 'liberation from the bondage of rebirth'.[112] But, when later questioned by the narrator if he has solved his 'long quest' of 'the problem of evil', Larry recognizes the ultimate conclusion that he had always missed: 'I'm not clever enough to find it.'[113] Even before this, the narrator had observed how Larry had changed, how his calm and focus seemed to seep into those around him. As Larry describes it, his demeanour following his enlightenment is one of 'calmness, forbearance, compassion, selflessness, and continence'.[114] Larry develops a non-dualistic, apophatic vision of divinity in which

> you can't say what it is; you can only say what it isn't. It's inexpressible. The Indians call it Brahman. It's nowhere and everywhere. All things imply and depend upon it. It's not a person, it's not a thing, it's not a cause. It has no qualities. It transcends permanence and change; whole and part, finite and infinite. It is eternal because its completeness and perfection are unrelated to time. It is truth and freedom.[115]

Larry's revelation to the narrator, however, grows and develops, claiming that even the notion of the world as an illusion, which he takes as a common misconception of Indian philosophy, is just a technique for encouraging people to move closer towards a recognition that the divine is infinite. 'Why should we of the West, we Americans especially, be daunted by decay and death, hunger and thirst, sickness, old age, grief, and delusion? The spirit of life is strong in us.'[116] In spite of Larry's realization, he continues to feel, in an echo of the opening lines of the novel about his Americanness, that 'I don't think it's possible for us Occidentals to believe in it as implicitly as those Orientals do. It's in their blood and bones. With us it can only be an opinion.'[117]

There is no way for the reader to grasp a material sense of what Larry experienced, and that seems to be precisely part of the point. Ramana Maharshi

---

[111] Maugham, p. 286.
[112] Maugham, p. 290.
[113] Maugham, p. 303.
[114] Maugham, p. 304.
[115] Maugham, p. 291.
[116] Maugham, p. 301.
[117] Maugham, p. 288.

did not record much of his teachings. Throughout the dialogues contained in the *Teachings of Ramana Maharshi in His Own Words*, both Maharshi and the devotee speak of him in the third person, distancing even the living person from the philosophical teachings. Something approximately the teachings that Larry experienced can be extracted from this text, which is very clear that on the path of liberation, 'personal example and instruction are the most helpful aids':

> As for intuitive understanding, a person may laboriously convince himself of the truth to be grasped by intuition, of its function and nature, but the actual intuition is more like feeling and requires practical and personal contact. Mere book learning is not of any great use. After Realization all intellectual loads are useless burdens and are to be thrown overboard.[118]

What the primary aim should be is to learn from the model of a guru 'who at all times abides in the profound depths of the Self [, who] never sees any difference between himself and others and is quite free from the idea that he is the Enlightened or the Liberated One, while those around him are in bondage or the darkness of ignorance'.[119] The portrayal of occult spiritual traditions from India and Tibet became, in the work of David-Neel, Brunton and Maugham, an emblematical wish to draw down the ineffable insight of gnosis, flatten it out and reconstitute it through the discursive practice of narrative language. But in each of their cases came the early recognition that language could do little to portray the insights and wisdom gained and that their works, if they achieved anything, could hope only to point readers towards the source of the *philosophia perennis*. The modernist period not only saw the expanding awareness in Western culture of the spiritual traditions of Hinduism and Buddhism but also a radical reassessment of individual subjectivity and the opportunity of being plucked from the nameless, faceless mass of modernity through spiritual enlightenment. One of Blavatsky's greatest contributions to the history of global occult philosophy is her early recognition of this, and although her meetings with the Tibetan Mahatmas were apocryphal, her movement towards a combinatory lineage of spiritual practice rooted in direct observation would invigorate future generations in their search for embodied knowledge of the perennial philosophy.

---

[118] Maharshi, pp. 1–2.
[119] Maharshi, p. 93.

Conclusion

In Dion Fortune's *The Sea Priestess*, the transcendent revitalization of the miserable and infirm Wilfred is instigated by a collection of books that offers him an initial glimpse into a world that will soon come to life. 'What with my dope dreams and Theosophical reading', he explains to the reader,

> I began to get on to Peter Ibbertson's idea of 'dreaming true'. … I also developed my power of 'feeling-with' nature things. I had had my first experience of this when I accidentally got in touch with the Moon during my first attack; later I read some of Algernon Blackwood's books; also *The Projection of the Astral Body* by Muldoon and Carrington. These gave me ideas.[1]

But these books must be hidden away from prying eyes, particularly from those of his watchful sister, not because he fears repercussions but because 'there is something very intimate and personal about one's books. They reveal so much of one's private soul'.[2] When Le Fay Morgan enters his life, her collection of books offers him new material to explore, and their 'fascinating smell' which lingers from a distant cedar-wood shelf assures him of the validity and value of their provenance.[3] Given the hugely suggestive presence of books within Wilfred's life and throughout Fortune's narrative as a whole, it is not at all surprising that Le Fay Morgan leaves her books to Wilfred in her will as a tangible record of his vast spiritual inheritance.

Words and language have been the material of occultists for hundreds of years, and many of the writers explored in this book were regular customers of one or both of two famous London occult bookshops. Watkins Books was founded in 1897 on the Charing Cross Road at the behest of Helena Blavatsky who understood the function of books in the dissemination of magical ways

---

[1] Dion Fortune, *The Sea Priestess* (1938; repr. York Beach, ME: Red Wheel/Weiser, 2003), pp. 13–14.
[2] Fortune, *The Sea Priestess*, p. 9.
[3] Fortune, *The Sea Priestess*, p. 83.

of thinking, and, twenty-five years later, Michael Houghton and Paul Brunton would open Atlantis Books on Museum Street which served as a central meeting place for leading occultists throughout the rest of the twentieth century. Both shops are still in existence and, today, convey the indelible impressions of generations of readers, writers and magicians who have sought wisdom from the books on their shelves. In 2003, the historian Christina Oakley Harrington opened Treadwell's Books, first in Covent Garden and now in Bloomsbury, which carries on the tradition of the occult bookshop as a meeting place and salon. Although the central premise of the preceding chapters has been that the modernists influenced by occult philosophy sought ways to resist the powerful command of narrative language in order to open up new potentials for cooperative knowledge and divine manifestation, the reiteration of the significance of words, language and texts is the unanticipated yet unmistakable conclusion.

The curious paradox which has run throughout the previous chapters of this book is that even while modern occult traditions were captivated by the prospects of the untold and unsayable, their most portable and lasting explications came in textual form. The notion that language could be yoked to an unchanging meaning and signification was a distinctly modern innovation, resisting the practices of premodern spiritual traditions which relied upon continual explication and exegesis of divine texts written in vibratory languages. The *Yoga Sutras* of Patanjali (*c.*500 BCE), for instance, comprise 196 fleeting aphorisms rooted in the sacred oral traditions of the Vedic period but require commentary and revelation in order to open up the full insinuations; Christopher Isherwood's commentary with Swami Prabhavananda, published in 1953, is one such modern instance of the necessary elaboration of meaning within the *Yoga Sutras*. To give just another example, a Kabbalist tradition contained within the *Shummushe Torah* indicates that when Moses received Torah, he was granted a second text which contained an esoteric formulation of the letters conveying the unknowable hidden message of the divine, leaving humanity to search for this message within the exoteric holy books.[4] For this reason, the Kabbalah is particularly interested in the ineffable signifiers of god – construed through the tetragrammaton יהוה ('YHVH'), rendered speakable in English with vowels that transform it into 'Jehovah' – and the associated practice of gematria, the assignment of numerical value to letters in order to reform and reconstitute meaning. 'What happens

---

[4] Elliot R. Wolfson, 'The Mystical Significance of Torah Study in German Pietism', *Jewish Quarterly Review*, 84.1 (1993), 43–78.

when a mystic encounters the holy scriptures of his tradition is briefly this', Kabbalah scholar Gershom Scholem explains:

> The sacred text is smelted down and a new dimension is discovered in it. ... The holiness of the texts resides precisely in their capacity for such metamorphosis. The word of God must be infinite, or, to put it in a different way, the absolute word is as such meaningless, but it is *pregnant* with meaning.[5]

Far from insisting on holy texts that are unyielding and immovable, Jewish mysticism views all human expression as merely an attempt at meaning-making, something which Scholem recognizes in the mystical traditions of other religions as well: 'One cannot but be fascinated by the unbelievable freedom with which Meister Eckhart, the author of the *Zohar*, or the great Sufi mystics read their canonical texts, from which their own world seems to construct itself.'[6] Indeed, for Scholem, any mystical experience must necessarily be recognized as a living tradition 'precisely because a mystic is what he is, precisely because he stands in a direct, productive relationship to the object of his experience, he transforms the content of the tradition in which he lives'.[7] In Old English, the word 'spel' denotes 'discourse, narration, speech', a meaning most clearly maintained in the Yiddish word 'spiel', 'a speech intended to persuade or advertise, patter'.[8] While the contemporary usage of 'spell' connotes a form of enchantment (such as the spell that Antoin Artaud had intended to cast on Lise Derharme), the magic, linguistically speaking, does not materialize from the spellcaster but from the incantation and the 'speech intended to persuade' of the spell itself.

The occult has always walked the perilous line between desiring a textual form while resisting the possibility that this form can ever be completely achieved. 'When we begin looking at the Western esoteric traditions,' Arthur Versluis writes, 'we find that the written word is often seen not only as a means of transmitting spiritual understanding, but even as a vehicle for attaining spiritual understanding. This is not to say that the written word is privileged over the oral tradition, but neither is it to say that the written word is disparaged.'[9] Like many modern prophets from William Blake to Aleister Crowley, Joseph Smith understood his temporal authority as invested principally in the textual

---

[5] Gershom Scholem, *On the Kabbalah and Its Symbolism*, trans. Ralph Manheim (New York: Schocken Books, 1969), pp. 11–12.
[6] Scholem, p. 13.
[7] Scholem, p. 9.
[8] *OED*.
[9] Arthur Versluis, *Restoring Paradise: Western Esotericism, Literature, Art, and Consciousness* (Albany: State University of New York Press, 2004), p. 5.

figurations of gnosis embodied by his divinely received *Book of Mormon*.[10] Peter Levenda traces considerable influence of Francis Barrett's epic work of ritual magic *The Magus* (1801) on Smith's early thinking, indicating a curious slippage in Smith's personal spiritual practice between the ritual magic described by Barrett (and Barrett's principle source in the fifteenth-century occultist Heinrich Cornelius Agrippa) and a form of Old Testament seership which involved Smith looking through a 'shew stone' to find the locations of buried golden plates containing a divinely conveyed text.[11] The Urim and Thummim, stones which form the breastplate of Aaron, become decisive physical symbols in Smith's mystical discovery of a sacred text and are patently echoed in the stone spectacles of Tony Kushner's *Angels in America* (1992) which enable the culmination of Prior Walter's visions. Written at a time when the personal and public traumas of HIV/AIDS had brought into focus an array of excruciating issues surrounding artistic impact, historical record and collective identity, *Angels in America* ultimately resists the positivism which had become the most compelling artistic and academic response to the health crisis. Undoubtedly the most poignant gesture made within Kushner's play is the positioning of a former drag queen currently living with AIDS as the prophetic voice of his generation. The late revelation that Joe Pitt had been ghost-writing bigoted court rulings brings sharply into focus the play's most significant theme of textual revelation. As Prior's boyfriend Louis finally realizes, 'These gems were ghostwritten. By you: his obedient, eager clerk.'[12] Like Prior, Joe was receiving his dictates from a higher source, and in a play about mystical textual exegesis, it is hugely sarcastic that Louis is a legal word processor. It is an almost too-perfect thematic culmination to a play which is concerned not merely with the long theological history of exegesis and textual revelation but also with the fantastical, camp promises that such revelation holds in a post-Enlightenment world predicated on scientific positivism. Prior's apocalyptic visions and access through the stone spectacles to an embodied revelation designate him as a prophet rather than merely a mystic, and, as such, shown the shadowy outlines of a *prisca theologia*. In spite of Kushner's clear investment in the identity politics of the final decade of the twentieth century, the play provides equally compelling evidence for a vision of origination and continuity inspired by the Western occult traditions.

[10] See, in particular, Richard Bushman, *Joseph Smith and the Beginnings of Mormonism* (Chicago: University of Illinois Press, 1984); Terry Givens, *By the Hand of Mormon: The America Scripture That Launches a New World Religion* (Oxford: Oxford University Press, 2002); Robert Gottlieb and Peter Wiley, *America's Saints: The Rise of Mormon Power* (New York: Putnam, 1984).
[11] Peter Levenda, *The Angel and the Sorcerer* (Lake Worth, FL: Ibis, 2012), p. 82.
[12] Tony Kushner, *Angels in America* (London: Nick Hern Books, 2007), p. 240.

In doing so, *Angels in America* underscores the outsider positions inherent in the development of Western religion and the esoteric currents which run beneath it and polemically defines mystical experience as a form of textual camp which has historically ascribed questionable alterity to the receiver.

The stories that we tell are among the most sacred acts humans have ever undertaken. When books were in short supply and reading was limited to monasteries and palaces, there was no room for pleasure reading – only the most enduringly important texts were copied and recopied so that the experience of readership implied that any text approached was greater, and usually more divinely connected to the word of god, than the individual reader. This receptivity of early readers was lost in the rise of egalitarian modernity. Even with the invention of script, the printing press, mass-produced paperbacks and the internet, the nature of stories is such that their physical presence is never their reality. We consume imaginative writing in order to think the incomprehensible, but, even so, we subject it to academic scrutiny as a means by which to either evaluate historical or philosophical hypotheses or to provide further evidence once the hypothesis has already been proven. The study of literature must therefore become essentially comparative in the sense that literary scholars evaluate the shifting historical and cultural influences that give meaning to a particular text, and which illuminate its hologram to portray a shared cultural understanding of what a work 'means'. This is not to say that texts are not real – in fact it is to say exactly the opposite.

The most significant challenge that scholars of literature face is that texts do not do anything: they are the directions for creating an exclusively subjective experience that will by necessity be different for every reader. Their low fidelity (i.e. their non-existent ability to reproduce identical copies of themselves) is one of their most significant features. While modernism has, since its beginnings, been understood as an explicitly rationalizing and liberating force, many of the most momentous expressions of modern frailty and discontent have been contained within the contexts of enchanted epistemologies. It is undeniable that numerous modernists were occultists committed to practices including ceremonial magic, trance possession and Kabbalistic pathworking (and why should not they be?), but, beyond these most obvious examples, it begins to become clear that the foundations of modernist literature and of the modern world at large are unmistakably fused with magical ways of thinking.

Bibliography

Acker, Barbara 'The Verse Delivery Experiments of William Butler Yeats and Florence Farr', *Voice and Speech Review*, 5.1 (2007), 192–200.

Adams, David, 'Rudolf Steiner's First Goetheanum as an Illustration of Organic Functionalism', *Journal of the Society of Architectural Historians*, 51.2 (1992), 182–204.

Almond, Philip, *The British Discovery of Buddhism* (Cambridge: Cambridge University Press, 1988).

Apollinaire, Guillaume, 'Programme for *Parade*, 18 May 1917', in *Modernism: An Anthology of Sources and Documents*, ed. Vassiliki Kolocotroni, Jane Goldman and Olga Taxidou (Chicago: University of Chicago Press, 1998), pp. 212–13.

Appadurai, Arjun, *Modernity at Large: Cultural Dimensions of Globalization* (London: University of Minnesota Press, 1996).

Arata, Stephen, 'Occidental Tourist: *Dracula* and the Anxiety of Reverse Colonization', *Victorian Studies*, 33.4 (1990), 621–45.

Aristotle, *The Poetics of Aristotle*, trans. S. H. Butcher (London: Macmillan, 1902).

Artaud, Antonin, *Apocalypse*, trans. and ed. Stephen Barber (London: Infinity Land Press, 2018).

Artaud, Antonin, *The Theatre and Its Double*, trans. Victor Corti (1938; repr. Croydon: Alma Classics, 2014).

Barrie, J. M, *Dear Brutus* (1917; repr. London: Oberon Modern Plays, 2017).

Bates, Brian, *The Way of the Actor* (London: Century Hutchinson, 1987).

Bauman, Zygmunt, 'From Pilgrim to Tourist – or a Short History of Identity', in *Questions of Cultural Identity*, ed. Stuart Hall and Paul du Gay (London: Sage, 1996), pp. 18–36.

Bax, Clifford (ed.), *Letters: Florence Farr, Bernard Shaw, W. B. Yeats* (London: Home & Van Thal, 1946).

Bell, Catherine, *Ritual: Perspectives and Dimensions* (Oxford: Oxford University Press, 1997).

Belsey, Catherine, *Critical Practice*, 2nd edn (London: Routledge, 2002).

Benjamin, Walter, 'Theses on the Philosophy of History', in *Illuminations*, trans. Harry Zohn (1940; repr. New York: Schocken, 1968).

Berger, Peter L., *The Many Altars of Modernity* (Berlin: De Gruyter, 2014).

Bergson, Henri, *Creative Evolution*, trans. by Arthur Mitchell (1911; repr. Mineola, NY: Dover, 1998).

Besant, Annie, *Initiation: The Perfection of Man* (London: Theosophical Publishing House, 1918).
Blavatsky, H. P., *The Key to Theosophy* (1889; repr. Los Angeles: Theosophy Company, 1987).
Blavatsky, H. P., *The Secret Doctrine: The Synthesis of Science, Religion and Philosophy*, vol. 1 (London: Theosophical Publishing Company, 1888).
Boll, Theophilus E. M., 'May Sinclair and the Medico-Psychological Clinic of London', *Proceedings of the American Philosophical Society*, 106 (1962), 310–26.
Booth, Wayne C., *The Rhetoric of Fiction*, 2nd edn (1960; repr. Harmondsworth: Penguin, 1987).
Boyle, John, 'Esoteric Traces in Contemporary Psychoanalysis', *American Imago*, 73.1 (2016), 95–119.
Boym, Svetlana, *The Future of Nostalgia* (New York: Basic, 2001).
Bramble, John, *Modernism and the Occult* (Basingstoke: Palgrave Macmillan, 2015).
Brook, Peter, *The Empty Space* (1968; repr. London: Penguin, 2008).
Brunnhölzl, Karl, *Center of the Sunlit Sky: Madhyamaka in the Kagyu Tradition* (Ithaca, NY: Snow Lion, 2004).
Bruton, Paul, *A Hermit in the Himalayas: The Journal of a Lonely Exile* (1937; repr. Bombay: B. I. Publications, 1974).
Bruton, Paul, 'A Pioneer Western Buddhist', *Ceylon Daily News, Vesak Number* (1941).
Bruton, Paul, *A Search in Secret India* (1934; repr. York Beach, ME: Samuel Weiser, 1997).
Bushman, Richard, *Joseph Smith and the Beginnings of Mormonism* (Chicago: University of Illinois Press, 1984).
Butler, E. M., *The Myth of the Magus* (Cambridge: Cambridge University Press, 1948).
Butts, Mary, *Armed with Madness* in *The Taverner Novels* (New York: McPherson, 1992).
Byrd, Rudolph P., *Jean Toomer's Years with Gurdjieff: Portrait of an Artist, 1923–1936* (Athens: University of Georgia Press, 1990).
Caputo, John D., *The Mystical Element in Heidegger's Thought* (New York: Fordham University Press, 1986).
Carlson, Maria, *No Religion Higher Than Truth: A History of the Theosophical Movement in Russia, 1875–1922* (Princeton, NJ: Princeton University Press, 1993).
Carver, Craig, 'James Joyce and the Theory of Magic', *James Joyce Quarterly*, 15.3 (1978), 201–14.
Clausson, Nils, 'Degeneration, *Fin-de-Siécle* Gothic, and the Science of Detection: Arthur Conan Doyle's *The Hound of the Baskervilles* and the Emergence of the Modern Detective Story', *Journal of Narrative Theory*, 35 (2005), 60–87.
Clement, Christian, 'Weimar Classicism and Modern Spiritual Drama: Rudolf Steiner's Theatre of Spiritual Realism', in *Weimar Classicism: Studies in Goethe, Schiller, Forster, Berlepsch, Weiland, Herder, and Steiner*, ed. David Gallagher (Lewiston, NY: Edwin Mellen Press, 2011), pp. 135–54.

Coats, Jason M., 'H. D. and the Hermetic Impulse', *South Atlantic Review*, 77 (1/2), 79–98.
Cocking, John, *Imagination: A Study in the History of Ideas* (Abingdon: Routledge, 1991).
Colucciello Barber, Daniel, *Deleuze and the Naming of God: Post-Secularism and the Future of Immanence* (Edinburgh: Edinburgh University Press, 2015).
Conrad, Joseph, 'Henry James: An Appreciation', in *Notes on Life and Letters*, ed. J. H. Stape (Cambridge: Cambridge University Press, 2004), pp. 15–20.
Corbett, Lionel, 'Jung's *The Red Book* Dialogues with the Soul: Herald of a New Religion?', *Jung Journal*, 5.3 (2011), 63–77.
Coward, Harold, *Jung and Eastern Thought* (Albany: State University of New York Press, 1985).
Creekmore, Betsey B., 'The Tarot Fortune in The Waste Land', *ELH*, 49.4 (1982), 908–28.
Creese, Robb, 'Anthroposophical Performance', *Drama Review*, 22.2 (1978), 45–74.
Crow, John L., 'Taming the Astral Body: The Theosophical Society's Ongoing Problem of Emotion and Control', *Journal of the American Academy of Religion*, 80.3 (2012), 691–717.
Crowley, Aleister, 'How to Write a Novel! (After W. S. Maugham)', *Vanity Fair* (30 December 1908), 838–40.
Crowley, Aleister, *Magick in Theory and Practice* (1929; repr. New York: Castle Books, 1970).
Crowley, Aleister, *The Simon Iff Stories and Other Works* (Ware: Wordsworth, 2012).
Currie, Robert, 'Eliot and the Tarot', *ELH*, 46.4 (1979), 722–33.
Cusack, Carol M., ' "And the Building Becomes Man": Meaning and Aesthetic in Rudolf Steiner's Goetheanum', in *Handbook of New Religions and Cultural Production*, ed. Carole M. Cusak and Alex Norman (Leiden: Brill, 2012), pp. 173–92.
David-Neel, Alexandra, *Magic and Mystery in Tibet* (1932; repr. London: Souvenir Press, 2007).
David-Neel, Alexandra, and Lama Yongden, *The Secret Oral Teachings in Tibetan Buddhist Sects* (San Francisco, CA: City Lights Books, 1967), p. 12.
Davis, Erik, *Techgnosis: Myth, Magic, and Mystery in the Information Age* (Berkeley, CA: North Atlantic Books, 2015).
Delap, Lucy, 'The Superwoman: Theories of Gender and Genius in Edwardian Britain', *Historical Journal*, 47.1 (2004), 101–26.
Deleuze, Gilles, 'The Conditions of the Question: What is Philosophy', trans. Daniel W. Smith and Arnold I. Davidson, *Critical Inquiry*, 17.3 (1991), 471–78 (p. 474).
Eagleton, Terry, *Literary Theory: An Introduction* (Oxford: Basil Blackwell, 1983).
Eliade, Mircea, *Patterns in Comparative Religion*, trans. Rosemary Sheed (Lincoln: University of Nebraska Press, 1996).
Eliade, Mircea, *The Sacred and the Profane: The Nature of Religion*, trans. Willard R. Trask (New York: Harvest, 1959).
Engell, James, *The Creative Imagination: Enlightenment to Romanticism* (New York: Harvard University Press, 1981).

Faivre, Antoine, *Western Esotericism: A Concise History*, trans. Christine Rhone (Albany: State University of New York Press, 2010).

Faivre, Antoine, and Karen-Claire Voss, 'Western Esotericism and the Science of Religions', *Numen*, 42.1 (1995), 48–77.

Farr, Florence, *Modern Woman: Her Intentions* (London: Frank Palmer, 1910).

Farr, Florence, 'Superman Consciousness', *The New Age*, 1.6 (6 June 1907).

Farr, Florence, and Olivia Shakespear, *The Beloved of Hathor and the Shrine of the Golden Hawk* (Croydon: privately published, 1902).

Ferguson, Christine, 'Introduction', in *The Occult Imagination in Britain, 1875–1947*, ed. Christine Ferguson and Andrew Radford (Abingdon: Routledge, 2018), pp. 1–20.

Fortune, Dion, 'Ceremonial Magic Unveiled', repr. in Gareth Knight, *Dion Fortune's Rites of Isis and of Pan* (Cheltenham: Skylight, 2013), pp. 82–93.

Fortune, Dion (as Violet M. Firth), *Machinery of the Mind* (1922; repr. Abingdon: Routledge, 2018).

Fortune, Dion, 'The Novels of Dion Fortune', repr. in Gareth Knight, *Dion Fortune's Rites of Isis and of Pan* (Cheltenham: Skylight, 2013), pp. 94–102.

Fortune, Dion (as Violet M. Firth), *The Problem of Purity* (New York: Samuel Weiser, 1985).

Fortune, Dion, *Psychic Self-Defense* (1930; repr. San Francisco, CA: Red Wheel/Weiser, 2001).

Fortune, Dion, *The Rite of Pan*, repr. in Gareth Knight, *Dion Fortune's Rites of Isis and of Pan* (Cheltenham: Skylight, 2013).

Fortune, Dion, *The Sea Priestess* (1938; repr. York Beach, ME: Red Wheel/Weiser, 2003).

Fortune, Dion, *The Secrets of Doctor Taverner* (San Francisco, CA: Red Wheel/Weiser, 2011).

Foster, Barbara, and Michael Foster, *The Secret Lives of Alexandra David-Neel* (New York: Overlook Press, 1998).

Foster, R. F., *W. B. Yeats: A Life, Volume 1: The Apprentice Mage* (Oxford: Oxford University Press, 1998).

Franke, William, *On What Cannot Be Said: Apophatic Discourses in Philosophy, Religion, Literature, and the Arts*, vol. 2 (London: University of Notre Dame Press, 2007).

Freeman, Nick, 'Wilde's Edwardian Afterlife: Somerset Maugham, Aleister Crowley, and the Magician', *Literature and History*, 16.2 (2007), 16–29.

Freud, Sigmund, *Beyond the Pleasure Principle* in *Complete Psychological Works of Sigmund Freud*, vol. 18 (London: Vintage, 2001).

Galton, Francis, *Inquiries into Human Faculty and Its Development* (1883; repr. London: J. M. Dent & Sons, 1919).

Garrigan Mattar, Sinéad, 'Yeats, Fairies, and the New Animism', *New Literary History*, 43 (2012), 137–57.

Garrity, Jane, *Step-Daughters of England: British Women Modernists and the National Imaginary* (Manchester: Manchester University Press, 2003).

Gavrilyuk, Paul, and Sarah Coakley (eds), *The Spiritual Senses: Perceiving God in Western Christianity* (Cambridge: Cambridge University Press, 2011).

Gilbert, R. A., *The Golden Dawn Scrapbook: The Rise and Fall of a Magical Order* (York Beach, ME: Samuel Weiser, 1997).

Gilbert, R. A. (ed.), *The Magical Mason: Forgotten Hermetic Writings of William Wynn Westcott, Physician and Magus* (Wellingborough: Aquarian Press, 1983).

Givens, Terry, *By the Hand of Mormon: The America Scripture That Launches a New World Religion* (Oxford: Oxford University Press, 2002).

Gomes, Daniel, 'Reviving Oisin: Yeats and the Conflicted Appeal of Irish Mythology', *Texas Studies in Literature & Language*, 56 (2014), 376–99.

Goodrick-Clarke, Nicholas, *Helena Blavatsky: Western Esoteric Masters* (Berkeley, CA: North Atlantic Books, 2004).

Gordon, Mel, 'Mikhail Chekhov's 1931 Occult Fantasy', *Performing Arts Journal*, 17.1 (1995), 110–12.

Gottlieb, Robert, and Peter Wiley, *America's Saints: The Rise of Mormon Power* (New York: Putnam, 1984).

Grainger, Roger, *Ritual and Theatre* (London: Austin Macauley, 2014).

Granholm, Kennet, 'Locating the West: Problematizing the Western in Western Esotericism and Occultism', in *Occultism in a Global Perspective*, ed. by Henrik Bogdan and Gordan Djurdjevic (London: Routledge, 2013), pp. 17–36.

Grant, Mark, 'Steiner and the Humours: The Survival of Ancient Greek Science', *British Journal of Educational Studies*, 47.1 (1999), 56–70.

Greene, Liz, *The Astrological World of Jung's* Liber Novus: *Daimons, Gods, and the Planetary Journey* (Abingdon: Routledge, 2018).

Greene, Liz, *Jung's Studies in Astrology: Prophecy, Magic, and the Qualities of Time* (Abingdon: Routledge, 2018).

Greer, Mary K., *Women of the Golden Dawn: Rebels and Priestesses* (Rochester, VT: Inner Traditions, 1995).

Grimes, Ronald, 'Religion, Ritual, and Performance', in *Religion, Theatre, and Performance: Acts of Faith*, ed. Lance Gharavi (New York: Routledge, 2012).

Grotowski, Jerzy, *Towards a Poor Theatre* (London: Methuen, 1968).

Guénon, René, *The Crisis of the Modern World*, trans. by Marco Pallis, Arthur Osborne and Richard C. Nicholson (1942; repr. Hillsdale, NY: Sophia Perennis, 2004).

Gunn, Joshua, 'An Occult Poetics, or, the Secret Rhetoric of Religion', *Rhetoric Society Quarterly*, 34.2 (2004), 29–51.

H. D., *Notes on Thought and Vision & the Wise Sappho* (San Francisco, CA: City Lights Books, 1982).

Habermas, Jürgen, *The Philosophical Discourse of Modernity*, trans. Frederick Lawrence (Cambridge: Polity, 1987).

Hallward, Peter, *Out of This World: Deleuze and the Philosophy of Creation* (London: Verso, 2006).

Hammer, Olav, *Claiming Knowledge: Strategies of Epistemology from Theosophy to the New Age* (Leiden: Brill, 2001).

Handley, William R., 'The Housemaid and the Kitchen Table: Incorporating the Frame in *To* the Lighthouse', *Twentieth Century Literature*, 40.1 (1994), 15–41.

Hanegraaff, Wouter J., 'Beyond the Yates Paradigm: The Study of Western Esotericism between Counterculture and New Complexity', *Aries*, 1.1 (2001), 5–37.

Hanegraaff, Wouter J., et al. (eds), *Dictionary of Gnosis and Western Esotericism* (Amsterdam: Brill, 2006).

Hanegraaff, Wouter J., *Esotericism and the Academy: Rejected Knowledge in Western Culture* (Cambridge: Cambridge University Press, 2012).

Hanegraaff, Wouter J., *New Age Religion and Western Culture: Esotericism in the Mirror of Secular Thought* (Albany: State University of New York Press, 1998).

Hanegraaff, Wouter J., *Western Esotericism: A Guide for the Perplexed* (London: Bloomsbury, 2013).

Hanley, Catriona, *Being and God in Aristotle and Heidegger: The Role of Method in Thinking the Infinite* (Oxford: Rowman & Littlefield, 2000).

Hannah, Barbara, *Encounters with the Soul: Active Imagination as Developed by C. G. Jung* (Cambridge, MA: Sigo, 1981).

Harris, Elizabeth J., 'Ananda Metteyya: Controversial Networker, Passionate Critic', *Contemporary Buddhism: An Interdisciplinary Journal*, 14.1 (2013), 77–92.

Harris, Elizabeth J., *Theravada Buddhism and the British Encounter* (London: Routledge, 2006).

Hesse, Hermann, *Demian*, trans. W. J. Strachan (London: Penguin, 2017).

Hesse, Hermann, *The Journey to the East*, trans. Hilda Rosner (London: Peter Owen, 2001).

Hesse, Hermann, *Siddhartha*, trans. Hilda Rosner (New York: New Directions, 1951).

Hesse, Hermann, *Steppenwolf*, trans. David Horrocks (London: Penguin, 2012).

Hillman, James, and Sonu Shamdasani, *Lament of the Dead: Psychology after Jung's Red Book* (London: W. W. Norton, 2013).

Hilton, James, *Lost Horizon* (1933; repr. Chichester: Summersdale, 2005).

Hodge, Alison, 'Introduction' to *Twentieth-Century Actor Training*, ed. Alison Hodge (London: Routledge, 2000), pp. 1–9.

Hoeller, Stephan A., *The Gnostic Jung and the Seven Sermons to the Dead* (London: Theosophical Publishing House, 1982).

Holroyd, Michael, *Bernard Shaw: Volume 1, 1856–1898, The Search for Love* (London: Penguin, 1988).

Holroyd, Michael, 'George Bernard Shaw: Women and the Body Politic', *Critical Inquiry*, 6.1 (1979), 17–32.

'Home of Theosophy Burns: Incendiarism Suspected in Destruction of Steiner's Temple Near Basle' [*sic*], *New York Times*, 2 January 1923.

Hood, Ralph W., 'The Construction and Preliminary Validation of a Measure of Reported Mystical Experience', *Journal for the Scientific Study of Religion*, 14.1 (1975), 29–41.

Howe, Ellic, *The Magicians of the Golden Dawn: A Documentary History of a Magical Order, 1887–1923* (York Beach, ME: Samuel Weiser, 1972).

Hugo, Leon, *Bernard Shaw: Playwright and Preacher* (London: Methuen, 1971).

Hutchins, Eileen, *Introduction to the Mystery Plays of Rudolf Steiner* (Forest Row: Rudolf Steiner Press, 2014).

Hutton, Ronald, *Stations of the Sun: A History of the Ritual Year in Britain* (Oxford: Oxford University Press, 2001).

Hutton, Ronald, *The Triumph of the Moon: A History of Modern Pagan Witchcraft* (Oxford: Oxford University Press, 1999).

Huyssen, Andreas, *After the Great Divide: Modernism, Mass Culture, Postmodernism* (Bloomington: Indiana University Press, 1986).

Ingelbien, Raphael, 'Metres and the Pound: Taking the Measure of British Modernism', *European Review*, 19.2 (2011), 285–97.

Innes, Christopher, *Modern British Drama: 1890–1990* (Cambridge: Cambridge University Press, 1992).

Irwin, Robert, *For Lust of Knowing: The Orientalists and Their Enemies* (London: Penguin, 2007).

James, William, *The Varieties of Religious Experience* (1902; repr. London: Penguin, 1982).

Johnson, Allan, *Masculine Identity in Modernist Literature: Castration, Narration, and a Sense of the Beginning, 1919–1945* (London: Palgrave Macmillan, 2017).

Johnson, Anthony L., ' "Broken Images": Discursive Fragmentation and Paradigmatic Integrity in the Poetry of T. S. Eliot', *Poetics Today*, 6.3 (1985), 399–416.

Johnson, Josephine, *Florence Farr: Bernard Shaw's New Woman* (Gerrards Cross: Colin Smythe, 1975).

Johnson, K. Paul, *The Masters Revealed: Madame Blavatsky and the Myth of the Great White Lodge* (Albany: State University of New York Press, 1994).

Johnston Graf, Susan, 'The Occult Novels of Dion Fortune', *Journal of Gender Studies*, 16.1 (2007), 47–56.

Jung, C. G., *Analytical Psychology: Its Theory and Practice* (London: Routledge, 1982).

Jung, C. G., *Memories, Dreams, Reflections* (London: Fontana, 1995), p. 207.

Jung, C. G., *Modern Man in Search of a Soul* (1933; repr. Abingdon: Routledge, 2001).

Jung, C. G., *Psychology and Religion: West and East, Collected Works*, vol. 11, trans. Gerhard Adler and R. F. C. Hull (Princeton, NJ: Princeton University Press, 1969).

Jung, C. G., *The Red Book: A Reader's Edition*, ed. Sonu Shamdasani, trans. Mark Kyburz, John Peck and Sonu Shamdasani (London: W. W. Norton, 2009).

Jung, C. G., *The Seven Sermons to the Dead*, in Stephan A. Hoeller, *The Gnostic Jung and the Seven Sermons to the Dead* (London: Theosophical Publishing House, 1982).

Kalogera, Lucy, 'Yeats's Celtic Mysteries', unpublished doctoral dissertation, Florida State University, 1977.

Kane, Julie, 'Varieties of Mystical Experience in the Writings of Virginia Woolf', *Twentieth Century Literature*, 41.4 (1995), 328–49.

Kibble, Matthew, 'Sublimation and the Over-Mind in H.D.'s "Notes on Thought and Vision"', *English Literature in Transition, 1880–1920*, 41.1 (1998), 42–57.

Kingsland, William, *The Real H.P. Blavatsky: A Study in Theosophy, and a Memoir of a Great Soul*, 2nd edn (London: Theosophical Publishing House, 1985).

Knight, Christopher, *Modern Apophaticism from Henry James to Jacques Derrida* (Toronto: University of Toronto Press, 2010).

Knight, Gareth, *Dion Fortune's Rites of Isis and of Pan* (Cheltenham: Skylight, 2013).

Kraft, Siv Ellen, '"To Mix or Not to Mix": Syncretism/Anti-Syncretism in the History of Theosophy', *Numen*, 49.2 (2002), 142–77.

Kripal, Jeffrey, *The Flip: Epiphanies of Mind and the Future of Knowledge* (New York: Bellevue Literary Press, 2019).

Kushner, Tony, *Angels in America* (London: Nick Hern Books, 2007).

Lachman, Gary, *Jung the Mystic: The Esoteric Dimensions of Carl Jung's Life and Teachings* (New York: Tarcher, 2010).

Latham, Sean, *Am I a Snob?: Modernism and the Novel* (Ithaca, NY: Cornell University Press, 2003).

Levenda, Peter, *The Angel and the Sorcerer* (Lake Worth, FL: Ibis, 2012).

Levenson, Michael, *Modernism* (London: Yale University Press, 2011).

Lévi-Strauss, Claude, *The Savage Mind* (London: Weidenfeld and Nicolson, 1966).

Lewis, Bernard, 'The Question of Orientalism', *New York Review of Books*, 24 June 1982.

Lewis, Pericles, *Religious Experience and the Modernist Novel* (Cambridge: Cambridge University Press, 2010).

Lingan, Edmund, *The Theatre of the Occult Revival: Alternative Spiritual Performance from 1875 to the Present* (London: Palgrave Macmillan, 2015).

Lorraine, Tamsin, *Deleuze and Guattari's Immanence Ethics* (Albany: State University of New York Press, 2011).

Lukács, György, 'The Ideology of Modernism', in *The Meaning of Contemporary Realism*, trans. John Mander and Necke Mander (London: Merlin Press, 1963).

Mahaffey, Vicki, *Modernist Literature: Challenging Fictions* (Oxford: Blackwell, 2007).

Maharshi, Ramana, *The Teachings of Ramana Maharshi*, ed. by Arthur Osborne (1962; repr. London: Rider, 2014).

Main, Roderick, *The Rupture of Time: Synchronicity and Jung's Critique of Modern Western Culture* (New York: Brunner-Routledge, 2004).

Mao, Douglas, and Rebecca L. Walkowitz, 'The New Modernist Studies', *PMLA*, 123.3 (2008), 737–48.

Marinetti, F. T., 'Contempt for Women', in *Modernism: An Anthology*, ed. Lawrence Rainey, trans. Lawrence Rainey (1911; repr. Oxford: Blackwell, 2005), pp. 9–11.

Marinetti, F. T., 'Destruction of Syntax – Wireless Imagination – Words-in-Freedom', in *Modernism: An Anthology*, ed. Lawrence Rainey, trans. Lawrence Rainey (Oxford: Blackwell, 2005), pp. 27–34.

Marinetti, F. T., 'The Founding and the Manifesto of Futurism' (1909), in *Modernism: An Anthology*, ed. Lawrence Rainey, trans. Lawrence Rainey (Oxford: Blackwell, 2005), pp. 3–6.

Marinetti, F. T., 'Technical Manifesto of Futurist Literature', in *Modernism: An Anthology*, ed. Lawrence Rainey, trans. Lawrence Rainey (1912; repr. Oxford: Blackwell, 2005), pp. 15–19.

Marinetti, F. T., 'The Variety Theatre', in *Modernism: An Anthology*, ed. Lawrence Rainey, trans. Lawrence Rainey (1913; repr. Oxford: Blackwell, 2005), pp. 34–8.

Martin, Wallace, *The New Age under Orage: Chapters in English Cultural History* (Manchester: Manchester University Press, 1967).

Martz, Louis L., *Many Gods and Many Voices: The Role of the Prophet in English and American Modernism* (London: University of Missouri Press, 1998).

Materer, Timothy, *Modernist Alchemy: Poetry and the Occult* (Ithaca, NY: Cornell University Press, 1995).

Mather, Jeff, 'Captivating Readers: Middlebrow Aesthetics and James Hilton's *Lost Horizon*', *CEA Critic*, 79.2 (2017), 231–43.

Maugham, W. Somerset, *The Magician* (1908; repr. London: Vintage, 2000).

Maugham, W. Somerset, *The Razor's Edge* (1944; repr. London: Vintage, 2000).

McLaurin, Allen, *Virginia Woolf: The Echoes Enslaved* (Cambridge: Cambridge University Press, 1973).

McMahan, David L., 'Modernity and the Early Discourse of Scientific Buddhism', *Journal of the American Academy of Religion*, 72.4 (2004), 897–933.

Merivale, Patricia, 'Learning the Hard Way: Gothic Pedagogy in the Modern Romantic Question', *Comparative Literature*, 36.2 (1984), 146–61.

Mileck, Joseph, *Hermann Hesse: Life and Art* (London: University of California Press, 1980).

Miller, Jeffrey C., *The Transcendent Function: Jung's Model of Psychological Growth through Dialogue with the Unconscious* (Albany: State University of New York Press, 2004).

Mills, Sara, *Discourses of Difference: An Analysis of Women's Travel Writing and Colonialism* (London: Routledge, 1991).

Mutter, Matthew, '"The Power to Enchant That Comes from Disillusion": W. H. Auden's Criticism of Magical Poetics', *Journal of Modern Literature*, 34.1 (2010), 58–85.

Nagal, Thomas, *Mind and Cosmos: Why the Materialist Neo-Darwinian Conception of Nature Is Almost Certainly False* (Oxford: Oxford University Press, 2012).

Nietzsche, Friedrich, *The Gay Science*, trans. Walter Kaufmann (1882; repr. New York: Random House, 1974).

Nietzsche, Friedrich, *Thus Spoke Zarathustra*, trans. R. J. Hollingdale (London: Penguin, 2003).

Nietzsche, Friedrich, *Twilight of the Idols and the Anti-Christ*, trans. R. J. Hollingdale (London: Penguin, 2003).

Noll, Richard, *The Jung Cult: Origins of a Charismatic Movement* (London: Fontana, 1996).

Nott, C. S., *Teachings of Gurdjieff: The Journal of a Pupil* (London: Routledge & Kegan Paul, 1961).

Olcott, Henry Steel, 'The Ordination of Allan Macgregor', *Theosophist*, 23.11 (1902), 683–8.

O'Mara, John, *The New School of the Imagination: Rudolf Steiner's Mystery Plays in Literary Tradition* (Ottawa: Heart's Core, 2005).

Orage, A. R., *Friedrich Nietzsche: The Dionysian Spirit of the Age* (London: T. N. Foulis, 1906).

Orage, A. R., *The New Age*, vol. IV (28 January 1909), p. 280.

Orage, A. R., *On Love and Psychological Exercises* (York Beach, ME: Samuel Weiser, 1998).

Owen, Alex, *The Place of Enchantment: British Occultism and the Culture of the Modern* (London: University of Chicago Press, 2004).

Peters, Margot, *Bernard Shaw and the Actresses* (New York: Doubleday, 1980).

Peters, Sally, *The Ascent of the Superman* (London: Yale University Press, 1996).

Pinkerton, Steve, *Blasphemous Modernism: The 20th-Century Word Made Flesh* (Oxford: Oxford University Press, 2017).

Pound, Ezra, 'Psychology and Troubadours', *Quest: A Quarterly Review*, 4.1 (1912), 37–58.

Pound, Ezra, 'Vortex', *Blast*, 1.1 (1914), 153–4 (p. 153).

Progoff, Ira, *Jung, Synchronicity, and Human Destiny: Noncausal Dimensions of Human Experience* (New York: Delta, 1973).

Prothero, Stephen, 'From Spiritualism to Theosophy: "Uplifting" a Democratic Tradition', *Religion and American Culture: A Journal of Interpretation*, 3.2 (1993), 197–216.

Prothero, Stephen, 'Henry Steel Olcott and "Protestant Buddhism"', *Journal of the American Academy of Religion*, 63.2 (1995), 281–302.

Radford, Andrew, 'Anxieties of Mystical Influence: Dion Fortune's *The Winged Bull* and Aleister Crowley', in *The Occult Imagination in Britain, 1875–1947*, ed. Christine Ferguson and Andrew Radford (Abingdon: Routledge, 2018), pp. 165–80.

Radford, Andrew, 'Defending Nature's Holy Shrine', *Journal of Modern Literature*, 29.3 (2006), 126–49.

Radford, Andrew, 'Excavating a Secret History: Mary Butts and the Return of the Nativist', *Connotations: A Journal for Critical Debate*, 17.1 (2007), 80–108.

Rainey, Lawrence, *Modernism: An Anthology* (Oxford: Blackwell, 2005).

Raitt, Suzanne, 'Early British Psychoanalysis and the Medico-Psychological Clinic', *History Workshop Journal*, 58 (2004), 62–85.

Regardie, Israel, *The Golden Dawn: The Original Account of the Teachings, Rites and Ceremonies of the Hermetic Order of the Golden Dawn*, 6th edn (St Paul: Llewellyn, 1989).

Richardson, Alan, *Aleister Crowley and Dion Fortune: The Logos of the Aeon and the Shakti of the Age* (Woodbury, MN: Llewellyn, 2009).

Robinson, Ken, 'A Brief History of the British Psychoanalytical Society', in *100 Years of the IPA : The Centenary History of the International Psychoanalytical Association, 1910–2010*, ed. Peter Loewenberg and Nellie L. Thompson (London: Routledge, 2011), pp. 196–230.

Roukema, Aren, and Allan Kilner-Johnson, 'Time to Drop the "Western"', *Correspondences*, 6.2 (2018), 109–15.

Rowan, John, 'Dialogical Self and the Soul', in *Jungian and Dialogical Self Perspectives*, ed. Raya A. Jones and Masayoshi Morioka (Basingstoke: Palgrave Macmillan, 2011), pp. 152–66.

Said, Edward W., *Orientalism* (New York: Vintage, 1979).

Saler, Michael, 'Modernity and Enchantment: A Historiographic Review', *American Historical Review*, 111.3 (2006), 692–716.

Scarry, Elaine, *Dreaming by the Book* (New York: Farrar, Straus and Giroux, 1999).

Schefer, Olivier, 'Variations on Totality: Romanticism and the Total Work of Art', in *The Aesthetics of Total Artwork: On Borders and Fragments*, ed. Anke Finger and Danielle Follett (Baltimore, MD: Johns Hopkins University Press, 2011).

Scholem, Gershom, *On the Kabbalah and Its Symbolism*, trans. Ralph Manheim (New York: Schocken Books, 1969).

Schuré, Edouard, *The Genesis of Tragedy and The Sacred Drama of Eleusis*, trans. Fred Rothwell (London: Rudolf Steiner, 1936).

Sedgwick, Mark, *Against the Modern World: Traditionalism and the Secret Intellectual History of the Twentieth Century* (Oxford: Oxford University Press, 2004).

Shakespeare, William, *Julius Caesar* (1599; repr. London: Penguin, 2015).

Shamdasani, Sonu, 'Introduction' to C. G. Jung, *The Red Book: A Reader's Edition*, ed. Sonu Shamdasani (London: W. W. Norton, 2009).

Shaw, Bernard, 'Christianity and Equality', in *The Religious Speeches of Bernard Shaw*, ed. Warren Sylvester Smith (University Park, PA: Penn State University Press, 1963).

Shaw, Bernard, *Heartbreak House: A Fantasia in the Russian Manner on English Themes* (1919; repr. London: Penguin, 2000).

Shaw, Bernard, *Man and Superman* (1903; repr. London: Penguin, 1946).

Shaw, Bernard, 'Modern Religion I', in *The Religious Speeches of Bernard Shaw*, ed. Warren Sylvester Smith (University Park, PA: Penn State University Press, 1963).

Shaw, Bernard, *Plays Pleasant* (1898; repr. London: Penguin, 2003).

Shaw, Bernard, 'The Religion of the Future', in *The Religious Speeches of Bernard Shaw*, ed. Warren Sylvester Smith (University Park, PA: Penn State University Press, 1963).

Shaw, Bernard, *Saint Joan* (1923; repr. London: Penguin, 2003).

Shils, Edwards, 'The Intellectuals and the Powers: Some Perspectives for Comparative Analysis', *Comparative Studies in Society and History*, 1.1 (1958), 5–22.

Sinnett, A. P., *Esoteric Buddhism* (London: Truber & Co., 1883).

Slattery, Dennis, 'Thirteen Ways of Looking at *The Red Book*: C. G. Jung's Divine Comedy', *Jung Journal*, 5.3 (2011), 128–44.

Smith, Warren Sylvester, *Bishop of Everywhere: Bernard Shaw and the Life Force* (London: Pennsylvania State University Press, 1982).

Speakman, Charles, *Lancet*, 20 December 1913, pp. 1, 803.

Stanislavski, Constantin, *An Actor Prepares*, trans. Elizabeth Reynolds Hapgood (London: Geoffrey Bliss, 1937).

Stein, Murray, 'The Gnostic Critique, Past and Present', in *The Allure of Gnosticism: The Gnostic Experience in Jungian Psychology and Contemporary Culture*, ed. Robert A. Segal (Chicago: Open Court, 1995), pp. 39–53.

Steiner, Rudolf, 'The Ahrimanic Deception', trans. by M. Cotterell (1919), http://wn.rsarchive.org/Lectures/AhrDec_index.html, accessed 23 February 2018.

Steiner, Rudolf, 'Christian Initiation, in *The Essential Steiner*, ed. Robert McDermott (San Francisco, CA: Floris, 1996), pp. 255–65.

Steiner, Rudolf, *The Guardian of the Threshold* in *Four Mystery Dramas*, trans. Ruth and Hans Pusch (Great Barrington, MA: Steiner Books, 2007).

Steiner, Rudolf, *An Outline of Esoteric Science*, trans. by Catherine E. Creeger (1909; repr. Hudson, NY: Anthroposophic Press, 1997).

Steiner, Rudolf, *The Portal of Initiation* in *Four Mystery Dramas*, trans. Ruth Pusch and Hans Pusch (Great Barrington, MA: Steiner Books, 2007).

Steiner, Rudolf, 'The Raising of Lazarus', in *The Essential Steiner*, ed. Robert McDermott (San Francisco, CA: Floris, 1996), pp. 234–54.

Steiner, Rudolf, 'Self-Knowledge in Relation to the Mystery Play *The Portal of Initiation*', trans. G. A. Kaufmann (1910), http://wn.rsarchive.org/Lectures/19100917p02.html, accessed 23 February 2018.

Steiner, Rudolf, *The Soul's Awakening* in *Four Mystery Dramas*, trans. Ruth Pusch and Hans Pusch (Great Barrington, MA: Steiner Books, 2007).

Steiner, Rudolf, *The Soul's Probation* in *Four Mystery Dramas*, trans. Ruth Pusch and Hans Pusch (Great Barrington, MA: Steiner Books, 2007).

Steiner, Rudolf, *The Theosophy of the Rosicrucian* (1907; repr. London: Rudolf Steiner Press, 1966).

Sterenberg, Matthew, *Mythic Thinking in Twentieth-Century Britain: Meaning for Modernity* (London: Palgrave Macmillan, 2013).

Stock, Brian, *Augustine's Inner Dialogue: The Philosophical Soliloquy in Late Antiquity* (Cambridge: Cambridge University Press, 2010).

Styers, Randall, *Making Magic: Religion, Magic, and Science in the Modern World* (Oxford: Oxford University Press, 2004).

Surette, Leon, *The Birth of Modernism: Ezra Pound, T. S. Eliot, W. B. Yeats, and the Occult* (Quebec: McGill-Queen's University Press, 1993).

Sword, Helen, *Ghostwriting Modernism* (London: Cornell University Press, 2002).
Thomas, Ronald R., *Detective Fiction and the Rise of Forensic Science* (Cambridge: Cambridge University Press, 1999).
Thompson, Jon, *Fiction, Crime, and Empire* (Chicago: University of Illinois Press, 1993).
Thurschwell, Pamela, *Literature, Technology, and Magical Thinking, 1880–1920* (Cambridge: Cambridge University Press, 2001).
Tillet, Gregory, 'Modern Western Magic and Theosophy', *Aries*, 12.1 (2012), 17–51.
Tryphonopoulos, Demetres, *Celestial Tradition: A Study of Ezra Pound's* The Cantos (Waterloo: Wilfrid Laurier University Press, 1992).
Turner, Alicia, Laurence Cox and Brian Bocking, 'A Buddhist Crossroads: Pioneer European Buddhists and Globalizing Asian Networks 1860–1960', *Contemporary Buddhism: An Interdisciplinary Journal*, 14.1 (2013), 1–16.
Tweed, Thomas A., 'Toward a Translocative History of Occult Buddhism: Flows and Confluences, 1881–1912', *History of Religions*, 54.4 (2015), 423–33.
Uhrmacher, P. Bruce, 'Uncommon Schooling: A Historical Look at Rudolf Steiner, Anthroposophy, and Waldorf Education', *Curriculum Inquiry*, 25.4 (1995), 381–406.
Underhill, Evelyn, *Mysticism* (London: Methuen, 1911).
Versluis, Arthur, *Restoring Paradise: Western Esotericism, Literature, Art, and Consciousness* (Albany: State University of New York Press, 2004).
Viswanathan, Gauri, 'Secularism in the Framework of Heterodoxy', *PMLA*, 123.2 (2008), 466–76.
Wallraven, Miriam, *Women Writers and the Occult in Literature and Culture: Female Lucifers, Priestesses, and Witches* (Abingdon: Routledge, 2015).
Watts, Alan, 'Foreword', in *The Secret Oral Teachings in Tibetan Buddhist Sects* (San Francisco, CA: City Lights Books, 1967).
Weber, Max, 'Science as a Vocation', in *From Max Weber: Essays in Sociology*, trans. H. H. Gerth and C. Wright Mills (1917; repr. Oxford: Oxford University Press, 1946).
Weston, Jessie L., *From Ritual to Romance* (1920; repr. New York: Anchor, 1957).
Whitman, Robert, *Shaw and the Play of Ideas* (London: Cornell University Press, 1977).
Wilber, Ken, *Sex, Ecology, Spirituality: The Spirit of Evolution* (London: Shambhala, 1995).
Wilson, Colin, *The Occult* (1979; repr. London: Watkins, 2003).
Wilson, Leigh, *Modernism and Magic: Experiments with Spiritualism, Theosophy and the Occult* (Edinburgh: Edinburgh University Press, 2012).
Wiseman, Sam, 'Cosmopolitanism and Environmental Ethics in Mary Butts's Dorset', *Twentieth-Century Literature*, 61.3 (2015), 373–91.
Wolfson, Elliot R., 'The Mystical Significance of Torah Study in German Pietism', *Jewish Quarterly Review*, 84.1 (1993), 43–78.
Woolf, Virginia, *To the Lighthouse* (1927; repr. New York: Harcourt, 1981).
Yates, Frances, *The Rosicrucian Enlightenment* (1972; repr. St Albans: Paladin, 1975).

Yeats, W. B., 'Magic', in *The Major Works*, ed. Edward Larrissy (Oxford: Oxford University Press, 2001), pp. 344–9.

Zhang Longxi, *Unexpected Affinities: Reading across Culture* (London: University of Toronto Press, 2007).

Zwerdling, Alex, *Virginia Woolf and the Real World* (London: University of California Press, 1986).

Index

Abraxas 82–3
Ahriman 69–73
alchemy 9, 35, 51, 57–8, 75
ambiguity 24, 45
anthroposophy 56, 65–7, 72
apophaticism 5, 28, 32, 49, 109–10, 153
Aristotle 58, 110
Artaud, Antonin 57–8, 73
Atlantis Books 130, 156
author surrogate 39, 149

Basilides 82
Bennett, Alan 52, 128–9
Bergson, Henri 98–101, 107–9
Besant, Annie 53, 65–6, 105–6, 119
blasphemy 15–16, 82
Blavatsky, Helena 52, 55, 127–32, 139–45, 154–5
Brook, Peter 57–9
Brunton, Paul 25, 27, 128–31, 140, 147–9
Buddhism 65, 127–9, 133, 140–6, 154
Bulwer-Lytton, Edward 140
Butts, Mary 43–7

cantillation 60, 62
Carrington, Leonora 59
Celtic Revival 14–15, 46, 54
ceremonial magic 13, 62, 79, 95
Chekhov, Michael 49, 56, 59, 64
Chrétien de Troyes 40
Christianity 10, 15–16, 66, 76, 107, 116
Christian mysticism 8, 25, 67, 72, 112, 146
Conan Doyle, Arthur 88–90
Crowley, Aleister 18, 21, 52, 54–5, 89–90, 96–7, 101, 128

David Neel, Alexandra 25–7, 130–1, 137, 142–7, 154
decadence 95, 121
degeneration 27, 88, 118
Durkheim, Émile 5, 50

Eckhart, Meister 8, 20, 157
Egypt 61–4, 72
Eliot, T. S. 4, 12, 15–16, 25, 31, 35, 37, 40–6
elision 5, 26, 29–33, 42–3
Enlightenment, The 5, 7–8, 19–21, 158
eugenics 98, 117
eurhythmy 56, 64, 66–7
evolution 6, 107–9, 114, 118, 120

Fabian Society 27–8, 61, 99, 101, 106
Farr, Florence 25, 50, 52, 59–64, 101–2, 105–7, 113, 119
Fellowship of the Three Kings 60
feminism 11, 63–4, 101–2
First World War 26–9, 40, 50, 77, 79, 83–4, 91, 102, 120, 130–40, 150–2
Fisher King 41, 43, 123
Fortune, Dion 21, 27, 84–93, 97–9, 119–26, 155
Fraternity of the Inner Light 9, 85–6, 119, 123, 146
Frazer, James 19, 41, 50
Freemasonry 51, 52–4, 87, 140, 142
Freud, Sigmund 2, 45, 77, 85, 87, 91, 110
futurism 33–7

Gnosticism 5, 23, 33, 79, 82, 107–8, 125, 132
Goethe, Johann Wolfgang 66–7, 98, 100
Goetheanum 63–5, 67
gothic 88, 96, 139
Grotowski, Jerzy 26, 49, 57
Gurdjieff, G. I. 25, 59, 98, 101–5, 140

Heidegger, Martin 5, 20, 29
Hermetic Order of the Golden Dawn 9–10, 12–13, 25, 52–5, 59–61, 84, 97, 101, 105, 128, 140
Hermeticism 8–10, 13, 56, 107, 132
Hesse, Hermann 27, 79–84, 135–7

Hinduism 65, 144, 154
Holy Grail 26, 40–6
Horniman, Annie 25, 52, 60
hypnotism 75, 78

I Ching 75, 131, 133
imagination 17, 37, 73, 76, 78
India 25, 27, 65–6, 129–30, 139–54
initiation 10, 39, 53, 61, 64–5, 68–78
Inner Light Magazine 85, 123
Institute for the Harmonious Development of Man 9, 25, 103
Irish Nationalism 14, 116
Isherwood, Christopher 150, 156

James, Henry 21, 31, 96
James, William 50, 112–13, 150
Joyce, James 31–2, 136
Jung, Carl 7, 18, 27, 75–9, 82–3, 86–7, 93, 110, 132, 133

Kabbalah 8–9, 34, 75, 96, 123, 142, 156–7
Krishnamurti, Jiddu 66

Leeds Arts Club 99
Levi, Eliphas 55, 89, 96
liberalism 2, 11, 28, 99
Life Force 98, 106, 108–9, 111, 114
Lucifer 69–73

Maharshi, Ramana 130, 142, 148–9, 152–4
Mahatmas 52, 139–42, 154
Maitreya 66, 127
Mansfield, Katherine 25, 101, 103
Marinetti, F. T. 34–7, 99
Marx, Karl 2, 5
Mathers, Samuel Liddell Macgregor 51–2, 96–7
Matter of Britain 26, 40
Maugham, W. Somerset 27, 95–7, 130–1, 137, 149–54
Mead, G. R. S. 38, 41
Medico-Psychological Clinic of London 79, 84–6, 91
mesmerism 75, 77, 79
method acting 26, 56–7
Meyerhold, Vesolod 49, 59
Moscow Arts Theatre 56, 64
mystery drama 50, 64–73

mysticism 6, 23, 38, 36–8, 104, 109, 112–13, 144, 146, 157
myth 10–15, 17–20, 50, 54

narrative theory 4, 24, 43, 90, 108, 130, 138, 147, 149
Neoplatonism 9, 28, 132
New Drama 49–50, 59
Nietzsche, Friedrich 2, 7, 11, 27–8, 81, 98–101, 106, 113
nostalgia 13–15

Occult Revival 9–10, 55, 96
occulture 16
Olcott, Henry Steel 127–8
Orage, A. R. 25, 27, 97–107
orientalism 133–4
Ouspensky, P. D. 102–4

Petronius 42
Pound, Ezra 3–4, 12, 15, 25, 32, 37–43, 101
psychoanalysis 11, 26, 76–9, 84–93
psychophysical reductionism 22

Quest Society 9, 25, 38, 41

religionism 18
ritual 36, 41–3, 49–54, 60, 62, 90–1, 95, 123
Rosicrucian Manifestos 34, 71
Rosicrucianism 8, 26, 34–5, 51, 67, 71–2, 136, 140

Second World War 123, 131
sexuality 11, 46, 119, 125
Shakespear, Olivia 50, 61–4
Shaw, Bernard 11, 24–5, 27, 59–60, 98–101, 105–19, 126
shell shock 85, 91–2
Sinnett, A. P. 139–42
Society for Psychical Research 78, 105, 141
Socitas Rosicruciana in Anglia 51
Spiritualism 16–17, 39, 75, 106, 142
Stanislavski, Konstantin 49, 56, 57, 64
Steiner, Rudolf 50, 56, 59, 64–73
Stella Matutina 9, 52
Stoker, Bram 96, 121
surrealism 2, 73
symbolism 13, 56

tarot 43, 51
The New Age 25, 98–106
Thelema 43, 89, 97
Theosophical Society 9–10, 18, 25, 38, 64–6, 102, 105–6, 127–33, 139, 143
Tibet 129–30, 137–40, 142–7, 154
Toomer, Jean 104
traditionalism 131
Treadwell's Books 156

Underhill, Evelyn 25, 38, 113

Waite, A. E. 38, 52, 96–7
Waldorf schools 66
Weber, Max 2–3, 5–7, 19, 117
Western esotericism 7–9, 131, 146
Williams, Charles 43
Woolf, Virginia 29–32, 46–7

Yeats, W. B. 4, 12–15, 25, 38, 52, 60, 99
yoga 78, 131, 146–8, 156

Zoroastrianism 69, 98, 115, 136

www.ingramcontent.com/pod-product-compliance
Lightning Source LLC
Chambersburg PA
CBHW061837300426
44115CB00013B/2420